Parliaments and Legislatures Series

SAMUEL C. PATTERSON
General Advisory Editor

## Parliaments and Legislatures Series
General Advisory Editor
SAMUEL C. PATTERSON, OHIO STATE UNIVERSITY, USA

The aims of this series are to enhance knowledge about the well-established legislative assemblies of North America and western Europe and to publish studies of parliamentary assemblies worldwide—from Russia and the former Soviet bloc nations to Asia, Africa, and Latin America. The series is open to a wide variety of theoretical applications, historical dimensions, data collections, and methodologies.

### Editorial Board
David W. Brady, Stanford University, USA
Gary W. Cox, University of California, San Diego, USA
Erik Damgaard, University of Aarhus, Denmark
C. E. S. Franks, Queen's University, Canada
John R. Hibbing, University of Nebraska, USA
Gerhard Loewenberg, University of Iowa, USA
Thomas F. Remington, Emory University, USA
Suzanne S. Schüttemeyer, Universität Lüneburg, Germany
Itler Turan, Koç University, Turkey

### Other books in the series
Cheap Seats:
*The Democratic Party's Advantage in U.S. House Elections*
James E. Campbell

Coalition Government, Subnational Style:
*Multiparty Politics in Europe's Regional Parliaments*
William M. Downs

Creating Parliamentary Government in Bulgaria:
*The Transition to Democracy*
Albert P. Melone

Politics, Parties, and Parliaments:
*Political Change in Norway*
William Shaffer

# Citizens as Legislators

## Direct Democracy in the United States

SHAUN BOWLER
TODD DONOVAN
CAROLINE J. TOLBERT

Editors

Ohio State University Press
*Columbus*

Library of Congress Cataloging-in Publication Data
Citizens as legislators : direct democracy in the United States /
  edited by Shaun Bowler, Todd Donovan, and Caroline J. Tolbert.
      p.   cm. — (Parliaments and legislatures series)
   Includes bibliographical references and index.
   ISBN 0-8142-0777-4 (cloth : alk. paper). — ISBN 0-8142-0778-2
(pbk. : alk. paper)
   1. Referendum—United States—States.   I. Bowler, Shaun, 1958– .
   II. Donovan, Todd.   III. Tolbert, Caroline J.   IV. Series.
JF494.C57   1998
328.2'73—dc21                                                    98-13863
                                                                       CIP

Type set in Adobe Trump Medieval and Optima by Nighthawk Design.
Printed by Thomson-Shore.

9  8  7  6  5  4  3  2  1

# Contents

## Part III  State Public Policies and Direct Democracy

# Foreword

Making laws is not the only activity in which parliaments engage, and lawmaking may be done without parliament. *Direct democracy* is a political process in which the law of the land is made by citizens firsthand. In the experience of most democratic countries, direct legislation takes place in the form of a *referendum*, a procedure through which parliament passes on an issue of public policy to the citizens for their participatory approval or disapproval. British membership in the European Community was effectuated through a referendum in 1975; referenda brought about ratification of the Maastricht Treaty in Denmark, France, and Ireland in the mid-1990s, further integrating the countries of the European Community; a celebrated proposed constitutional settlement to resolve the status of French Quebec was defeated in Canada in 1992; fundamental majoritarian political reforms were approved through referenda in Italy in 1991 and 1993; and new constitutions have been put into effect through referenda in as many as fifty-five countries.

The *initiative*, a procedure in which citizens directly propose public policies which are then voted on, is a much rarer form of direct legislation than the referendum. Only in Switzerland, and in twenty-six of the American states, is the initiative regularly practiced. A Swiss initiative in 1990 imposed a decade-long moratorium on the construction of nuclear power plants, and another in 1993 declared a national workers' holiday in August to commemorate the creation of the Swiss confederation. National initiatives (or referenda) have never been conducted in the United States, but state ballots can be replete with proposals of direct legislation. Outside of the Swiss case, to study initiatives is to study American state politics and elections.

Since the thirteenth century, and perhaps before that, the process of making laws for a political society has unfolded mainly in the form of *representative* democracy. Representative democracy is a form of government in which citizens elect representatives who, in turn, meet as a parliament to enact laws. Accordingly, this two-step system of parliamentary government can be said to constitute *indirect* democracy. Beginning in the nineteenth century, in some American states populism took the form of rejecting indirect, or representative, democracy, at least for some purposes such as changing the state constitution, or substituting electoral devices to permit direct democracy by citizens.

Direct democracy may take various forms, including the town meeting, in which all citizens meet together to adopt laws (as has been practiced in New England towns), the referendum, in which legislative enactments must get citizen-voter approval before taking effect; the initiative, in which citizens may directly propose legislation for a popular vote; and the recall, in which public officials may be removed from office by popular vote. This book treats only one of these instances of "citizens as legislators"—the initiative as it is practiced in the American states.

The initiative is provided for preponderantly in the constitutions of states west of the Mississippi River (the notable exceptions being Maine, Massachusetts, and Florida). Among these states, application of the initiative varies considerably. The chapters of this book illustrate many variations in the use of the initiative to make constitutional or statutory changes. The paradigmatic case is California, where typically election ballots burgeon with initiated proposals—so-called propositions like the infamous Proposition 13 in 1978 that signaled a tax revolt among many California citizens. More recently, in 1994 California voters were persuaded to adopt Proposition 187, which prohibited the provision of educational, medical, or social services to illegal immigrants or their children.

The contributors to this interesting collection present several different analyses of initiatives like those adopted by California voters. One group of contributions focuses upon the campaigns seeking adoption of initiative proposals. Often, initiative campaigns today are highly professionalized, media-intensive, public relations efforts. Once considered mainly a political process for amateurs, contemporary initiative campaigns are frequently lavishly funded by well-heeled special interests. Given the armamentarium of modern political campaigning, it is not easy in the large urban states to mount an initiative effort without first amassing an enormous campaign fund. But even special interest initiative campaigns may arouse and activate large numbers of citizens to participate in the policy-making process.

A second cluster of contributions in this book concern initiative elections in the light of what the editors call "the rise of the initiative industry." These chapters provide penetrating results showing how campaign spending influences the outcomes of initiative elections, how voters' preferences and ideological orientations affect voting, and how much endorsements by leaders (such as the celebrated leadership of former U.S. House Speaker Tom Foley against the term limits initiative in Washington State) affect initiative outcomes.

Finally, these authors analyze and appraise the public policies that are the tangible product of state initiatives. This leads one contributor to focus upon recent initiative campaigns seeking to change "state governance policies" epitomized in efforts to restrict the taxing and expenditure powers of government or to lay limits on the terms of public officials. Other contributors carefully dissect the strategies of interest groups manipulating the initiative process, the voting behavior of racial and ethnic minority groups, and the impact of initiative outcomes upon toleration of unpopular or defenseless minorities.

This sensitive, theoretically interesting, methodologically savvy collection puts the use of the initiative in America on a much surer empirical footing. Moreover, these studies allow the authors to raise important normative questions about the efficacy of direct legislation. Their work stimulates reflection about the propriety of passing laws without the benefit of legislative deliberation and debate. Above all, taken together, these contributions underscore the importance of the initiative as a policy-making process, and demonstrate the significant impact of direct democracy on the politics and policies of the American states.

SAMUEL C. PATTERSON

# Acknowledgments

This book is the product of the skill, energy, and patience of many people. The editors are particularly grateful to all the contributors to the volume. They have provided us with interesting, accessible, original scholarship, some while having to bear with neurotic proddings of the editors.

Nearly all of the material here was written specifically for this book, yet each of the chapters has a slightly different history of origin. Some began as projects that were presented over the last few years at numerous panels at annual meetings of the Western Political Science Association (WPSA), the American Political Science Association, and the Pacific Northwest Political Science Association. We are thankful for the opportunities to receive feedback on research in these forums and are grateful to WPSA organizers, who provide a continuing forum for discussion of direct democracy. We thank fellow panelists, discussants, and audience members who contributed to the development of these papers.

The editors also thank Max Neiman, Dave McCuan, and the Center for Social and Behavioral Research of the College of Humanities, Arts, and Social Sciences at UC Riverside for organizing a workshop on direct democracy that brought many of the contributors together. We also thank Bruce Cain for his comments and interest in this project.

Donovan and Bowler were assisted with research funds from their respective universities. Donovan expresses his appreciation to the Western Washington University Department of Political Science, the College of Arts and Sciences, and the Bureau for Faculty Research for their support. Help has come from many at Western Washington, including Ken Hoover, Gene Hogan, Mohib Ghali, and

Pete Elich. Donovan is also grateful to Jack Vowles for an opportunity to complete some of this work while visiting at the University of Waikato.

Susan Brumbaugh, Lucky Tedrow, and Jim Wenzel have provided assistance with data and computing resources. At WWU, Kevin Short assisted with graphics. The Washington State Federation of Employees provided data from a survey they had conducted by the Greenburg-Lake firm. This was used in Chapter 7. We are highly indebted to numerous individuals involved in initiative campaigns who took valuable time from their busy schedules in order to be interviewed for this book.

The people at the Ohio State University Press have been tremendously helpful in bringing this book together. Our thanks go to Samuel Patterson for help in getting the project started. Charlotte Dihoff was a great advocate of the project, and we are sincerely appreciative of her concern for the book. Beth Ina worked to make sure the book made it through the production stage and has no need to apologize for "nit-picking." Her efforts have been outstanding. The editors would also like to thank our daughters: Jessica Bowler, Verity Bowler, Fiona Donovan, Jacqueline Dowling, and Eveline Dowling.

# 1

# An Overview of Direct Democracy in the American States

## TODD DONOVAN AND SHAUN BOWLER

Direct democracy devices such as the initiative, referendum, and recall were adopted by many states during the Progressive Era, a period of radical redesign and reform for many American political
institutions. The unique institutions emerging from this era were
expected to give citizens a greater voice in state-level policy making
and weaken the hold of wealthy interests over state legislatures.
Early-twentieth-century reformers hoped that by gaining more direct access to the legislative process, citizens would be able to control public affairs and thereby "insure responsive as well as responsible government" (Howe 1967, 171). This book is a modest attempt
to assess direct democracy and to determine how it might make
government more responsive or responsible.

Direct democracy clearly was not part of America's original constitutional design. In practice it was virtually unknown when the
Constitution of 1787 was drafted, and it was abhorred by the Feder-
alists (Eule 1990). For the authors of the Constitution, the ideal
form of democracy was representative (or republican) government,
in which the control of legislation, in practice and theory, was insulated from popular majorities by representative institutions. As
Thomas Cronin notes (1989, 43–46), forceful agitation for greater direct citizen involvement in legislation began later in the nineteenth
century with disaffected groups and social movements such as

1

grange organizations, single-taxers, socialists, labor groups, prohibitionists, and evangelists—groups that often had their greatest political influence in the western United States. Whatever differences existed over the particular cause of each group's disaffection, they could agree that unreformed state legislatures and political parties were corrupt, beholden to "moneyed interests" and "trusts" (Cronin 1989, 45). The direct citizen's initiative would be the "gun behind the door" that would force state legislatures to be responsive to the public's will. Taking this western metaphor further, advocates argued that insulated legislatures needed the "spur in the flanks" of the initiative and the "bit in the mouth" of the referendum (Johnson 1944, 291).

To its advocates, then, direct democracy would provide an end-run around partisan legislatures, mitigating the corrupting influences thought to operate within them, and would also improve the quality of public life. Voter interest would be stimulated as citizens participated directly in drafting and approving legislation. The new, open process would thus instill civic virtue by simultaneously educating and involving the mass public (Haynes 1907; Barnett 1915; Beard and Schultz 1912; Key and Crouch 1939).

Although unique direct-democracy coalitions formed in each state that adopted these devices, it was the Populists, prolabor Democrats, and middle-class Progressive reform groups who finally secured amendments to many state constitutions in the early twentieth century. In California, the Progressives launched the direct democracy movement to break Southern Pacific Railroad's hold on the state legislature (Sutro 1994, 945; Lee 1978, 88). In Oregon, the initiative and referendum emerged from a coalition of dissident free-silver Republicans, some Democrats, and Henry George–inspired Populists (Mason 1994, 26–29). In Washington, a coalition of labor, farmers, and urban Progressives fought for direct democracy (Warner 1995, 54; Benedict 1975). In all, 24 states adopted some form of the citizen's initiative, with only a handful being enacted after the Progressive period.

The institutions of direct democracy provide the opportunity for groups and individuals to draft legislation directly, to overturn laws adopted by legislatures, and to recall recalcitrant representatives. This book focuses primarily on one commonly used feature arising from the Progressive Era: the citizen's initiative. With this device, broad-based, "grassroots" groups outside of the legislative arena can draft their own laws, then petition to have citizens vote directly on the proposed legislation in a statewide election. In adopting this device, states opened a door to the legislative process for groups who had previously failed to gain access. In the next section, we provide a sketch of how direct democracy works, since the process will only be familiar to those who live in states that allow it. Then we address some of the theoretical and normative issues that direct democracy presents—issues that we examine further in the chapters that follow.

## Use of the "Citizen's" Initiative

Since South Dakota adopted the initiative in 1898, hundreds of these "citizen"-drafted laws have appeared on ballots in American states. David Magleby notes that from 1898 to 1992, over 1700 initiatives were placed before U.S. voters. Among states using initiatives, the most during this period, 274, appeared in Oregon, with 232 appearing in California, 160 in North Dakota, 150 in Colorado, 133 in Arizona, and 91 in Washington (Neal 1993). Hundreds of additional petitions were filed yet failed to qualify, and hundreds of additional referenda were placed before voters by legislatures. Most initiatives were rejected by voters, yet 38% passed from 1898 to 1992 (Magleby 1994, 231).

As we will show, voters have approved many initiative proposals that have had great impact on state politics and policy, and in various chapters in this volume we assess how direct democracy makes the politics in these states somewhat unique. One reason to expect differences between direct and representative democracy states is that the initiative creates an additional point of access to the policy process—not only for "narrow" or "special" interests that have traditionally enjoyed influence within an elected legislature, but also for broad-based groups. Direct democracy states provide an arena in which broad-based popular groups and well-financed interests can compete in a different setting than in representative states, and where major policy conflicts can take place outside of the legislature and beyond party politics.

It has probably been like this since the earliest days of the initiative. States such as Oregon and Washington witnessed the immediate use of the device by broad-based, populist reform groups working outside of the legislature to promote policies extending women's suffrage, limiting child labor, establishing the eight-hour work day, and enacting Prohibition. At the same time, there were numerous direct legislation attempts by some of the era's dominant industries—such as fishing and brewing—to establish their own industry regulations. Conflicts between industry and broad-based reform groups were also contested outside of the legislature. For example, several initiatives were placed on ballots by railroad and liquor interests in response to laws drafted by newly influential reform groups (Mason 1994, 196–97; Washington Secretary of State 1994).

Although the players have changed since the earliest days of American direct democracy, the contemporary era also demonstrates that broad-based and narrow groups continue to use the initiative in tandem. In a single California election in 1988, voters were presented five separate, competing initiatives dealing with automobile insurance and drafted by industry groups, trial lawyers, and consumer activists (Banducci 1992; Lupia 1994b). In 1996, labor unions and citizen activists laying claim to populist roots placed initiatives on California's ballot that would raise the minimum wage, limit and regulate campaign contribution, and repeal affirmative action. At the same time, one group qualified initiatives that would allow casino gambling in a limited area, and another qualified a measure drafted on behalf of a San Diego attorney that would rewrite rules regarding the type of lawsuits in which he specialized (Scott 1996).

## Variations in Provision for Use of the Initiative

Not all states have used the initiative in the same way. Considerable variation exists across states in the conditions under which the process can operate. According to the Council of State Governments, 16 states that use *direct* initiatives allow citizens to amend the state's constitution.[1] Most of these states also allow direct initiatives dealing with statutes. In direct initiative states, once the required number of signatures are verified, initiatives are placed on the ballot without being submitted to the legislature for a decision or revision.

Two more states, Massachusetts and Mississippi, allow *indirect* constitutional initiatives only, with Massachusetts also providing for indirect statutory initiatives. These must be submitted to the legislature before being placed on a ballot. The legislature may adopt the law, send the original proposal to the people for a vote, or revise the law and put their version before the people for a vote.

A few state constitutions allow citizens to change statutes but not to amend the constitution. Some allow this only by direct initiative (Alaska, Idaho). Others allow only direct and indirect statutory initiatives (Washington and Utah), while Maine and Wyoming allow only indirect statutory initiatives. Table 1.1 lists states that allow the popular initiative and the types of initiatives used in each state. Figure 1.1 illustrates the geographic distribution of states using the initiative.

**Table 1.1** Types of Initiatives in the U.S. States

| State | Direct Constitutional | Indirect Constitutional | Direct Statute | Indirect Statute |
|---|---|---|---|---|
| Alaska | | | X | |
| Arizona | X | | X | |
| Arkansas | X | | X | |
| California | X | | X | |
| Colorado | X | | X | |
| Florida | X | | | |
| Idaho | | | X | |
| Illinois | X | | X | |
| Maine | | | | X |
| Massachusetts | | X | | X |
| Michigan | X | | | X |
| Mississippi | | X | | |
| Missouri | X | | X | |
| Montana | X | | X | |
| Nebraska | X | | X | |
| Nevada | X | | X | X |
| North Dakota | X | | X | |
| Ohio | X | | X | X |
| Oklahoma | X | | X | |
| Oregon | X | | X | |
| South Dakota | X | | X | |
| Utah | | | X | X |
| Washington | | | X | X |
| Wyoming | | | | X |

**Figure1.1** The Geographic Distribution of States Using the Initiative

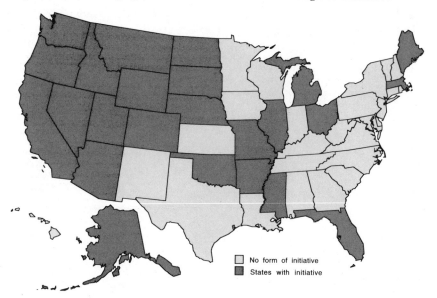

Apart from restricting initiatives to constitutional or statutory measures, almost anything that could be considered by a legislature can also be placed on a state ballot by petition. Half of the states that allow initiatives place no substantive restrictions on the policies that direct legislation may address. The restrictions that do exist typically prohibit measures involving state revenues and spending, and measures dealing with health and public safety. In theory each initiative can deal with only a single subject, but as we see in chapter 2, many state courts have interpreted this rule fairly liberally.

Given the few restrictions on subject matter and the wide latitude granted for drafting statutes and amending state constitutions, the topics addressed by initiatives have varied widely. According to Magleby, in the early 1990s nearly 30% of qualified initiatives dealt with governmental or political reform (i.e., term limits and campaign finance measures). This number represents an increase in the use of such measures from previous decades, when reform measures represented 19% of initiatives. In chapters 7 and 8 we pay particular attention to the adoption of these increasingly important reform initiatives.

Of the remaining initiatives on modern ballots, Magleby determined that over 25% dealt with revenue and tax measures, 15% with "public morality" (issues such as abortion and gambling), and nearly 10% with environmental and land-use issues. Initiatives affecting the regulation of business—a category of measures often eliciting the largest campaign expenditures—accounted for 16% of qualified initiatives (Magleby 1994, 238; see also S. Thomas 1984).

There is some consistency across states regarding the initial phases of the direct legislation process. Requests for circulating an initiative petition are typically submitted to the secretary of state, or in some states the attorney general or lieutenant governor, who then sets an official title and description to appear on the public petition. Typically, the state's attorney, or the attorney general or secretary of state, sets ballot titles and ballot summaries for initiatives once they are qualified.[2] Only four states actually allow the proponent of the initiative to develop the title and summary of the proposal as they will be listed on the petition.[3]

Beyond this, there is substantial variation across states in the procedural rules affecting the number of initiatives that can appear on the state's ballots in any given election. Each state's constitution sets provisions for how petitions are circulated, how long petitions may circulate, and how many signatures are needed to qualify. As we see in chapter 5, these factors explain some of the variation in initiative use across states.

We should note here that as the population of some direct democracy states has exploded, these qualification requirements have tended to remain static. Where thousands of signatures were once sufficient to qualify a measure, today hundreds of thousands must now be gathered in the same time period. The rise of for-profit petition management firms has corresponded with new demands for gathering greater numbers of signatures. In response to paid signature gathering, some states passed rules banning its use (see chapter 2); however, a 1988 U.S. Supreme Court ruling nullified these regulations. This means that no state can ban the operation of for-profit petition firms. For groups with sufficient financial resources, these firms provide an opportunity for ballot access. They are also responsible in part for the first resurgence in initiative use since the low point of the 1940s–1950s (Magleby 1994; Lee 1978), and could provide a means for future accelerated use in states where initiatives have rarely appeared.

Signature requirements vary greatly across states. Within each state, constitutional measures typically require that proponents obtain more signatures than are needed for statutes. The number required for placing a proposal on state ballots ranges from the equivalent of 3% to 15% of the votes cast in the previous general election. At the lower end, Massachusetts requires 3% of votes cast in the previous gubernatorial election (with the requirement that no more than 25% of signatures be gathered in any one county), and Colorado requires 5% of votes cast in the secretary of state election. Petitions for statutes in North Dakota can qualify with signatures of only 2% of the resident population. At the higher end, Utah statutes require signatures equal to 10% of the votes cast in the governor's race, with 10% of that number from a majority of each of the state's counties. Wyoming has perhaps the most onerous qualification hurdle, requiring signatures equivalent to 15% of the vote total from the previous general election, with signatures obtained from at least two-thirds of the state's counties. Oklahoma and Arizona also require 15% of general election votes for a petition to be qualified (*The Book of the States, 1994–95*).

Time constraints can also present a significant challenge to placing direct legislation on a state's ballot. At least 11 states allow proponents to have a petition in circulation for a year or more. Some, however, limit efforts to only a few months: Oklahoma restricts petitioning to three months after the initiative is filed; California, to five months; and Colorado and Washington, to six months.

To place these demands into perspective, consider the raw numbers of signatures needed to get an initiative on ballots in various states. Using election turnout from 1994, a proposed law could reach the ballot in Idaho—a state where only 14 initiatives have been listed since 1912—with just under 40,000 signatures. In Oregon, the most initiative-prone of the American states, a constitutional initiative petition would require roughly 75,000 signatures (fewer are required for statutes). Missouri, a state having only 10 more initiatives in its history than Idaho, requires 117,000 signatures collected over the course of 20 months for an initiative statute to be placed on the ballot. These modest requirements are perhaps not radically different from the Progressives' goal of establishing a system that could allow ill-funded "popular" groups to place issues before the public for a vote.

In contrast, given Michigan's requirements and population in 1994, just over 300,000 signatures would have to have been gathered within 6 months in order to place a measure on the ballot. In California, proponents needed to collect 630,000 signatures in 150 days to propose an amendment to the constitution in 1996. Clearly, in these states the effort to qualify an initiative will require substantial financial resources, organizational skill, and massive volunteer efforts. In all states, these efforts are further complicated by the need to "overqualify," obtaining excess signatures to compensate for the invalid signatures inevitably detected when any petition is filed.

Apart from highlighting the difficulties involved with ballot access, these signature requirements also illustrate an issue that we will discuss in greater detail in a later chapter. While signature requirements affect how many initiatives reach the ballot, there are other state-level factors that explain why states such as Oregon and Missouri, in spite of relatively low hurdles for qualifying direct legislation, have radically different experiences with the use of it, the initiative being more common in Oregon than in Missouri.

It is important to understand that the rules and conditions facilitating the use of the initiative vary from state to state, and that these factors in turn play some role in affecting how much the state comes to rely upon direct rather than representative procedures when setting policy. As we illustrate in chapter 8, in "populist" states where initiatives are used most frequently, public policy is more likely to constrain the discretion of elected legislatures. In various chapters, we examine how this creates differences between direct and representative democracy states. In the end, we suggest that use of the initiative may cause governments to be more responsive to *some* public demands, but that it is another matter to say that the resulting policies are more "responsible."

## Variations in Initiative Use Over Time

Use of the initiative declined in the middle part of the twentieth century, only to be revived in recent decades. Virginia Graham's

(1976) compilation of statewide initiative use from 1900 to 1976 illustrates that initiatives were used with great frequency between 1910 and 1920, when over 250 reached state ballots, and use remained close to this level through the 1930s. However, as the population of western states expanded during and after World War II, the use of popular initiatives plunged. In the politically tumultuous decade of the 1960s, fewer than 90 initiatives appeared on all state ballots. Magleby (1994) and Thomas (1984) noted an upswing in initiative use by the 1970s and 1980s, with Magleby (1994) estimating that rates in the 1990s would exceed those of the Progressive Era. It would seem that state-level direct democracy has been rediscovered near the end of the twentieth century.

Several factors are associated with the expanded use of popular initiatives in the 1980s and 1990s. One reason is that opponents of some initiatives are now much more likely to resort to the initiative process themselves. As we discuss in chapters 3–5, the evolution of opposition tactics has led to much greater use of *counterpropositions*, a rapidly qualified initiative designed to deflect attention from an opponent's initiative. Dozens of these measures have reached state ballots, particularly since the late 1980s. In Oregon, for example, a tax on tobacco to support health care and antismoking programs (Measure 44) qualified for the 1996 ballot and quickly attracted a rapidly qualified counterproposition backed by the tobacco industry. By qualifying measures that would, among other things, require insurers to pay for the services of chiropractors and "alternative healers," the industry hoped that health care providers would have to deflect resources away from the anti-tobacco measure to defend their own interests.

Rapid qualification of these counterproposals would not be possible without petition management firms and the maturation of a campaign industry that has made it easier for "grassroots" and industry alike to get on ballots in populous states (see chapter 3). Using subcontractors who specialize in hiring clipboard-wielding crews paid by the signature (or sometimes by the hour), these firms can estimate costs for qualification given the subject, the number of other initiative petitions in circulation, and the time remaining in the qualification period. Firms can virtually guarantee qualification (and do so in trade advertisements) if a proponent is willing to pay top price per signature.

Magleby notes an additional factor contributing to the renewal of initiative politics: the rediscovery of direct democracy by conservative and liberal issue-activists since the 1970s (Magleby 1994, 233). Groups that might look more akin to the non-elite (or nonindustry) "citizens" that the Progressives had hoped to empower have used the initiative to qualify a variety of measures, including coastal management (Sabatier and Mazmanian 1983); statewide land-use measures; antitax measures (Sears and Citrin 1982); nuclear freeze proposals; public expenditure limitations; abortion measures; "death with dignity" proposals; victims rights policies; medical marijuana use; "three strikes," tough-on-crime laws; and term limitations—to name a few.[4]

## Critiques of Direct Democracy

At the time direct democracy was adopted, not all observers were as sanguine about its prospects as the early Populists and Progressives were. Early critics chose several lines of attack. Echoing classical democratic theorists, some feared that direct democracy would produce policies hostile to the interests of unpopular minorities, or simply further the political nostrums of "faddists" (Lowrie 1911; Croly 1914). Others feared that direct democracy would increase the power of narrow interests as it weakened parties, leaving groups with money to control the political agenda, defeating initiatives that threatened them while placing their own legislation on ballots (Eaton 1912).

As the debates continued over adoption of the initiative in the American states, additional questions were raised about voter competency (see Haynes 1907; Barnett 1915). In 1915, for example, Barnett observed that "to submit these matters to popular vote is to strain the interest and intelligence of the citizen and invite the most haphazard way of legislation" (1915, 538; also Renisch 1912). Voters, the critics argued, will be uninterested or unable to learn enough about propositions to vote intelligently (Haynes 1907).

Contemporary critics of the process have echoed all of these concerns (e.g., Lawrence 1995; Eule 1990; Bell 1978). Citing changes in politics over the course of the twentieth century, in addition to the original critiques of direct democracy, these critics see reason to doubt that the process might create responsive and responsible

politics at the end of this century. Perhaps the most significant new
critique is that American direct democracy has fallen short of the
Populist-Progressive goal—the creation of a process whereby broad-
based groups can create public policy that better serves the public.
Some critics point to the professionalization of what was supposedly an "amateur" process. An "initiative industry" has evolved,
seemingly supplanting the original ideal of a populist system that
provides access to the legislative process. Composed of law firms
that draft legislation, petition management firms that guarantee
ballot access, direct-mail firms, and campaign consultants who specialize in initiative contests across several states, the industry is
visible in nearly all states where initiatives are used frequently. Although the "industry" has been active in California since at least
the 1930s (Lee 1978; McWilliams 1951), it has evolved and grown in
importance as campaigns have relied more heavily upon electronic
media and direct mail.

Thus, in addition to reflecting confusion or randomness, critics
note that voter choices might reflect outright manipulation by well-
financed "industry" campaigns. If this is the case, we should not
necessarily expect that public policy in direct democracy states reflects any heightened responsiveness to popular preferences. In this
book, particularly in chapters 3 and 4, we detail the evolution of the
initiative industry in order to examine how grassroots democracy—
or anything akin to the Populist-Progressive vision—can coexist
with it.

Many studies of American direct democracy voting have provided empirical evidence to support the old contention that voters
may be unable to deal with the complexity of choices placed before
them (see Bowler and Donovan n.d.; Magleby 1984; and Cronin
1989 for reviews). Nearly 70 years after the early critics expressed
concern about voter ignorance and apathy, a major contemporary
study of voting on ballot measures (Magleby 1984) suggests in its
conclusion that most voters who have not learned about a measure
"before entering the booth will play a form of Russian roulette, casting affirmative and negative votes at random" (198). These conclusions are based on the view that, lacking an informed understanding
of the factual and legal details of an initiative, voters will be ill
equipped to make decisions that reflect their underlying preferences
about policies—if they indeed have some consistent preferences

that can be expressed in initiative voting (see also Hensler and Hensler 1979; Wolfinger and Greenstein 1968, 767).

This is not to say that voters in direct democracy never figure out what they are for or against, but that they might be forced to choose on the basis of racist feelings, ethnic ethos, undefined moods, whims, campaign manipulation, alienation, symbolism, and a host of factors only indirectly related to their understanding of how policies affect their own personal interests (see for example Gamson 1961; Horton and Thompson 1962; McDill and Ridley 1962; Wilson and Banfield 1963; Boskof and Zeigler 1964; Mueller 1965; Wolfinger and Greenstein 1968; Mueller 1969; Durand 1972; Lowery and Sigelman 1981; Cataldo and Holm 1983).

Yet not all research has been dismissive of the idea that ill-informed voters can figure out how to cast votes for initiatives that further their policy preferences. Lupia (1994, 1992) has shown that poorly informed initiative voters can emulate the behavior of well-informed voters if they simply have cues about who is backing an initiative (also see Bartels 1996). Such cues can help voters sort through several measures dealing with the same topic that appear on a ballot simultaneously. Bowler and Donovan (1994c, n.d.) also show that many voters make use of elite cues (such as endorsements) to figure out what they are for or against, and that these cues can even help voters to evaluate issues in terms of their underlying partisanship. The emerging research on initiative voting, however, has yet to establish if voters' preferences have any coherent structure (or ideological constraint) across multiple initiatives. Nor have scholars fully examined the sources of the elite cues that people use to figure out how to vote for their preferred policies.

In chapters 6 and 7 in this volume, we reexamine the voter's ability to reason in direct democracy. Chapter 6 demonstrates that electoral choices across multiple ballot propositions can be constrained by some underlying attitudes, and chapter 7 demonstrates that voters are able to learn elite positions from various media sources, then vote on the basis of such cues.

## Institutional Effects of Direct Democracy

One central question structuring much of this volume is, What difference does direct democracy make? The "rediscovery" of institutions by political scientists, and the development of tools by which to analyze them, have led to widespread interest in and examination of the effects of institutional forms. As a unique institution that creates its own set of incentives and opportunities for political actors at the mass and elite levels, the initiative process can be expected to create substantial differences in policy outcomes between direct and representative democracy states. One primary effect of direct democratic institutions, for the Progressives, was that state policies would be made more responsive to mass preferences.

As Riker (1982) notes, many formal theories consider political institutions as vehicles for aggregating the preexisting preferences of citizens into policy outcomes. Given the same set of underlying mass preferences, different political institutions can produce different policy outcomes.[5] Some research on legislative organization portrays legislatures as an arena where logrolling can produce policies that deviate from the preferences of the median voter. Logrolling in legislatures allows a member to gain support for her preferred programs by trading votes with others who support programs she might not prefer—thus creating legislative majorities for some programs where electoral majorities might not exist. This perspective suggests that a legislative setting can sometimes produce policies different from those that mass preferences might otherwise demand (Weingast and Marshall 1988; Weingast, Shepsle, and Johnsen 1981).

Conversely, one of the main claims of the Populist and Progressive advocates of the initiative was that direct legislation should make politics more responsive, that is, more reflective of mass preferences for policy. In practical terms, voters in two states might be equally disposed to support term limits, or tax limitations, or abortion rights. If variation in institutional design affects policy outcomes such that initiatives translate preferences into policy, we might expect different policy outcomes when we compare initiative states to pure representative states. As we see in chapters 8 and 9, there are reasons to expect that public policies will more closely match citizen preferences in direct democracy states. Both institutional rules (direct v. representative government) as well as the nature of citizen preferences about policies affect the policies that a government might adopt.

In some policy arenas, the relationship between direct democracy and policy outcomes is less than straightforward. As Matsusaka (1995) illustrates, institutions of direct democracy create a policy process that largely nullifies logrolling and vote trading, creating a different fiscal environment from that found in states with pure representative government. He finds evidence that government spending is lower in initiative states than noninitiative states. Conversely, Zax (1989) found that initiatives lead to greater spending, as they allow citizens to punish legislatures for any "sins of omission" when popular items are left out of the state budget (see Blair 1967).

Finding different spending levels between direct and representative democracy states says little about an institution's ability to translate preferences into policies, however. Lascher et al. (1996) conducted a study of state budgets that included an actual measure of each state's mass preferences for policy. Like Matsusaka, Lascher et al. show that initiative states might have less-progressive taxes than would purely representative states. Initiative states also spend less on Aid to Families with Dependent Children and public education, and have less-liberal policy outcomes overall. However, the data actually suggest that the citizen's initiative might cause spending policy to be *less* responsive to mass preferences in these areas, in spite of initiative advocates' pronouncements to the contrary.[6]

Lascher et al. do not attribute this to direct democracy's muting or distorting the translation of spending preferences into policy, but their findings do suggest a possible conservative policy bias associated with direct democracy institutions,[7] something which we examine further in chapter 12. Their results also conflict with what is demonstrated in chapter 9—that state policies about parental consent for abortion more closely reflect public preferences in direct democracy states. In chapter 12, we also examine why these studies might draw contradictory conclusions about the effects of direct democracy.

In addition to affecting policy outcomes directly, or indirectly by influencing how legislators behave, direct democracy is also able to shape the institutions that produce policy. Direct democracy states appear more likely to adopt governance policies—laws that change the way legislatures do business. The process can therefore possibly be seen to reflect the influence of mass preferences over institutions, not just over policy. Some of these "governance" issues include term limits or tax and expenditure limits. In at least some of these areas it seems reasonable to suppose that legislators will have a hard time reforming and regulating themselves. Hence, the direct democracy process provides, at least in principle, some means by which institutional changes can be introduced.

As an institution, then, direct democracy is an interesting one, for not only can it shape policy outcomes directly but it can also shape future institutions. In our concluding chapter we suggest that direct democracy, in being fairly responsive to demands to cut taxes, can create a paradoxical outcome by rendering initiative states less able to respond to mass preferences for public spending.

## Direct Democracy and Minorities

Any evaluation of direct democracy's responsiveness to mass preferences must face the issue of majority abuse of unpopular minorities. Fearing majoritarian tyranny, America's original republican institutions were designed with a measure of protection for minority rights, and included institutional safeguards (elections staggered over time, indirect elections, separation of powers, judicial review, etc.) that offered minorities broad protection from popular majorities. Direct democracy's critics have long stressed that legislatures (or republican government) are better equipped for accommodating minorities, given that legislatures provide an environment that facilitates face-to-face contact and bargaining. Much of the contemporary disdain for direct democracy centers on the fear that it is abusive of minorities (Magleby 1984, 182; Gamble 1997; Linde 1994; 1992; Eule 1990; Bell 1978). Critics point to highly contentious ballot measures affecting the civil rights of immigrants, gays and lesbians, and racial minorities as an example of abuse, while implying that representative government will better protect minorities. Gamble (1997, 262) reflects this perspective in concluding that direct legislation "separates us as a people" and "only weakens us as a nation." Others note that state courts—being subject to voter confirmation in nearly all direct democracy states—provide little refuge for minorities targeted by initiatives (Eule 1994, 1990).

Cain (1992b, 270) has suggested further that minorities lose by initiative what they might gain in the legislature. Minority electoral legislative districts created in the spirit of the Voting Rights

Act have accounted for substantial policy gains by racial and ethnic minorities; however, these gains are repeatedly threatened by the popular initiative (i.e., California's anti-immigrant Proposition 187 of 1994; California's civil rights initiative, Proposition 209 of 1996).

The latter part of the twentieth century does provide numerous examples of initiatives targeting unpopular minorities. We will examine the political dynamics of these initiatives in several chapters. In our conclusion, we examine evidence about antiminority policies and state-level direct democracy. We argue that it is wrong to point to these high-profile initiatives and conclude that policy outcomes from direct democracy are more abusive of minorities than are outcomes from legislatures. State and federal courts have struck down nearly every state initiative that critics cite as being abusive of minorities. In many cases, state voters are less likely to pass initiatives targeting minorities than they are to approve initiatives in general. We also concur with Richard Briffault (1985), who suggests that comparisons between direct and representative processes are often flawed, since critics may have overly idealized views of state legislatures. Cronin (1989) has illustrated that elected legislatures can produce policies that are also outrageously abusive to minority rights.

This does not mean that we find state-level direct democracy flawless in its treatment of minorities. The act of deliberating about the fate of minorities can have a negative effect on the mass public's attitudes toward the group targeted by the initiative. It is important to note that in the real world, citizen preferences about policies—or about groups of people—might not always be stable or preexisting. In contrast to the assumption of many formal models that preferences are exogenous to the process of deciding on policies, preferences might not be totally independent of political institutions. March and Olsen, for example (1984, 739), suggest that institutions—that is, the rules and processes by which policies are debated and adopted—have an important role in the formation of citizens' attitudes and preferences about policies.

Just as elites might use representative assemblies, elections, or political parties to move mass opinions (Carmines and Stimson 1989; Zaller 1992; Gerber and Jackson 1993), so too might campaigns associated with ballot initiatives. This possibility adds another dimension to the criticism that direct democracy breeds majority tyranny of unpopular minority groups. If the institutions of direct democracy can shape preferences as well as policies, then we must be concerned about how initiatives affect opinions about unpopular minorities. The initiative device allows citizen groups to draft legislation singling out unpopular minorities, then wage campaigns that subject these groups to scrutiny, criticism, and moral judgment. Direct democracy can thus create an environment where public attitudes about these groups (and attitudes about policies associated with the group) become more hostile.

The courts might block policies from being implemented, but they cannot easily undo shifts in opinions about minorities brought about by some campaigns. Most statewide antigay initiatives in the 1980s and 1990s failed (Donovan and Bowler 1997), and much of California's anti-illegal immigrant Proposition 187 was overturned in the courts. But for the groups targeted by these initiatives, the significance of direct legislation might not be the actual policy outcomes but the way in which ballot contests stigmatize certain minorities.

In chapter 11, we present evidence that mass opinions about immigrants (and policies associated with gays and immigrants) turn more hostile over time in places where the groups were targeted by popular initiatives. We preface this in chapter 10 with an examination of the contextual/racial forces affecting support for English Only measures and California's anti-immigrant Proposition 187.

## Direct Democracy: More Responsive and Responsible?

In the end, we wish to assess how well contemporary direct democracy matches up to the Progressive vision of reform. We have noted that the Progressives hoped that direct democracy would produce policies that were more responsive to public opinion, and more responsible than what legislatures would produce. There is no easy way to determine whether this is the case. We can begin by asking questions about the sort of groups that are able to use direct democracy today. This can bring us some way toward assessing *whom* the process might be responsive to. The process is clearly professionalized, but this is not an entirely new development. In the chapters that follow, we illustrate that from the earliest days of American direct democracy, there existed elements of what is now referred to as the modern "initiative industry."

Yet the contemporary era is marked by changes that might further remove this "citizen"-legislation process from the grassroots. As the initiative industry matures and as gaining ballot access becomes more costly for all groups, it becomes increasingly difficult for an observer to distinguish the efforts of "citizen" groups from the methods used by narrow "interest" groups. Put differently, while direct democracy provides access to legislation for groups who might lack influence in a legislature, we find that many of the major players in initiative politics are often the same actors who wield influence in legislatures. Vast amounts of money involved with these campaigns might lead some to conclude that narrow interests can buy favorable legislation through direct democracy.

But we will argue that the process is not particularly responsive to the best-financed interest groups—at least not in a way that lets them pass policies furthering their goals. Money is critically important in affecting outcomes, as we show in chapter 5. However, if we examine the role of well-financed interests in the direct legislation arena, we find that their primary advantages are defensive. Big money might affect how the process translates the public's preferences into policy by facilitating the defeat of measures that might have otherwise appealed to broad interests. It is far more difficult—and takes far more cash—for big money to buy a victory.

Another aspect of responsiveness involves how well the process of direct legislation translates mass preferences into policy. We can ask, Do voters who show up at the polls make decisions in a way that is informed? If this is the case, we might assume votes can reflect their preferences. But do they have coherent preferences? We offer some evidence that suggests the answer to each of these questions is yes.

In spite of the professionalization and commercialization of the process, several chapters in this volume demonstrate that it does have a substantial effect on state politics and policy. The effect, moreover, occasionally appears to be one that makes these states more responsive to the mass electorate in certain policy arenas.

Perhaps the most noteworthy examples of this effect are the modern political reforms we call "governance" policies, such as term limitations, tax and expenditure limitations, and supermajority requirements that affect the way representative legislatures can govern. Furthermore, it is only in direct democracy states that voters go to the polls to decide the fate of minorities—a process that can change mass opinions. Direct democracy thus remains a unique vehicle for institutional change, opinion change, and policy making.

A process that is responsive to certain mass preferences, however, is not necessarily one that produces *responsible* policy. Highly effective responsiveness to majority opinions that are hostile to a minority, for example, should not be seen as leading to responsible policy. But what is responsible public policy? It is easier to document responsiveness—in terms of who uses the process, how people are motivated to vote, which things pass—than it is to assess how responsible the outcomes might be. Indeed, in the chapters that follow we do not really address this issue of responsible policy. There is simply no easy, straightforward way to define responsible policy without offering normative considerations.

In our concluding chapter, we suggest that outcomes can be considered responsible if, *over the long haul,* they are consistent with democratic principles of tolerance of minorities, and if they are not fiscally imprudent. This is but one possible definition of responsible policy, and it is likely a narrow one. But on these terms, we will suggest that state-level direct democracy at the end of the twentieth century has produced mixed results, and that irresponsible outcomes might be more evident in the fiscal arena than in the treatment of minorities. We conclude that it is hard to support the argument that outcomes under direct democracy, while unique and potentially more responsive to public preferences, are vastly more responsible or irresponsible than those of elected legislatures.

NOTES

1. These states are Arizona, Arkansas, California, Colorado, Florida, Illinois, Michigan, Missouri, Montana, Nebraska, Nevada, North Dakota, Ohio, Oklahoma, Oregon, South Dakota (*The Book of the States, 1994–95,* table 5.16).

2. Alaska and Vermont place these responsibilities with the lieutenant governor.

3. These states are Florida, Maine, Nevada, and South Dakota (*The Book of the States, 1994–95*).

4. With three of these examples, there is also evidence that the "grassroots" initiative efforts were eventually financed by deep-pocket contributors. On term limits in Washington, the billionaire Koch brothers of Kansas funded qualification after activists' initial efforts floundered. See Olson (1992). The National Rifle Association financed "three strikes" efforts in some states after efforts were started independently by citizens. And medical marijuana was given a financial boost by a single wealthy donor.

5. Riker (1982) also points out that where preferences are ill formed, stable political outcomes result only under certain representative designs, rather than under direct democracy.

6. Some of the relationships we discuss from the Lascher et al. study (1996) are based on significance tests of $p < .10$, though the authors did not discuss relationships at this level of significance. In the areas of education and spending, their data indicate a $p < .05$ relationship, but this was not noted in their article.

7. Although their data suggest this, Lascher and Matsusaka do not draw this conclusion.

# Part I

# The Context of Direct Legislation Campaigns

This book covers three stages of the initiative process and is divided into parts dedicated to each stage of the process. In part 1, we examine rules that regulate how various policies reach the ballot, and provide information about the industry and actors involved with drafting initiatives and waging direct democracy contests. In part 2, we examine election results and assess how voters behave when making decisions on some of these issues. These chapters examine when initiatives are used, when they pass, how voters cope with competing propositions, whether there is consistency in voter evaluations of propositions, and what sources of information are used by voters. In part 3, we examine policy outcomes that often distinguish direct democracy states from non-direct democracy states. We examine the direct effect of the use of initiatives on the adoption of term limits and tax and expenditure limitations, and the indirect effects associated with the initiative's constraint of legislative behavior. This part also gives special emphasis to prominent antiminority initiatives that reached state ballots in the 1990s. We conclude by discussing the long-term consequences of these policies for direct democracy states and compare direct to non-direct democracy states.

Election law defines how direct democracy may be used, but federal court decisions affect how the process is used in every state, particularly in terms of how campaigns may be regulated. Rulings about campaign spending and paid signature gathering have, to some extent, created national standards that prevent or substantially limit state regulation in these areas. But direct democracy still looks quite different from one state to the next. Much of this variation is a function of state law and state court rulings. Chapter 2 provides a basic overview of the electoral rules that determine how direct democracy may be used. Readers interested in discovering the nuances of each state's rules should consult the literature

25

referred to in chapter 2, as well as Daniel Lowenstein's book on election law.

In chapter 3, we begin to look at how initiative proponents operate within these rules. We trace the rise of California's initiative campaign "industry," and then interview people within the industry to assess the specialization of tasks that has developed. California's campaign professionals reveal that there is little left—if anything—of the pure amateurism or grassroots politics that many associate with direct legislation.

In chapter 4, we examine the initiative campaign industry's role in various types of direct democracy contests. We suggest that for a large portion of "majoritarian" policies, which place broad groups in opposition to each other, the industry might have a fairly muted role in affecting outcomes. We find that the campaign industry can provide well-financed interests with some defensive advantages, but that narrow interests rarely pass "clientele" policies that diffuse costs at the general public's expense. In fact, there are more examples of broad interests defeating narrow interests than of narrow defeating broad.

# 2

# Election Law and Rules for Using Initiatives

CAROLINE J. TOLBERT,
DANIEL H. LOWENSTEIN,
AND TODD DONOVAN

As with most political institutions, the nature and consequences of the initiative depend in large measure on the legal rules that define and govern it. Under American federalism, it is up to each state to decide whether it will include the initiative among its legislative procedures and, if so, what the ground rules will be. Approximately half the states do provide for the initiative in one form or another, and in those states the rules governing the process vary considerably. In this chapter, we consider the rules governing the qualification of initiatives for the ballot; the subject matter that may be included in an initiative proposal; the effects of spending in initiative election campaigns and the efforts that have been made to regulate the flow of campaign finance; and the review of initiatives by the judiciary when they are challenged on constitutional grounds.

Although each state can set its own rules and procedures for the initiative, all such rules are subject to the constraints of the United States Constitution. As we shall see in this chapter, the Constitution, as interpreted by the United States Supreme Court, precludes certain forms of regulation of the initiative process, particularly regulation of the use of money.

# Qualification of Initiative Measures

## Signature Requirements

The most basic requirement for qualifying an initiative measure for the ballot is obtaining a specified number of signatures on petitions. The rules and procedures for obtaining signatures vary from state to state, including, most fundamentally, how many signatures are required. Typically, the required number of signatures is defined by law as a percentage of the vote for governor or secretary of state in the most recent general election. Signature requirements sometimes vary depending on whether the measure is a proposed statute or constitutional amendment. The percentage ranges from a low of 2% in North Dakota to a high of 15% in Wyoming, in each of these cases for statutory initiatives (see table 2.1).

The data in table 2.1 suggest that the stringency of a state's petition requirement is, not surprisingly, inversely related to the frequency of measures qualifying for the ballot. Massachusetts and Arizona are exceptions, but in general the initiative is used more frequently in the states with lower signature requirements. As we shall see in chapter 5, multivariate analysis suggests that other structural and political factors also affect frequency of initiative use.

## Time Limitations

The length of time permitted for gathering signatures also affects the difficulty of qualifying an initiative. As indicated in table 2.2, states vary greatly in how much time they allow. Five states—Arkansas, Idaho, Nebraska, Oregon, and Utah—have no time limit for signature gathering. Theoretically, a petition drive in one of these states could begin in 1998 and be completed in 2098. Ohio requires a two-stage petition drive, with the first stage of unlimited duration and the second limited to 90 days. At the other extreme, Oklahoma, California, and Massachusetts have the briefest signature-gathering periods. Six states—Arizona, Colorado, Massachusetts, Missouri, Nevada, and Washington—require all initiative petitions to be circulated simultaneously (Public Affairs Research Institute of New Jersey 1992a). One study asserts that in these states, each initiative campaign must compete with every other initiative campaign for volunteers, and signature-gathering firms may

**Table 2.1** Stringency of Signature Requirements

| State | Statutory Initiative | Constitutional Initiative | Year of Adoption | No. since Adoption (to 1994) | Avg. No. per Cycle since Adoption |
|---|---|---|---|---|---|
| North Dakota | 2 | 5 | 1914 | 160 | 4.0 |
| Massachusetts | 5 | 5 | 1918 | 41 | 1.1 |
| Colorado | 5 | 8 | 1910 | 150 | 3.6 |
| California | 5 | 8 | 1911 | 232 | 5.5 |
| Oregon | 6 | 8 | 1902 | 274 | 6.0 |
| Missouri | 5 | — | 1908 | 60 | 1.4 |
| Washington | 8 | 10 | 1918 | 91 | 2.2 |
| Montana | 5 | 10 | 1906 | 56 | 1.3 |
| South Dakota | 5 | 10 | 1898 | 42 | 0.9 |
| Ohio | 6 | 10 | 1912 | 58 | 1.4 |
| Nebraska | 7 | 10 | 1912 | 35 | 0.9 |
| Michigan | 8 | 10 | 1913 | 54 | 1.3 |
| Arkansas | 8 | 8 | 1910 | 80 | 1.9 |
| Florida | — | 8 | 1968 | 12 | 0.9 |
| Illinois | — | 15 | 1970 | 4 | 0.3* |
| Oklahoma | 8 | — | 1907 | 79 | 1.8 |
| Alaska | 10 | 15 | 1959 | 22 | 1.2 |
| Arizona | 10 | — | 1911 | 133 | 3.2 |
| Idaho | 10 | — | 1912 | 17 | 0.4 |
| Maine | 10 | 10 | 1908 | 27 | 0.6 |
| Nevada | 10 | — | 1912 | 27 | 0.7 |
| Utah | 10 | 12 | 1900 | 16 | 0.3 |
| Mississippi | — | — | 1992 | 0 | 0.0 |
| Wyoming | 15 | 10 | 1968 | 3 | 0.2 |

*Source:* "Historical Use of the Initiative Process," in Tolbert 1996 and Neal 1993. Signature thresholds from *The Book of the States, 1994–95*. Average signature threshold from Magleby 1994. Year of adoption from Cronin 1989.

*Illinois has unusual restrictions on initiative use. See text.

be able to charge premium rates if there is sufficient demand (Kehler and Stern 1995). However, in some instances the effects may be the opposite, because a single circulator can efficiently carry several different petitions at once.

## Geographic Distribution Requirement

Table 2.3 identifies 10 states that require some form of a geographic distribution of signatures. The goal of a geographic distribu-

**Table 2.2** Maximum Period of Time to Gather Signatures
to Qualify a Statutory Initiative

| State | Signature-Gathering Period |
|---|---|
| Alaska | 1 year |
| Arizona | 20 months* |
| Arkansas | Unlimited |
| California | 150 days |
| Colorado | 6 months* |
| Florida | No statutory initiatives |
| Idaho | Unlimited |
| Illinois | 2 years |
| Maine | 1 year |
| Massachusetts | 3 months, then 1 month* |
| Michigan | 180 days |
| Missouri | 20 months* |
| Montana | 1 year |
| Nebraska | Unlimited |
| Nevada | 289 days* |
| North Dakota | 1 year |
| Ohio | Unlimited, then 90 days |
| Oklahoma | 90 days |
| Oregon | Unlimited |
| South Dakota | 1 year |
| Utah | Unlimited |
| Washington | 6 months* |
| Wyoming | 18 months |

*Source:* Public Affairs Research Institute of New Jersey survey of
election officials, in *Initiative Petitions* 3 (June 1992).

*All initiative petitions are circulated during a single designated
time period.

tion requirement is to ensure that a proposal has broad support
across the state and to force proponents to extend their efforts outside the most highly populated counties. The effect in several
states, however, is an antiurban bias in the signature-gathering
process (Kehler and Stern 1995). The presence of a geographic distribution requirement appears to hamper proponents' efforts to place
their measures on the ballot.

The geographic signature requirement is probably vulnerable to
constitutional challenge under the "one-person, one-vote" principle. Although some state courts have upheld such requirements

**Table 2.3** Geographic Distribution Signature Requirements
for Statutory Initiative Petitions

| State | Requirement |
| --- | --- |
| Alaska | At least one signature must be provided by voters resident in each of at least two-thirds of Alaska's 27 election districts. |
| Arkansas | Signatures equal to 4% of the total votes cast for governor in the previous gubernatorial general election must be gathered in each of at least 15 counties (out of a total of 75 counties). |
| Massachusetts | No more than 25% of the required number of signatures can be provided by voters of any single county. |
| Missouri | Signatures equal to 5% of the total votes cast for governor in the previous gubernatorial general election must be gathered in each of at least 6 congressional districts. Missouri has a total of 9 congressional districts. |
| Montana | Signatures equal to 5% of the total votes cast for governor in the previous gubernatorial general election must be gathered in each of at least 34 legislative districts. Montana has a total of 100 legislative districts. |
| Nebraska | Signatures equal to 5% of the total votes cast for governor in the previous gubernatorial general election must be gathered in each of at least 38 counties. Nebraska has 93 counties. |
| Nevada | Signatures equal to 10% of the total votes cast in the previous general election held in an even numbered year must be gathered in each of at least 13 counties. Nevada has a total of 17 counties. |
| Ohio | Signatures equal to 1½% of the total votes cast for governor in the previous gubernatorial general election must be gathered in each of at least 44 counties. Ohio has a total of 88 counties. |
| Utah | Signatures equal to 10% of the total votes cast for governor in the previous gubernatorial general election must be gathered in each of at least 15 counties. Utah has a total of 29 counties. |
| Wyoming | At least one signature must be provided by voters resident in each of at least 8 of Wyoming's 23 counties. |

*Source:* Public Affairs Research Institute of New Jersey survey of election officials, in *Initiative Petitions* 3 (June 1992).

*Note:* Florida does not provide for the statutory initiative, but does impose a signature distribution requirement for constitutional initiative petitions.

(Public Affairs Research Institute 1992a), the issue has not yet reached the Supreme Court. In *Moore v. Ogilvie,* 394 U.S. 814 (1969), the Supreme Court declared unconstitutional an analogous geographic distribution requirement for nominating petitions for candidates for public office.

## Title and Summary

Because the text of an initiative measure is that of a proposed statute or constitutional amendment, it can be very lengthy and technical. All states provide a short summary of the proposal and a short title to appear on the ballot, written in most states by public officials. Not surprisingly, the language of the title and summary is often controversial and, in states such as California and Colorado, frequently becomes the subject of litigation (Smith 1996; Legislative Council of the Colorado General Assembly 1992).

One example occurred in 1996 in connection with California's Proposition 209. Proponents wanted the title to describe the measure as a prohibition of racial and gender "preferences," while opponents wanted the title to refer to "affirmative action." Survey evidence suggests "affirmative action" is more popular than "preferences," but the text of the measure prohibited preferences and said nothing at all about affirmative action. In a display of common sense not always seen when judges intervene in elections, a California court let stand the title written by state officials, which referred to "preferences."

## Circulating Petitions

### Circulators and Their Activities

In most initiative states, the person gathering signatures must attest that he or she witnessed each signing. Typically, the circulator must meet certain requirements, such as being a registered voter or residing in the county in which he or she is circulating the petition. However, in eight states—Alaska, Arkansas, Colorado, Maine, Massachusetts, Montana, Oklahoma, and Washington—the separate signature of a circulator is not required.

The requirement that each petition part be signed by a circulator does not necessarily interfere with innovative methods of circulation. For example, proponents of a few propositions in California have had good success collecting signatures by mail (Magleby 1984, 64–65; Lowenstein and Stern 1989, 205–9). Even if only a single addressee signs the petition part and mails it back, the addressee can also sign as the circulator. On a measure that draws unusually intense support, such as the Proposition 13 property tax initiative, the mailings can serve the dual functions of circulation and fund raising. In Washington, petitions are sometimes printed as advertisements in newspapers for voters to clip, sign, and mail to the measure's sponsors.

What typically happens when a circulator solicits signatures? We shall present two dramatically different accounts. The first is taken from the testimony in *Meyer v. Grant*, discussed below, of Paul Grant, the proponent of a Colorado initiative to deregulate the trucking industry.

> [T]he way we go about soliciting signatures is that you ask the person—first of all, you interrupt the person in their walk or whatever they are doing. You intrude upon them and ask them, "Are you a registered voter?["]
>
> [. . .]
>
> If you get a yes, then you tell the person your purpose, that you are circulating a petition to qualify the issue on the ballot in November, and tell them what about, and they say, "Please let me know a little bit more." Typically, that takes maybe a minute or two, the process of explaining to the person that you are trying to put the initiative on the ballot to exempt Colorado transportation from [State Public Utilities Commission] regulations.
>
> Then you ask the person if they will sign your petition. If they hesitate, you try to come up with additional arguments to get them to sign.
>
> [. . .]
>
> [We try] to explain not just the deregulation in this industry. . . . [Two paragraphs follow summarizing the substantive arguments that, according to Grant, were used to try to get people to sign.]
> (*Meyer v. Grant*, 486 U.S. 414, 421–22 n. 4 (1988).

The following contrasting account is by the late Ed Koupal, the most successful manager of volunteer petition drives in California during the 1970s:

"Generally, people who are out getting signatures are too god-damned interested in their ideology to get the required number in the required time," Koupal said. "We use the hoopla process. First, you set up a table with six petitions taped to it and a sign in front that says, SIGN HERE. One person sits at the table. Another person stands in front. That's all you need—two people.

"While one person sits at the table, the other walks up to people and asks two questions. (We operate on the old selling maxim that two yesses make a sale.) First, we ask if they are a registered voter. If they say yes, we ask them if they are registered in that county. If they say yes to that, we immediately push them up to the table where the person points to a petition and says, 'Sign this.' By this time the person feels, 'Oh, goodie, I get to play,' and signs it. If a table doesn't get 80 signatures an hour using this method, it's moved the next day."

Koupal said that about 75 percent of the people sign when they're told to. "Hell no, people don't ask to read the petition and we certainly don't offer," he added. "Why try to educate the world when you're trying to get signatures?" (Duscha 1975)

### The Issue of Professional Circulators

Because the number of signatures required is typically a percentage of turnout in specified statewide elections, the difficulty of qualifying initiatives increases over time as the population of a state grows. Furthermore, recruiting and motivating volunteers to circulate petitions is more difficult in a society that lacks the cohesive urban neighborhoods and strong political organizations of the early part of the twentieth century. For these reasons, initiative proponents have increasingly turned to the use of paid circulators in several states, most notably California.

Paid circulators are recruited and organized by a small number of specialized commercial firms. These firms make up the most distinctive portion of what is now known as "the initiative industry" (Magleby 1992; Cronin 1992; Citrin 1996). The initiative industry has professionalized the politics of direct democracy with specialized professionals to draft measures, circulate petitions, manage campaigns, provide polling, and produce commercials (California Commission on Campaign Financing [CCCF] 1992; Magleby 1988; Neiman and Gottdiener 1985; Bowler, Donovan, and Happ 1991).

Professional signature-gathering firms in California date back at least to the 1930s, but through about the end of the 1970s they co-existed with frequent initiative-circulation drives that relied entirely or primarily on volunteer circulators. In the past two decades, virtually all successful drives have relied, at least predominantly, on professional circulation firms. One study concluded, "Professional signature-gathering firms now boast that they can qualify *any* measure for the ballot (one "guarantees" qualification) if paid enough money for cadres of individual signature gatherers, and their statement is probably true. Any individual, corporation or organization with approximately $1 million to spend can now place any issue on the ballot" (CCCF 1992, 265).

As the same report pointed out, the money to qualify the 1984 initiative that created the California lottery was put up almost entirely by one company, Scientific Games of Atlanta—a vendor of lottery materials—which contributed $1.1 million, or 99.6% of the total raised for the qualification effort. But the reliance on paid circulators is now universal. Groups that have relied on professionals include not only businesses, but environmental, consumer, antitobacco, education, and, perhaps ironically, campaign finance groups. As stated in the California report, "Qualifying an initiative for the statewide ballot is thus no longer so much a measure of general citizen interest as it is a test of fundraising ability" (CCCF 1992, 265).

It is not surprising, then, that a few states banned the use of paid circulators in initiative qualification drives. However, in *Meyer v. Grant*, 486 U.S. 414 (1988), the Supreme Court ruled that such bans violate the First Amendment. Writing for a unanimous Court, Justice Stevens stated that the paid circulator ban infringed upon speech in two ways. First, circulators engage in political speech when they solicit signatures. As in the case of campaign spending, it is just as unconstitutional to suppress speech indirectly by prohibiting payment for dissemination of the speech as it would be to prohibit the speech directly. Second, by making it more difficult to qualify initiatives for the ballot, the ban suppresses the debate that occurs when measures are voted on.

Neither of these assertions can withstand scrutiny. On the first point, even circulators using the "hoopla method" described above by Ed Koupal can no doubt be said to engage in speech, and it surely would be unconstitutional to prohibit the employment of individuals to stand in public places and engage in such speech to passersby, including the solicitation of signatures on petitions that express views on issues or on desired legislation. But no such activity is prohibited by a ban on paid circulation of *initiative* petitions. What is distinctive about an initiative petition is that is a legally efficacious document that triggers state action, i.e., placing a measure on the ballot. The ban on paid circulators is no more than a decision by the state that its own ballot allocations will be influenced only by signatures obtained from volunteers. The speech activity is paying people to circulate petitions, and the ban does not prevent anyone from doing that. The ban simply establishes that the state's ballot allocation will be unaffected by the speech activity in question.

Justice Stevens's second point, that the political speech that would surround a measure is discouraged if the ban prevents the measure from qualifying, can hardly be taken seriously. The First Amendment prevents suppression of speech but does not require states to place measures on the ballot in order to encourage speech. As we have seen, a variety of procedural requirements impede the qualification of initiatives. Indeed, that is the very purpose of the requirements, since the state obviously is not required to place every measure that may be proposed by anyone on the ballot. We shall see below that various restrictions on the content of initiatives are in effect in different states. If Justice Stevens's position were correct, such content restrictions would be especially offensive to the First Amendment. Finally, about half the states do not allow for initiative measures at all. It is hard to see how making it more difficult to qualify a measure can violate the First Amendment in one state when another state is permitted to make it impossible.

Whatever the deficiencies of *Meyer v. Grant*, the ban on paid circulators is clearly not an option for states in the foreseeable future. Evidence suggests that, as Ed Koupal stated, a high percentage of individuals will sign a petition upon request (Lowenstein and Stern 1989, 194–200). The result is that positions on the ballot are for sale, with the proceeds not even going to the state. This is hardly a rational policy, nor one in tune with the original purpose of the initiative: to provide a more popular means of legislating.

*Meyer v. Grant* does not necessarily preclude all remedies. One proposal is for a two-tier system in which proponents could use both volunteer and paid circulators. However, a multiplier would be applied so that signatures obtained from volunteers would count more toward qualification. The use of volunteers would be encouraged, and it would be more difficult to succeed with paid circulators alone. Nevertheless, paid circulators could be used and the signatures they obtain would count, obviating any First Amendment problems (Lowenstein and Stern 1989, 219–23). A two-tier system was included in a package of initiative reforms considered by the Nebraska state legislature in 1995, but the package was ultimately defeated.

## Verification of Petition Signatures

After the signature-gathering process is complete, the initiative petitions are submitted to election officials for verification. In North Dakota, which has no voter registration, the state must assume that all of the signatures and names are legitimate. The remaining states allow only registered voters to sign petitions. Because a substantial number of signatures turn out to be those of nonregistered voters, or duplicates, or otherwise ineligible, proponents need to obtain substantially more than the actual required number of signatures, typically by a 25% to 50% margin.

States vary in how they verify petition signatures, ranging from verifying each signature to verifying a random sample of signatures. The latter is increasingly the more common procedure because of the large number of signatures necessary to qualify a measure for the state ballot.

Defining what constitutes a valid signature can be controversial. The voter's name must be the one listed on the voter registration statement, though states—and possibly counties within states—probably vary as to how close the match must be. In Colorado, signatures have been disqualified if an individual signed with a nickname or an abbreviated version of his or her name, rather than the name as it is listed on the voter registration rolls. In California, the petition signer is also required to provide his or address, and if the voter's address on the petition does not match the address on the voter registration rolls, the signature is presumed to be fraudulent and is invalidated (Public Affairs Research Institute of New

Jersey 1992a). Occasionally the verification process has brought to light fraud or other improper practices in the circulation of petitions, sufficient to warrant criminal prosecutions (Lowenstein and Stern 1989, 188–92).

### Vote for Enactment

The vote needed for enactment of an initiative also varies among states. Some states require a majority of those voting on the measures while others require a majority of those voting in the election. In 1996, a failed referendum on the Colorado statewide ballot would have required a supermajority (60%) vote of the electorate for adoption of constitutional initiatives. The intent of the legislation was to make it more difficult for sponsors to amend the constitution than to change statutory law. One study estimated that roughly half of all constitutional initiatives adopted in Colorado over the past century would not have passed if a 60% vote had been required (Legislative Council of the Colorado General Assembly 1996). No state currently requires a supermajority vote of the electorate for passage of constitutional or statutory initiatives. Yet the state of Nevada requires a majority vote in two consecutive elections for a constitutional initiative to take effect; thus, voters had to approve a term limit amendment in both the 1992 and 1994 statewide elections. When Minnesota voted on whether to adopt the initiative process in 1980, 53.2% of those voting on the question voted for the proposal, but a quarter of a million persons who voted in the election failed to vote on the ballot measure. Thus, only 46.7% of all voters in the election approved of the measure. Since Minnesota law requires that a majority of those voting in the election vote affirmatively to change the state constitution, the amendment failed.

## Subject Matter Constraints

In most states initiatives can and do cover a wide range of substantive issues. In recent years in California alone, initiatives have dealt with issues including taxation, political and governmental reform, civil rights, education, the environment, auto insurance, and tobacco policy. However, probably all states have at least some restrictions on what may be included in an initiative measure. In some states, an initiative cannot appropriate funds. Some states prohibit initiatives from dealing with "administrative" as opposed to "legislative" questions, and a few prohibit the reversal by initiative of a decision that already has been made by a legislative body. One state, Illinois, limits initiatives to a narrow range consisting of some aspects of the legislature. We begin by considering the Illinois limitation and then proceed to the two most important restrictions on content in some other states.

## The Case of Illinois

In Illinois, the initiative is permitted *only* for the purpose of altering the legislative process: "Amendments to Article IV [the legislative article] of this Constitution may be proposed by a petition signed by a [specified number of electors]. Amendments shall be limited to structural and procedural subjects contained in Article IV" (Illinois Constitution, art. 14, sec. 3). The rationale for this very limited scope has been explained as follows: "[The initiative provision in the constitution] recognizes that the General Assembly is unlikely to propose any changes in its basic structure, but that some changes may appear to be necessary. Thus, a method of constitutional revision other than through the General Assembly is necessary" (Helman and Whalen 1993).

Legislative term limits, adopted by Illinois voters in 1994, provide an example of the process being used to alter legislative institutions. But the success of the term limits initiative is the exception rather than the rule in Illinois. The Illinois provision for the initiative, narrow to begin with, has been interpreted strictly by the Illinois courts. In *Coalition for Political Honesty v. State Board of Elections*, 359 N.E. 2d 138 (1976), the Illinois Supreme Court ruled that an Illinois initiative must make both structural *and* procedural changes to the legislative process. On this basis it struck down three initiative proposals, including one that prohibited legislators from voting on bills in which they had conflicts of interest. Presumably, the court regarded that as a procedural but not a structural change. In *Chicago Bar Association v. State Board of Elections*, 561 N.E. 2d 50 (1990), the court struck down a proposal that would have required a three-fifths vote in each house for any bill that would increase revenues and would have required a special revenue committee to be created in each house. The court concluded that the proposal was not *limited* to structural and procedural changes, because "[w]rapped up in this structural and procedural package is a substantive issue not found in article IV—the subject of increasing State revenue or increasing taxes."[1]

Curiously, although in Illinois the initiative is *limited* to alterations of the legislative process, in at least two other states, California and Massachusetts, the courts have found ways to *prevent* an otherwise broad initiative power from being used to alter legislative rules (Lowenstein 1995, 271–277).

## Initiatives That Amend Rather Than Revise the Constitution

In some states the initiative may be used to *amend* the state constitution but not to *revise* it. This distinction, as explained in *Raven v. Deukmejian,* 276 Cal. Rptr. 326 (1990), is said to be "based on the principle that 'comprehensive changes' to the Constitution require more formality, discussion and deliberation than is available through the initiative process."

Not surprisingly, California's Proposition 13 was challenged on the ground that it revised rather than amended the constitution. Proposition 13, a constitutional initiative adopted by voters in 1978, sharply reduced the level and growth of state and local government expenditures by restricting the use of the property tax as a source of government revenue. Proposition 13 rolled back property tax rates and capped property assessments. The measure reduced local government revenue by $7 billion in just one fiscal year (Schmidt 1989; Sears and Citrin 1982; Tolbert 1996).

The California Supreme Court ruled that Proposition 13 was valid as a constitutional amendment. In *Amador Valley Joint Union High School District v. State Board of Equalization,* 149 Cal. Rptr. 239 (1978), the court ruled the proposition was not a revision of the constitution because its "changes operate functionally within a relatively narrow range to accomplish a new system of taxation which may provide substantial tax relief for our citizens."

However, in *Raven v. Deukmejian* (1990), the California court struck down as a "revision" a provision in Proposition 115 that required the state courts, in construing the rights of criminal defendants under the state constitution, to follow the U.S. Supreme Court's interpretations of corresponding rights under the federal Constitution. Although following the federal constructions had previously been a "general principle" for the California courts, the state supreme court regarded the transformation of that general principle into a mandatory rule as an improper constitutional revision. Two years later, in *Legislature v. Eu* 286 Cal. Rptr. 283, cert. denied 503 U.S. 919 (1992), the California Supreme Court considered Proposition 140, which limited the terms of legislators and statewide elected officials and which cut the state legislature's budget by about a third. Proposition 140, the court held, was an amendment rather than a revision.

In the three cases described above, the California court has found:

1. That Proposition 13, which dramatically lowered property taxes, greatly increased the difficulty of increasing taxes in the future, and predictably effected a major shift of power from local to state governments, is not a sufficiently "comprehensive change" to constitute a revision;
2. Proposition 115, which converted a general principle of interpretation of certain rights into a mandatory principle, is a revision; and
3. Proposition 140, which adopted term limits and slashed the legislative budget, is not a revision.

Perhaps judges are more sensitive to intrusions on their own powers than on those of the coordinate branches of government.

## The Single-Subject Rule

Most state constitutions provide that laws passed by the state legislature must be limited to one subject. Such provisions are only occasionally enforced by the judiciary. Several states have similar provisions applicable to initiative measures. Because initiatives are typically controversial and are often wide-ranging, serious single-subject challenges to initiatives are more common than those to statutes passed by legislatures and, in at least one major state, have had more success.

What is the purpose of the single-subject rule? Two answers are commonly given: to avoid voter confusion and to prevent logrolling. But the single-subject rule is at best an extremely crude means of achieving either of these purposes. Furthermore, if aggressively interpreted, the single-subject rule gives to the judiciary what for all practical purposes is a discretionary veto power, because the determination of what constitutes a "subject" is a function of convenience, not of applying some naturally predetermined taxonomy.

One of us has argued that a more plausible purpose of the single-subject rule is simply to avoid massively comprehensive initiatives. In this view, the rule serves a function analogous to that of the rule against constitutional "revisions," and it should be applied only against extremely comprehensive initiative measures (Lowenstein 1983).

Single-subject challenges to initiatives have had the greatest success in Florida. For example, in 1994, the Florida Supreme Court removed two tax-limitation initiatives from the ballot on single-subject grounds, though voters responded by passing a constitutional initiative setting aside the single-subject rule for initiatives dealing with fiscal policy (Tolbert 1994a). Also in 1994, the Florida court removed from the ballot a proposed constitutional initiative amendment that would have prevented new antidiscrimination laws based on characteristics other than "race, color, religion, sex, national origin, age, handicap, ethnic background, marital status, or familial status." Supporters of this proposal argued that it dealt with the single subject of discrimination. The Florida Supreme Court, illustrating our assertion that "subjects" exist in the eye of the beholder, saw it differently. In *In re Advisory Opinion*, 632 So. 2d 1018 (1994), the court stated that the proposal

> enumerates ten classifications of people that would be entitled to protection from discrimination if the amendment were passed. The voter is essentially being asked to give one "yes" or "no" answer to a proposal that actually asks ten questions. For example, a voter may want to support protection from discrimination for people based on race and religion, but oppose protection based on marital status and familial status. Requiring voters to choose which classifications they feel most strongly about, and then requiring them to cast an all or nothing vote on the classifications listed in the amendment, defies the purpose of the single-subject limitation.

In no other state have the courts applied the rule as strictly as in Florida. Indeed, Florida appears to be the only state in which the standard for applying the single-subject rule is overtly declared to be more strict for initiatives than for statutes passed by the legislature (Lowenstein 1995, 282–83). One commentator, in the course of criticizing the California courts for their permissive application of the single-subject rule, describes some of the techniques used by the courts: "The supreme court uses several artifices to avoid invalidating initiatives under the single-subject rule. Indeed, with these methods it can avoid altogether a meaningful application of the rule. These artifices include the broad manner of defining "subject," the loose relationship allowed between the measure's provisions and its "subject," the failure to distinguish between a measure's subject and objective, and the preference for delaying review until after an election. These artifices allow the court to sidestep serious review of complex initiative measures" (Minger 1991, 899–900).

Even in a state that interprets the rule liberally, anyone drafting an initiative—and anyone looking for a way to invalidate an initiative—should bear the single-subject rule in mind. For example, in *Chemical Specialties Manufacturers Association v. Deukmejian*, 278 Cal. Rptr. 128 (1991), a California appellate court struck down an initiative whose proponent defended it as addressing the single subject of "disclosure." The measure required labeling of household toxic products; disclosure of the affiliations of certain marketers of insurance to seniors; disclosures in contracts of nursing homes; disclosure of the major funding source in advertisements for or against statewide ballot propositions; and disclosure to investors if the issuer of securities was doing business in South Africa.

## Campaign Finance

The past quarter century has been a time of intense debate over regulation of campaign finance practices. Most attention has been given to the 1974 amendments to the Federal Election Campaign Act (FECA) of 1971, which created a system of publicly financed presidential elections and limits on campaign finance practices in all federal elections (Corrado 1996). There are no federal ballot measure elections; therefore, there has been no occasion for federal regulation of campaign finance in such elections. However, state regulation of campaign finance has been prolific, and in initiative states attempts have been made to extend the regulations to ballot measure campaigns. However, as we shall see, the United States Supreme Court has struck down regulations of ballot measure campaign finance that would have been upheld if applied to candidate elections. Accordingly, beyond public disclosure of receipts and expenditures, little regulation of campaign finance in initiative campaigns is presently in force.

## Limits in Candidate Races

Almost before the ink was dry on the FECA, virtually all of its provisions were challenged under a variety of constitutional theories. In *Buckley v. Valeo*, 424 U.S. 1 (1976), the Supreme Court handed down a treatise setting forth its view of the constitutional principles relating to campaign finance regulation, and upheld some while striking down other of the FECA provisions. The Court has decided several important issues in the past two decades, but *Buckley* remains the cornerstone of constitutional doctrine for campaign finance.[2]

The portion of *Buckley* most relevant for present purposes considered the extent to which limits on campaign contributions and expenditures are consistent with First Amendment rights of speech and association. The key principle established by the Court was a sharp distinction between limits on contributions and limits on expenditures. Although the Court found that both types of limits impinged on First Amendment rights, it found that expenditure limits did so to a far greater degree than contribution limits.

Given a large and technically advanced society in which all forms of mass communication are expensive, expenditure limits put a direct limit on the amount of permissible political speech, in the Court's view. Limiting contributions imposes no such direct restriction on speech. Although the Court conceded that making a contribution to a candidate communicates a message of support, it regarded the *amount* of the contribution as only tenuously related to the message. The Court denied that the FECA contribution limits would indirectly limit the amount candidates could spend, pointing out that candidates could make up for the lack of large contributions by soliciting more small contributions, and supported its conclusion by empirical analysis that might charitably be described as casual. On the other hand, the Court concluded that contribution limits impinge on freedom of association, though only to a limited degree, since the contribution as a means of association had been limited but not eliminated, and all other means of association were unaffected.

The result of this analysis was that both contribution limits and expenditure limits would be unconstitutional unless they could withstand "strict scrutiny" by the Court. However, because of the sharp difference the Court found in the degree to which the two types of limits affected First Amendment rights, the scrutiny applicable to expenditure limits appeared to be considerably stricter than that applied to contribution limits. In any event, the Court found contribution limits justified by the government's desire to prevent corruption or the appearance of corruption. The Court concluded that the anticorruption purpose was satisfied by contribution limits, such that expenditure limits were superfluous for that purpose. The Court rejected the contention that spending limits could be justified as a means of controlling campaign costs, on the ground that in a free-speech regime the government has no legitimate interest in controlling such costs. Finally, the Court rejected equality as a government interest that could justify expenditure limits. Supporters of FECA had argued that spending limits would narrow the gap between rich and poor in their ability to influence political debate. Equality presumably is not an improper objective, but in the Court's view it could not be achieved by limiting the speech of some in order to enhance the relative effectiveness of others.

In subsequent decisions involving candidate campaigns, the Supreme Court has reaffirmed both the permissibility of contribution limits, in *California Medical Association v. Federal Election Commission (FEC)*, 453 U.S. 182 (1981), and the unconstitutionality of spending limits, in *FEC v. National Conservative Political Action Committee*, 470 U.S. 480 (1985); has upheld the prohibition of contributions *and* expenditures by corporations, in *FEC v. National Right to Work Committee*, 459 U.S. 197 (1982), and *Austin v. Michigan Chamber of Commerce*, 494 U.S. 652 (1990); and, in a split decision whose implications are still uncertain, has suggested that campaign finance practices of political parties may receive special constitutional protection, in *Colorado Republican Federal Campaign Committee v. FEC*, 116 S. Ct. 2309 (1996).

## Limits in Ballot Measure Campaigns

Two years after its *Buckley* decision, the Supreme Court, in *First National Bank of Boston v. Bellotti*, 435 U.S. 765 (1978), struck down a Massachusetts statute that banned corporate expenditures in ballot measure campaigns. For First Amendment specialists, the *Bellotti* decision is noteworthy as the first decision that unequivocally extended free-speech rights to corporations, on the theory that such rights protect the public's right to receive speech as well as the individual's need for self-expression. For our purposes, *Bellotti* is more important as the Court's first opportunity to extend its constitutional doctrine on campaign finance to ballot measure elections.

It will be recalled that in *Buckley*, contribution limits had been upheld as a means of preventing corruption or the appearance of corruption. In *Bellotti*, Justice Powell, writing for the Court, pointed out that no such rationale could justify campaign finance regulation for ballot measures: "Referenda are held on issues, not candidates for public office. The risk of corruption perceived in cases involving candidate elections simply is not present in a popular vote on a public issue." In defense of its statute, Massachusetts argued that corporate expenditures needed to be controlled lest funds from enormous corporate treasuries dominate ballot measure campaigns. The Court rejected this argument as a defense of the Massachusetts statute because the state had produced no evidence that domination was a realistic threat.

The Court was oddly equivocal on whether such a defense could support future efforts to justify such regulations. Out of one side of his mouth Justice Powell said: "According to [the state], corporations are wealthy and powerful and their views may drown out other points of view. If [the state's] arguments were supported by record or legislative findings that corporate advocacy threatened imminently to undermine democratic processes, thereby denigrating rather than serving First Amendment interests, these arguments would merit our consideration." From the other side of Justice Powell's mouth came these words: "To be sure, corporate advertising may influence the outcome of the vote; this would be its purpose. But the fact that advocacy may persuade the electorate is hardly a reason to suppress it: The Constitution 'protects expression which is eloquent no less than that which is unconvincing.'" 435 U.S. at 790 (quoting *Kingsley International Pictures Corp. v. Regents*, 360 U.S. 684, 689 [1959]). In the ensuing decades, practitioners and scholars alike have spent many happy but not entirely fruitful hours contemplating what, if any, empirical showing might justify regulation of corporate spending in ballot measure campaigns, in light of these two passages (Shockley 1985).

Finally, in *Bellotti*, the Court considered and rejected two additional justifications proposed by the state: that the funds of the corporation belonged to the stockholders, some of whom might disagree with the position taken on a ballot measure by the corporate management; and that the state had the right to regulate a corporation's use of its assets because of the advantages—limited liability for stockholders, for example—conferred by the state's corporate law (Lowenstein 1992, 405–13).

*Bellotti* concerned the limit on corporate expenditures in ballot measure campaigns, and *Buckley* had made it clear that expenditure limits would be hard to justify. Would limits on contributions to ballot measure campaigns fare better? The Court answered this question in the negative in *Citizens Against Rent Control (CARC) v. City of Berkeley*, 454 U.S. 290 (1981), in which it struck down an ordinance limiting contributions to ballot measure campaign committees to $250. Unlike the statute in *Bellotti*, the *CARC* ordinance applied to all contributors, individuals as well as corporations and other organizations. As in *Bellotti*, the Court observed that the anticorruption rationale, which had provided the justification for contribution limits in *Buckley*, was inapplicable in ballot measure elections. Responding to the claim that the limit was "needed to preserve voters' confidence in the ballot measure process," the Court stated that there was no evidence in the record to support this contention.

In the 1990 *Austin* decision, noted above, the Supreme Court upheld on anticorruption grounds a state ban on independent spending by corporations in state legislature campaigns. But the idea of corruption underlying *Austin*—scornfully dubbed the "New Corruption" by Justice Scalia in dissent—was quite different from that in

*Buckley* and other earlier cases, of using campaign contributions to improperly influence elected officials. According to the *Austin* court, this new conception of corruption consists of "the corrosive and distorting effects of immense aggregations of wealth that are accumulated with the help of the corporate form and that have little or no correlation to the public's support for the corporation's political ideas" (*Austin v. Michigan Chamber of Commerce*, 494 U.S. 652, 660 (1990).

*Austin* undermines the rationale of *Bellotti* (Lowenstein 1992, 402–5). If the "corruption" that can justify limits is political distortion caused by aggregated corporate wealth rather than improper influence over public officials, then the corruption rationale is just as applicable to ballot measure campaigns as to candidate campaigns. However, it would be a mistake to assume that *Bellotti* and *Citizens Against Rent Control* will soon be overruled. The Court's campaign finance decisions have been characterized by consistency in their adherence to particular rules far more than by conceptual consistency. Still, *Austin* might open the door for certain forms of regulation that have not specifically been struck down in cases already decided. For example, a reasonably high limit on the size of corporate contributions to a ballot measure campaign committee would have a good chance of being upheld under the *Austin* rationale.

## The Effects of Spending in Direct Democracy

In *Bellotti* and *CARC*, the Court noted that there was no evidence in the record to defend the challenged regulations. Since those cases were decided, a substantial body of empirical research has addressed the issue and produced considerable evidence that large spending against a measure has significant influence on election results (Magleby 1994; Lowenstein 1982; Zisk 1987; Bowler and Donovan n.d.; CCCF 1992. Conversely, see Owens and Wade 1986). Chapters 3 and 4 of this volume also show that narrow interests—typically corporate interests—are likely to be the groups making greatest use of the costly "initiative industry" and associated campaign techniques in California. Chapter 5 provides additional evidence consistent with the findings of most earlier studies—that heavy spending against initiatives has a far greater impact on vote margins than spending in favor of measures. Whether such evidence would have changed the results in *Bellotti* or *CARC*, and whether it would result in the upholding of any future regulations is hard to say, given the delphic nature of Justice Powell's opinion for the majority in *Bellotti*.

Assuming that at least some forms of regulation might pass constitutional muster, is regulation desirable, and if so, what form should it take? Lowenstein (1982, 1992) notes two conceptions of fairness that might inform our evaluation of spending in campaigns. First, there is an equality standard of fairness that regards a campaign as fair when each side has an equal ability to advance its arguments, regardless of the group's size. Second, there is an intensity standard, under which the ability of one side to communicate its argument reflects the number of people (initially) supporting that side. Lowenstein writes that the two fairness standards may be incompatible. If one side is apathetic while the other side is actively campaigning, "under the intensity standard the result is regarded as fair although voters are exposed to a relatively one-sided debate. On the other hand, if measures are taken to assure a relatively even-handed debate, the intense feelings on one side will not significantly enhance that side's chances of success" (1982, 515–16).

If all groups had equal resources and were equally susceptible to or free from collective-action problems, then the intensity standard of fairness would be satisfied without the need for regulation. Since these conditions often are not present, regulation to promote the intensity standard would typically take the form of some limitation on the ability of well-organized groups with large resources to utilize these advantages. Such regulations could result in a move from one-sided campaigns to virtually no campaign at all. This is not a pleasant choice, but it is difficult to believe that the First Amendment or, indeed, the public interest, would tolerate a high degree of suppression, even in the name of fairness.

Public financing would be the most straightforward means of promoting the equality standard of fairness. In typical cases in which one-sided spending results from organizational and resource advantages rather than one-sided enthusiasm, public financing would also promote the intensity standard. Public financing of ballot measure campaigns would present certain technical problems that are not present in public financing given to candidates. These problems are soluble (Lowenstein 1982). Nevertheless, although some states have adopted public financing for candidates, there is no prospect that any state will do so for ballot measures in the foreseeable future.

Disclosure of the flow of money in ballot measure campaigns is an important and relatively noncontroversial means of regulation (Gerber and Lupia 1995; Lupia 1992). Most if not all states already have successful disclosure systems in place. The Supreme Court undoubtedly is an obstacle to further regulation, but perhaps no more so than the intrinsic difficulty of finding a solution that will work not only reasonably well and reasonably fairly, but that will be able to muster enough political support to be adopted.

## Judicial Review

Statutes passed by the initiative process are subject to judicial review under the state and federal constitutions, and state constitutional amendments passed by initiative are reviewed under the United States Constitution. Of course, the likelihood of a judicial challenge and, most important, of the success of such a challenge will depend on the content of the measure. Some highly visible recent examples illustrate the centrality of judicial review to the initiative process:

1. Colorado's 1992 Amendment 2 attempted to prevent municipalities from prohibiting discrimination based on sexual orientation. A challenge to Amendment 2 reached the United States Supreme Court, which struck down the measure in *Romer v. Evans*, 116 S. Ct. 1620 (1996).
2. California's Proposition 187, the 1994 Illegal Immigration Initiative, is discussed later in this book. The measure attempted to deny public education, nonemergency medical care, and other social services to illegal immigrants. Soon after Proposition 187 was passed, a federal judge enjoined its enforcement. As of this writing, almost three years after the election, major portions of Proposition 187 have yet either to go into effect *or* to be finally declared constitutional or unconstitutional.

3. California's Proposition 208, passed in 1996, imposed a variety of regulations on campaign finance and other election practices. Five separate lawsuits have been filed challenging various aspects of Proposition 208.[3] A federal judge declined to grant preliminary relief in March 1997, but set a consolidated trial for October. Depending on the outcome of the trial, all or parts of Proposition 208 might be suspended for the 1998 election campaign, though a final ruling on the constitutional issues will probably come later.

4. California's Proposition 209, approved in 1996, prohibits most preferences based on race or gender in public education, public employment, and public contracting. A federal judge enjoined implementation of Proposition 209 soon after the election, but his injunction was vacated in 1997 by the Ninth Circuit Court of Appeals. Proposition 209 thus was reinstated, but its ultimate fate must await a full trial and subsequent appeals.

## The Guaranty Clause

A threshold contention has been that the initiative process itself violates the Guaranty Clause, article 4, section 4, of the Constitution, which states that: "The United States shall guarantee to every state in this union a republican form of government, and shall protect each of them against invasion." Those who believe the initiative process violates the Guaranty Clause maintain, relying in part on Madison's *Federalist No. 10,* that the "republican form of government" guaranteed must consist of a representative government, in contrast with a "democratic" form relying on direct action by the voters. The constitutionality of a tax adopted by initiative in Oregon was challenged on this theory in *Pacific States Tel. & Tel. Co. v. Oregon,* 223 U.S. 118 (1912). The Supreme Court declined to reach the merits of this challenge, holding instead that questions raised under the Guaranty Clause are "nonjusticiable," i.e., not subject to judicial review.

State courts may not be required to follow the lead of the Supreme Court on questions of justiciability. Hans Linde, a distinguished scholar and former member of the Oregon Supreme Court, has argued that state courts should declare that the submission to the voters of certain types of measures, particularly those that stigmatize particular groups, violates the requirement of a republican form of government (Linde 1993, 1994). Colorado's Amendment 2 and California's Proposition 187 might be examples, though their supporters would emphatically disagree. Nevertheless, state courts to date have followed *Pacific States* and declined to pass on whether the initiative process violates the Guaranty Clause. A recent example was in Justice Linde's own state of Oregon, *Lowe v. Keisling*, 882 P. 2d 91 (Or. App. 1994).

## Standards of Judicial Review

A challenge to a particular initiative measure may take one of two forms, though both may be and frequently are combined in one action. The first, which we have already considered, contends that the measure is not a proper one for adoption by initiative. For example, the measure may be outside the subject matter contained within the initiative power in the state, or it may be a constitutional revision or contain more than one subject. The other form of challenge contends that the measure violates some substantive provision of the federal or state constitution.

Some critics of the initiative process have proposed that when initiatives are challenged for substantive unconstitutionality, they should be subjected to particularly rigorous review. In the words of the late Julian Eule (1990), they should receive a "hard look." Eule based his argument on the constitutional system of checks and balances, which he contended is largely circumvented by the initiative process: "Where courts are but *one* of many checks on majority preferences, they serve predominantly as a safety net to catch those grains of tyrannical majoritarianism that slip through when the constitutional filtering system malfunctions. . . . Where, however, the filtering system has been removed, courts must play a larger role—not because direct democracy is unconstitutional, nor because it frequently produces legislation that we may find substantively displeasing or short sighted, but because the judiciary stands alone in guarding against those evils incident to transient, impassioned majorities that the Constitution seeks to dissipate" (Eule 1990, 1525).

Eule proposes that the "hard look" is particularly important when opponents claim that an initiative measure infringes on individual rights or equality interests. In contrast, in initiatives where the electorate acts to improve the processes of legislative representation, the justification for heightened judicial vigilance is absent: "Measures to enforce ethics in government, regulate lobbyists, or reform campaign finance practices pose no distinctive threat of majoritarian tyranny" (1990, 1559–60).

A skeptic might suggest that Eule's position on when a "hard look" is desirable reflected his own political preferences. Certainly, many have believed, including many courts, that governmental ethics requirements and regulation of lobbyists and of campaign finance have seriously infringed on individual rights and equality interests. More generally, critics of Eule's "hard look" approach argue that it is unnecessary, a misplaced remedy for the defects of the initiative process, and may hinder rather than further the constitutional system of checks and balances (Charlow 1994; Baker 1991).

## Conclusion

In the last three or four decades, the field of election law has exploded, as legislatures have subjected major portions of the political process to regulation and courts have dramatically extended the ways in which the Constitution constrains that process. As this chapter has shown, the initiative process has by no means been immune from these trends.

Plainly, it behooves those who must deal with initiatives—whether as proponents, campaigners, or challengers—to inform themselves of all the applicable legal requirements in the particular state, in far more detail than this chapter has been able to provide.

Aside from its practical importance, consideration of the rules of the initiative game is central to the great normative and policy questions surrounding the process. The debate over whether the initiative should exist will no doubt continue into perpetuity, but for those who live in initiative states, the more immediate question is not whether the process should exist but how it does and should work. The ground rules have a major effect on how the process actually works. To change the ground rules is the most efficacious means of making it work better—or, if we are not very careful, of making it worse.

## NOTES

1. Rules requiring a legislative supermajority vote to raise state taxes have been adopted by initiative in Arizona, Colorado, California, and Washington (Tolbert 1994; see also chapter 8 of this volume).

2. For edited versions of the major decisions, together with commentary and extensive references to the large scholarly literature, see Lowenstein 1995, 507–797.

3. One of the coauthors of this chapter represents the plaintiffs in one of these actions.

# 3

# California's Political Warriors: Campaign Professionals and the Initiative Process

DAVID MCCUAN, SHAUN BOWLER,
TODD DONOVAN, AND KEN FERNANDEZ

Opponents of the initiative process have long criticized its amateurism. Direct democracy gives the power of writing laws over to ordinary citizens, as opposed to keeping it where many believe it can be sensibly wielded, in the hands of legislators. Whatever other flaws legislators may have, runs the argument, they are at least familiar with the demands of drafting, writing, and amending legislation in modern societies—while ordinary citizens are not. It should come as no surprise, then, to find a series of arguments that criticize the initiative process on the ground that voters are easily fooled by slick ad campaigns and the like, since they lack the depth of knowledge of professional legislators.

Somewhat surprisingly, some supporters of the initiative process can arrive at similar conclusions from a very different set of assumptions. For them, amateurism meant that "professional" politicians could be bypassed by citizen-sponsored initiatives, and that narrow and sectional interests could thus be defeated by supporters of the "common good." In fact, a major cause of dismay for contemporary supporters of the initiative process has been the perceived decline in its amateur status. From this perspective, what was once the province of good government amateurs has recently been taken over, and possibly subverted, by big-money special interests and their hired-gun campaign firms. In consequence, while critics of the initiative process target its amateurism, supporters bemoan its lost "innocence" and newfound professionalism.

As an example of the latter view, California's Jerry Brown, a supporter of political reform efforts and of the initiative process, declared that "[t]he initiative was an instrument to give the people the power to make their own laws, but it is very rapidly becoming a tool of the special interests" (California Elections and Reapportionment Committee 1972, 48).

The former view was expressed in the same hearings by a politician more sympathetic to representative than direct democracy. Henry Waxman, then a member of the California Assembly, commented that "PR firms and advertising agencies are packing these highly complex constitutional amendments and statutes with jingles challenging the creative witticisms of Alka-Seltzer commercials. Any legislator would be embarrassed to utter on the floor of the legislature the simplistic slogans we find on television, radio and billboards" (California Elections and Reapportionment Committee 1972, 2). Even more vehement were the words of Charles O'Brien, a representative of Citizens Against Higher Taxes (a populist antitax group): "It seems to me we are witnessing in proposition after proposition a repeated and deliberate misleading of the public and a debasement of the very . . . process" (California Elections and Reapportionment Committee 1972, 24).

These comments, from very different "players" in the California political system, speak to the same general argument; namely, that professionalism, especially professionalism in campaigning, somehow undermines the initiative process. These comments, moreover, have been frequently echoed since then. Outcomes of the initiative process, it is argued, may represent the impact of "big money" more than "good ideas" (Lawrence 1995, 74), and likely represent the triumph of the narrowly interested professional over the broad-based, grassroots amateur.

A crucial element in this unequal battle is the campaigning period. During this period, citizens, often facing complex constitutional and policy issues for the very first time, are subject to the blandishments of rival campaigns. How these campaigns are conducted, and by whom, might shape eventual election outcomes.

Given the absence of traditional guides to voting, such as party labels, the effects of ballot proposition campaigns will possibly be more consequential than the effects of candidate campaigns, where partisanship anchors loyalties and voter assessments.

In this chapter and the next, we shift our focus to the role of the campaign industry in direct democracy—both as a player in its own right, and as a vehicle through which battles between "special interests" and the "public interest" are fought. We examine three issues relevant to these debates. First, we offer a brief history of the evolution of the initiative campaign industry in California, the state best known for innovations in political campaigning. Second, through a series of interviews with professional campaigners engaged in the initiative process, we detail how these professionals perceive their own role in direct democracy. Third, we then examine how different types of groups make use of these professionals and suggest that, at least in California, seeing initiative campaigns as a fight between narrow professional interests who use the industry and broad-based amateurs who do not is too simple.

We begin with a look at the campaign industry itself. Although much of the discussion surrounding the influence of interest groups and their hired-gun campaigners becomes heated very quickly, little is known about the actual campaign industry. In particular, it is little recognized that the campaign industry has been a feature of the initiative process almost from the very start.

## Political Marketing in California: The Early Years

The contemporary criticism of excessive spending and excessive professionalism found a voice, as we saw, in assembly hearings held twenty-five years ago. As complaints in 1972 anticipated those heard today, they also echoed themes heard a full fifty years before. In the 1920s, investigations of direct democracy by the Jones Committee of the California Senate disclosed two outstanding features: "(1) Startlingly large expenditures in campaigns on such measures (2) Campaign methods and practices that constitute a menace to our electoral system" (California Senate Journal [CSJ] 1923, 1782).

By "startlingly large," the Committee was referring to seven propositions on the 1922 ballot that, combined, saw in excess of

$1 million being spent on campaign activity. Over $660,000 was spent that year contesting the Water and Power Act, mostly by the Pacific Gas and Electric Company's campaign against the proposal. In addition to these seven propositions, another six saw an additional $21,000 in spending. All figures, it should be stressed, are in 1922 dollars—which means that tremendous sums of money were being spent. These figures led the committee to conclude that "the power of money in influencing public opinion . . . presents a problem in direct legislation which the citizens of this State cannot safely ignore" (CSJ 1923, 1783).

In noting the expenditure of such large sums *before* the television era, it is intriguing to ask what kinds of campaign activities took place. Before TV, of course, there was radio, and radio broadcasts on propositions were advertised in the *Los Angeles Times* at least as early as 1928; but there were many other campaigning outlets. In 1936, for example, the chain stores and independent merchants organized into two groups to fight a chain-store license measure (Proposition 22 of that year): "Both [sides] spent huge sums on advertising in newspapers, on billboards, over the radio, from sound trucks, on motion picture screens, on automobile stickers, by airplane or dirigible trailers and sky-writing, and by premiums to customers in the various stores. Programs were broadcast with such headliners as Conrad Nagel as master of ceremonies" (Cottrell 1939, 44).

At this point we should make clear an important analytical distinction between political marketing techniques and the political marketing industry. Although the two are related, they are also distinct features on the electoral landscape. Marketing techniques, the use of pollsters, spin doctors, direct mailing, and the like can be used by party bosses, interest groups, corporations, or professional campaigners. But the existence of an enduring professional campaign industry provides a potential campaign organization to any episodic initiative contestant who wishes to fight in an election, whether he or she is part of the normal political structure or not.

The development of the political marketing industry was, of course, tied to the development of the commercial marketing sector, and the adoption of political marketing techniques closely paralleled the development of mass marketing in the commercial sector (Bowler, Donovan, and Fernandez 1996). Early on, many individuals found short-term paid employment conducting such campaigns: "[T]here were managers, party hacks and volunteers to stuff envelopes, raise money and write copy. But always, [after election day] the posters came down, the headquarters were swept out and campaign workers packed off to whatever fate awaited them 'off-year'" (Rapaport 1989, 418–19).

This seasonal rhythm changed with the formation of the first permanent organization devoted to political campaigning. Whitaker & Baxter's Campaigns Inc. was founded in California in 1930. One of the first campaigns the new firm worked on was a referendum on a Central Valley water project in 1933;[1] thereafter they handled five or six initiatives in each election (McWilliams 1951, 348; Kelley 1957, chap. 2). With this increase in professionalism came a series of initiative campaigns demonstrating the serious presence of what we now call political marketing techniques. In 1939 Cottrell wrote, "[T]here has grown up a professional class of persons who spend their entire time in managing campaigns for this or that [ballot] measure" (Cottrell 1939, 43). The phrase *has grown up* is quite revealing, since it implies the existence of firms that predate 1939.

Writing in 1936, V. O. Key also noted the existence of Campaigns Inc. He found the firm handling all phases of campaigns for candidates, as well as for organizations interested in constitutional amendments or other issues. Key viewed the establishment of such a firm operating successfully on a commercial basis as extremely significant, since it indicated a trend away from personal politics of the precinct variety toward a reliance on mass propaganda techniques (Key 1936, 719 n.15).

Key also noted that campaigning associated with initiatives such as Proposition 22 was not exceptional for the period. The same methods were employed in 1938 for and against the "$30 Every Thursday" plan, repeal of the sales tax and adoption of a form of single tax, the revenue bond act, the labor control initiative, and the highway and traffic safety commissions. The year of the chain-store tax initiative, total expenditures on all proposals exclusive of expenditures for candidates would exceed $2 million (Cottrell 1939, 44).

The industrial scale of initiative campaigning can be seen in just one 1948 California initiative that involved the distribution of 1 million pamphlets, 4.5 million postcards and 50,000 direct-mail targeted letters, and 3,000 radio spots on 109 stations, in addition to

bumper stickers, campaign buttons, sound trucks, outdoor billboards and posters, theater and cinema slides (which may have
played to as many as two million people), newspaper ads, and TV
spots. Through these means, such campaigns could reach the millions of voters necessary for a proposition or candidate to succeed
(McWilliams 1951, 420).

By the 1950s Whitaker & Baxter were not alone as political consultants in the state—perhaps "dozens" of firms were in operation
in California by this time (*California Commission on Campaign Financing* [CCCF] 1992, 199), at least several of whom started out as
employees of Whitaker & Baxter (Pritchell 1959). As the political
marketing industry matured, it also developed greater specialization. Whitaker & Baxter initially offered a one-stop shop for all
kinds of political consultations.[2] But specialization soon led to
more firms being formed. King Research, for example, provided
polling data to Whitaker & Baxter, while Robinson & Co. helped to
collect, for a fee, the signatures required to place an issue on the ballot for them—a service now termed petition management, but a
common feature of initiative campaigns even before World War I
(see Bowler, Donovan, and Fernandez 1996 for review).

A major factor in the rise of the modern campaign industry lies
in the effects of the initiative process and other election laws introduced by the Progressives that were directed at political parties
themselves. These reforms subverted the traditional electioneering
function of the party and provided the opportunity for private (i.e.,
nonparty) organizations to offer advice and conduct campaigns. As
V. O. Key wrote, "[T]he more intelligent campaign managers are
finding that money spent for radio time, newspaper space, billboards and direct mail advertising is more wisely invested than
money paid to self-styled potentates of petty bailiwicks [party
bosses]" (Key 1936, 720).

By adopting civil service reforms, direct democracy, nonpartisan
(local) elections, candidate primaries, cross-filing in primaries, and
other such laws, California's parties lost much of their influence as
organizations contesting elections (Bell and Price 1984). In fact, unless the major political parties were to line up as opponents on ballot propositions, then the role for parties in direct democracy was
strictly limited, more or less by design. Party organizations, particu-

larly those weakened by progressive reforms, are simply not as relevant when contesting ballot propositions as they are in contesting candidate contests. This left those who did support (or oppose) propositions without the traditional organizational infrastructure of campaigning. Weak party organizations and a steady demand for campaign services begat by frequent initiatives thus provided the basis for the development of an enduring campaign industry, independent of parties (see Bowler, Donovan, and Fernandez 1996 for a longer elaboration of this argument).

As this brief review has shown, critiques of the excessive professionalization of a supposedly amateur process have been around for a very long while, but so have the particular objects of criticism—the use of political marketing techniques and the existence of a political marketing industry. Thus, the critique of excessive professionalism and of the "special interest" nature of direct democracy legislation has been in existence almost as long as the initiative process itself. This is not entirely surprising, since the incentive to form a campaign industry is, at least in part, a consequence of the initiative process itself. Once formed, the campaign industry is difficult to disband. The large number of elections—both candidate and proposition—in places like California, Arizona, Colorado, and Oregon have meant a large number of paying customers desperate for advice on how to win their election.

## California's Initiative Campaign Professionals in the 1990s

Since the 1950s this initiative campaign industry has grown even more specialized—so much so that we may talk of it as a mature industry. Exact and consistent figures of the size of the California campaign industry in general, let alone that part of it devoted to direct democracy elections, are hard to come by. One reason for some uncertainty over exact numbers is that political professionals from out of state do play a prominent role in statewide candidate elections. In 1990, for example, Dianne Feinstein's gubernatorial campaign retained KRC Research & Consulting of New York for its polling services. Similarly, Pete Wilson's campaign hired Don Sipple

of Strategic Communications, Inc. to produce media advertisements (Hagstrom 1990). In our interviews with initiative campaign
consultants, none mentioned the presence of non-California-based
operations as significant players in the initiative business. It is important to keep in mind, though, that several firms maintain offices
in California as well as in Washington, D.C., or New York City.

General consultants include those who handle all aspects of a
campaign, typically contracting out with vendors for services such
as polling, direct mail, and field operations. By our estimates, there
are eighty-nine consultants in the state who fall into this category
(see appendix). Approximately three dozen polling firms throughout
the state engage in some form of survey research, voter contact list
generation, and targeting. For six of these firms, polling services are
secondary to primary services as general consultants, media and
communications duties, or direct-mail services. Firms engaged
solely in direct-mail production number in the mid-thirties as well.
Those professionals who advertise services solely as field operations
and organization consultants (activities often offered as part of a
complete package of services by full-service campaign firms) number less than ten.[3]

Consultants engaged solely as initiative and referendum consultants number less than twenty. There is some degree of overlap between those consultants employed as professional signature gatherers and those working as public-relations and issues-management
professionals. It is not uncommon for a consultant to develop an
area of campaign expertise as a by-product of other experience in the
political process. Thus, former press and legislative staff members
can find themselves employed with "public affairs" firms. These
concerns often handle the governmental relations of trade associations and narrowly based interests because of these groups' long association with politics generally, and campaigns specifically. Other
campaign professionals develop expertise in specific policy areas.
One consultant, for example, has become an expert on health and
tobacco issues. A colleague adds, "[T]he . . . process which gives rise
to initiatives, gives rise to consultants who get involved in initiatives who get real good at them. . . . One of my best friends has developed an expertise and reputation fighting tobacco concerns. He is
sought out by these people" (Interview, 18 January 1995).

As part of a general trend in the consulting industry nationwide, California's campaign professionals were able to regroup in the 1990s after several election cycles of consolidation and separation among firms. Opposition research, or "oppo" (others refer to this as "strategic research" or "competitive intelligence"), has appeared as a newer specialization as campaigns seek more information on issues and actors associated with ballot measures. Opposition researchers culling through fund-raising reports and campaign disclosure statements now number around half a dozen firms engaged solely in this business. Any organization can also contract with press-clipping services in order to analyze the number of times an issue has appeared in the print media. Others provide background information on key players of campaign committees or voting records (Guskind 1990). Two areas, fund-raising and opposition research, have emerged as campaigns have become more professional. By our estimates, more than two dozen fund-raising operations also conduct business in the state to help groups raise the resources to pay for these services.

One consultant interviewed for this project provides the following estimates for the size of the industry in California. "For 'hardcore' consultants, the number is probably in the fifty to seventy range, but there are a lot of local groups and activists out there" (Anonymous interview, 19 January 1996).

One area not included in this long list of firms and specializations is that of political law. This has become an important element of initiative campaigns. The California Political Attorneys Association (CPAA) is a loose-knit trade group of some fifty-five to sixty attorneys who provide legal advice on advertising disclaimers, campaign contribution compliance, conflict-of-interest law, and disclosure. These attorneys work with candidates and proposition coalitions often in a fee-for-service capacity. More often than not, these individuals work on and off with campaigns and are generally not as deeply involved as consultants themselves (Interview, 13 September 1996). Adding in these firms produces yet another layer of specialization to the overall picture of the campaign industry.

Most general consultants have a relationship with vendors such as pollsters, voter list providers, or signature-gathering firms. By our estimates, less than half a dozen firms operate professional signature-gathering operations, with Kimball Petition Management (KPM) and National Petition Management (NPM) carrying the bulk of the work. Grassroots organizations typically involve their members in registration drives, although this too is changing.

Paid signature gathering has been a part of the initiative process since the very first initiatives. Robinson's firm, dating from the late 1930s, was the first (and for a long time the only) for-profit full-time firm devoted to this business. By the 1990s two large firms (KPM and APM in particular) had established routines in which they contracted for signatures with subcontractors ("crew chiefs"), who in turn contracted with those who actually gathered the signatures outside supermarkets, inside malls, or in other public places. Those gathering the signatures are paid approximately 25 to 35 cents per signature; the crew chiefs earn 5 to 10 cents per signature. KPM and APM then add in their own percentage on top of this when charging their clients. Prices and payments rise as the fixed period draws to a close (Price 1992b).[4]

One common theme among both candidate-centered campaign personnel and direct-democracy campaign personnel is the homogeneity of their employers. Most consultants are typecast early on as working for one general ideological perspective or the other in campaigns, although some vendors might be less typecast this way. This is partly a product of the training received by consultants through their work experience. As careers take shape, elites—composed of party leaders, staffers, and contributors—steer candidates toward certain consultants. This arrangement continues throughout the campaign process. Media consultants with a track record in the state are joined by pollsters and direct-mail specialists they have worked with before, while field operatives, fund-raising specialists, and opposition researchers complete the formidable team. This team is usually hired by specific issue-group or corporate concerns.

In one narrow sector, for example, Larry Tramautola, a political consultant based in the San Francisco Bay Area, has carved out a niche statewide. After the passage of Proposition 13 by California voters in 1978, local property taxes that previously funded many local government functions became squeezed as municipalities struggled with the impact of fiscal stress. School districts were hit hard by this trend, notably in the areas of facility maintenance and new construction. The passage in 1986 of Proposition 62 required that local governments and districts obtain a two-thirds majority of votes in a referendum to approve new taxes or increases in taxes that were often used to service bonds. Many school districts, fearing further erosion of services, sought professional help after several early ballot measures did not clear the two-thirds majority hurdle. Tramautola stepped forward with his experience working for then State Superintendent of Public Instruction, Bill Honig (Lindsay 1996). With experience in more than thirty local bond campaigns from northern California to the southland, Tramautola became recognized as an expert in voter targeting and message delivery in local ballot measures. One observer relates, "Everybody uses Larry now, he's sort of cornered the market" (Lindsay 1996).

While most general consultants typically work for interests broadly located at only one "end" of the political spectrum, there are several vendors that provide fee-for-service operations regardless of ideology. These firms make up legal representation for reporting compliance, voter database and list generation, and signature gathering. One consultant adds, "We provide services to whoever generally wants to use our service. There are very limited circumstances under which we wouldn't provide services. . . . We always have to analyze conflict-of-interest situations" (Interview, 13 September 1996). Still another professional adds, "As a vendor, I work to provide resources to implement the poll numbers. I service consultants, and most consultants know that they can call me and I will talk to them" (Interview, 19 January 1996).

Thus, from its start in the 1930s the political marketing industry associated with the initiative process has matured substantially. The most important marketing innovation is perhaps not simply the use of commercial techniques in politics (TV ads, direct mail, polls, focus groups, Web pages), but rather the existence of this stand-alone industry, independent of parties. Once this industry developed, a major traditional function of political parties—contesting elections—was taken away and, to some extent, given to "hired guns."

The existence of this profession has led to criticism, as we saw, of excessive professionalism in what is supposedly a grassroots (amateur) political process. This has led to a related set of criticisms arguing that professional campaigners are readily able to manipulate public opinion, often against the general good and toward narrow, sectional, private interests. Needless to say, those who work in the campaign industry argue that their role is a largely passive and technical one. For example, at the same California Assembly hearings that decried the manipulative and dishonest behavior of political campaigns, Whitaker[5] stated that when they are hired

> we devise a plan of campaign. We lay it out for them and ask them is this the way that you would concur in going at the issue? Then we go through the total research, the independent analysis, shop it out, farm it out, bring it back, and then lay it out one, two, three, four, this is how we propose that this thing be done.
>
> In the campaigns that we are involved [in], we have two critical committees. One is the finance committee, the other is the steering committee. The steering committee approves every bit of copy that goes out that we propose: sometimes they change it or suggest that we go back and do it differently. So this is not something we conjure up in the middle of the night and drop on a billboard. (California State Assembly 1972, 125–26)

These, and similar, statements paint a picture of a large and sophisticated industry of professionals, devoted to supplying technical advice to anyone who may pay the bills. Against this, however, must be set the views of those critics who argue that this campaign industry is far from a passive actor, but rather is an active and damaging player in what was once an amateur process. In the next section, we focus upon the activities of the campaign industry to examine whether or not the initiative process is failing in its original intent. Among other things, we focus on how professionals see their services being used by "special" narrow interests as opposed to broad "public" or grassroots interests.

## Views from the Campaign Professionals

In order to assess the initiative campaign industry, we conducted structured interviews over an eighteen-month period with general consultants, pollsters, media producers, lawyers, and direct-mail specialists, many of whom specialize as initiative and referendum consultants in local and statewide races. All interviews were recorded and notes transcribed immediately afterwards, and some who spoke did so only on the condition of anonymity. Individuals' names are thus not listed with their quotations. The average interview was 55 minutes long.

## Waging Initiative Campaigns

In some ways, ballot proposition contests mark a very different campaign environment from candidate campaigns. In both kinds of election, however, consultants emphasize dealing with "the persuadables" in an election. While a special election campaign aims to garner the so-called "fourteen-percenters" or activists who most frequently vote, most campaigns concentrate on the remaining "eighty-six-percenters" for votes. A different campaign is required for each type of election and, often, for each type of proposition. This means there are no "cookie-cutter" campaigns, where a candidate or group can apply some type of standardized chart to navigate the waters of a campaign. Campaign conditions are often idiosyncratic, and typically very changeable. As one professional put it, the substance of the campaign can be determined by the policy issues in an initiative:

> Initiatives are a device for enacting legislation. . . . You are voting on an actual piece of state law and part of what the proponents or opponents of a measure do is . . . make an assessment of whether the public is going to be favorably or unfavorably disposed towards them. So, most initiatives' campaigns really are processes of both one side and then the other side attempting to educate voters about different aspects of the measure. And as people get more information that tends to influence their attitudes about them [the ballot measures]. There typically is considerable attitudinal flux during the course of an initiative campaign. (Interview, 13 February 1997, Santa Monica, Calif.)

A familiar refrain throughout our interviews was the important mutual relationship between consultants and the media. Campaign professionals seek to put their candidate or measure in the most positive light before the voters, while reporters become dependent on feeding the media's need to inform the public. In the words of one consultant, "I don't think that there would be any political news if it weren't for consultants . . . they [the media] need us, we need them" (Interview, 2 May 1996). But however much the media need or like campaign consultants, the campaigns these consultants work on also need media coverage. When working on a ballot measure campaign, one firm makes its Sacramento office responsible for "just going out and securing endorsements and arranging for editorial board meetings with newspapers. This is a major box that needs to get checked" (Interview, 19 January 1995).

Another commonalty between candidate-centered and direct democracy campaigns is the use of a baseline or *benchmark* poll early in the cycle, often prior to a campaign's official start. Noted pollster Bill Hamilton, commenting on the phases of a political campaign, has described this stage as "early, when the campaigns are getting organized, strategy is developed, staff is hired, and the candidate is reviewing his or her issue material, but the vast majority of voters are unaware of any candidate or campaign activity" (Thurber and Nelson 1995, 171). This poll is used to test voter reactions to issues and name recognition. Perhaps more important, though, is the drafting of messages designed to gain support or test likely objections for a ballot measure. Analysis of the content of answers provided by the sample, typically in the range of 500 to 1,500 registered voters, is exhaustive in order to provide as complete a view as possible of the challenges ahead. In the words of one consultant, "[W]e test what the public believes to matter" (Interview, 13 September 1996). This is a somewhat simpler matter in initiative campaigns than it is in candidate campaigns.

> There are fewer variables in a ballot measure campaign. You can do a benchmark poll with a ballot measure at the outset of the campaign, and pretty much devise a strategy and play it out without any significant alteration right through Election Day. With a candidate campaign, there is an additional variable of at least two candidates and their personalities which you have only a limited amount of control over. You never get through a candidate campaign without having to make some major adjustment in strategy. (Interview, 19 January 1995)

The campaign waged by activists against three major AIDS initiatives is a case in point. Gay and lesbian activists waged an exhaustive statewide campaign seeking out key endorsements to persuade voters of the dangers inherent in the passage of any of the three measures. These endorsements, from doctors representing the California Medical Association (CMA) and nurses representing the California Nurses Association (CNA), were used because of the public's respect for opinions offered by members of these professions. As one consultant relates, "Before we did a thing in the AIDS initiatives campaigns, we did extensive polling on the issue and we really found that the only people who really had credibility to the public on the issue of AIDS were the doctors and nurses. So, we ran a campaign, in all three cases . . . completely driven by the medical establishment" (Interview, 2 May 1996).

Without exception, the consultants we interviewed believe that an effective fund-raising base, combined with early access by the consultant to develop the framework of a ballot measure, provide the greatest potential for electoral success. These interviews further showed that the involvement of professional campaign advice came at a later stage for grassroots groups. Consultants in California are generally retained at an earlier period by trade and interest groups as compared to the practices of more amateur-based organizations. Based on our interviews, trade and industry groups, such as the CNA, the California Teachers Association (CTA), or the California Trial Lawyers Association (CTLA), approach a legal team to draft a proposal in order to clear the hurdle of the actual ballot language. For measures these groups are involved with, this process usually occurs twelve to eighteen months prior to the actual election. Most of the work at this stage includes coalition building and circulation of draft measures among the group's members. In some cases, this first stage can include the filing of incorporation or nonprofit status for tax purposes.

One organization that provides legal services on the actual ballot language used in statewide propositions has a multiphase campaign strategy. The first stage includes the drafting of the ballot measure. Typically, clients are presented with the motivations of likely opponents of the measure. These arguments are built from information gathered by pollsters and the findings of focus groups. In the words of one professional, "I draft the arguments for the 'no' side. Sometimes you'll see the clients' eyes open wide. I want to show them how nasty it could get out there" (Ainsworth 1990–91).

After ballot language has been drafted and agreed upon, "typically that is when you realize that you need some kind of professional help. And if you are serious, you end up with a consultant right around that juncture" (Anonymous interview, 19 January 1995). The next step includes organizing and further coalition-building activities.

The early stage of the process also includes presentation of the proposed measure to the state attorney general's office. At this step, the attorney general's office provides a title and summary of the measure. This critical juncture often involves group members in a long negotiating process with the state's attorneys. One consultant relates his experience: "The title and summary end up, for many measures, being critical to your ability to pass them. And if you can't get a title and summary that is satisfactory, oftentimes the supporters will go back and redraft the entire initiative just to try to get a more favorable title and summary from the attorney general" (Interview, 18 January 1995). Representatives of a measure's supporters work diligently to put the best face on the proposed initiative. In the words of one, "The whole idea is to try to draft something that is a fair description of the measure, but also shows that it [the draft initiative] would have a positive impact and would appeal to voters" (Ainsworth 1990–91).

A consultant who has been involved in numerous statewide ballot campaigns adds:

> In most instances, I am brought in before the drafting begins [of an initiative]. When people are doing what might be called a feasibility study I am asked, "If an initiative like this were on the ballot, would it be possible to win? What would be necessary to put together a winning campaign?" And those questions are usually asked before the initiative is written. I am there playing a role in the writing of the initiative itself. . . . It also depends on what capacity people bring me into a campaign for . . . if they bring me in as a campaign manager, then it is usual that I play a role in the drafting of the initiative; if they bring me in as a media consultant, I am often brought in after the initiative has been written and given the task of developing commercials to help pass or defeat it. (Interview, 19 January 1995)

Another important step in ballot measure campaigns involves the analysis offered by the legislative analyst on the fiscal impact of a proposed measure. By this point in a campaign, a substantial investment in resources has usually been made. Consultants claim to provide the strategic tools needed to ensure the goals of a group are met. As one relates, "It takes you a good year to get qualified for the ballot. You have to start a year ahead of time or more. We spend a great deal of time ensuring that the legislative analyst is presented with a fair and accurate picture of what the measure entails" (Interview, 13 September 1996).

## Is There Anything Left of Grassroots Democracy?

The traditional view of ballot propositions noted above can help us think about the type of groups that compete in the direct democracy arena. A major reason offered by advocates to explain why the initiative process is a good thing is that it helps provide a voice for the "grassroots," and for ordinary citizens. Such voices might not be heard by legislators who may be too timid, too insensitive, or too tied to special interests to respond to popular appeals. One of the main normative arguments in favor of the initiative process, then, is that it represents a means by which the amateur may best the professional politician. Direct democracy should thus provide access to "outside" groups.

However, election campaigns on behalf of candidates and ballot measures have become increasingly professionalized and ever more expensive as pollsters, media consultants, and PR people all take up their roles in campaigns. With an established but expensive industry available for waging campaigns, well-financed groups who have a presence in electoral politics also have a vehicle for competing in the direct democracy arena.

This might suggest that initiative campaigns are frequently likely to embody a clash between amateur "outsiders" pitted against established interests who rely on campaign professionals. "Citizen" initiatives would, from this perspective, be placed on the ballot by grassroots insurgents who are likely to resent a professionalized political elite, or who at least have different policy goals. Lacking many resources beyond their electoral size, the citizen groups would make minimal use of professional help. On the other hand, the "elite" or "special" interests would serve as the opposition, using the initiative industry to defeat "citizen" proposals.

From our interviews it did become clear that broad-based, "amateur" organizations have a different approach to campaigning when compared to many trade- and industry-based groups, but they too cannot avoid relying on the machinery of the campaign industry.

One difference lies in how early in the process either type of group hires professional help. Trade associations and those "backed by special interests or business interests, or groups that have been through the process before" usually involve consultants earlier than less-established groups (Interview, 19 January 1995). On the other hand, community-based "grassroots" groups, usually formed at the local level, are less likely to hire a consultant early. One consultant who has witnessed this notes that "the ones [groups] at the state level approach me way ahead of time . . . whereas at the local level, they may approach me only a few months out" (Interview, 19 January 1996). It is interesting to note, however, that both types of groups will use consultants.

Our interviews provided further insights into the advantages gained by involving professional consultants early, even for groups with a populist agenda. Asked about his role when approached by interests early on, one consultant related how he helped one group in a campaign: "In Proposition 186, which would have established a single-payer health care system, some people drafting that initiative wanted to make health services in California available to anyone who asked for them. And I felt that if that were the case, the opposition would point out that illegal aliens and people from other states would come here to get medical assistance that taxpayers would have to pay for. And as a result, it would be very easy to defeat the initiative if that clause were in it. So, that clause was changed and the initiative was written to cover only legal residents of California" (Interview, 19 January 1995).

Other interviews provided further insights into the differences between the use of the initiative industry by well-established and less-established groups. One of the deans of California elections expressed some of the frustration that professionals have when working with less-established groups. He observed that "sometimes when a interest doesn't know a lot about politics, they tend to get involved . . . but a lot of times they get involved in the nitty-gritty of the campaign, so they argue over every sentence of the press release. . . . [T]he small, amateur groups do tend to be more meddlesome than the professional groups, especially those who have been through the mill before. The amateur groups tend to think that they know as much or more than you do" (Interview, 24 February 1995).

However, other campaign professionals volunteered that changes in California's political environment no longer allow for any meaningful distinction between amateur "citizen" efforts and those "professional" campaigns that rely heavily on the services of the initiative industry:

> There is no such thing as an amateur one [initiative]. The best example is this affirmative action one [Proposition 209 of 1996]. Two amateurs came up with the concept. And they wrote it . . . but, behind the scenes there are a lot of professionals involved in making sure it happens. I don't remember the last "amateur" one [initiative]. Prop. 103, Rosenfield's insurance initiative from '88, well, 'he was an amateur.' [But] when you look at his background . . . it wasn't an amateur deal. . . . [Y]ou go to a local race . . . you have a district attorney who has been around a long time and has run campaigns, you have a sheriff who has done the same, you have three or four unions, I am coordinating, too. . . . [I]s this an amateur initiative or is this a professional one? The last amateur campaign was Prop.' 13. (Interview, 19 January 1996)

Putting these viewpoints together with the brief history of the campaign industry presented above, we can see an evaluation of direct democracy that blurs the distinction between an originally "amateur" process and a newly professional one. Not only have marketing techniques been used in initiative contests about as soon as they were used commercially, and not only has the political consulting industry existed since these early days, but modern campaigners of all stripes—grassroots and narrow interests—are often sophisticated enough and have enough resources to pay for the assistance of professionals. Contemporary differences between amateur and professional campaign efforts may thus be differences of degree rather than of kind. But some differences in approach do seem to exist between the two types of groups.

Overall, the results of different groups' use of campaign professionals can be surmised by the remarks of one consultant interviewed for this project. Such professionals, not surprisingly, see their importance in terms of affecting election results:

> A lot of times candidates don't bring you in until they file [but] initiatives usually come in before they start the whole process. . . . [B]ecause I am on the local level . . . I have seen the contrast between those that do [hire campaign professionals] and those that don't. . . . I can tell you that there is a huge difference. The possibility of winning when you have a consultant goes way up because it is not just what amount of money you spend, it is how you spend it. A lot of times "amateur" consultants or people who are very well intended that help someone, end up wasting a lot of money. . . . They don't know the value of taking the soul of that message and framing it in a way people will read. (Interview, 28 August 1996)

The desire to have a helping hand at the earliest stages of the process appears to be one of the primary factors affecting whom consultants choose to work with. Ansolabehere, Behr, and Iyengar (1993) argue that "most candidates . . . fall somewhere in between" on the degree of control given to campaign professionals (99). Consultants interviewed in our study do appear to appreciate discretion in running the campaign, if not control. After general ideological compatibility with a client, the most frequently mentioned factor in deciding whether to join a campaign was the consultant's degree of responsibility. This finding is in line with the work of others who have studied campaign professionals (Sabato 1981; Luntz 1988).

Through our interviews, consultants also noted that many local, less-established interests are generally not very knowledgeable about the role of political advisors in campaigns. In one telling interview, a consultant offered: "They [clients] usually come here like babes in the woods. They're really not too sure who does what . . . and even when we explain to them the process and who does what and how to do it and how it will work best, they still don't always get it. They are just unfamiliar with the process and how technical and detailed and professionalized it is, they really don't know exactly how best to do things. . . . Campaigns are really not mom and pop operations" (Interview, 13 September 1996).

Overall, then, campaign professionals see themselves as providing a technical service that they believe allows their clients—grassroots or narrow-interests—an enhanced opportunity of victory. They do not see their job as promoting good or bad legislation, but helping their clients win. Their clients may be anyone willing and able to buy their advice—given general ideological common ground.

We also get a sense from these interviews that campaign professionals might be more comfortable working with well-established interests, since those groups grant the consultant greater discretion in running the campaign. But less-established "amateur" groups frequently work with these professionals, even in local contests. "Grassroots" groups tend to ask for less help, and might ask later than more organized trade groups, but they do ask. The impact of these professionals may have as much to do with the timing of their intervention in campaigns as with the simple fact of intervention. At least so far as the campaign professionals themselves are concerned, the earlier they are hired, the more they can affect the election outcome.

Rigorous empirical research on the real impact of these campaign professionals on the success or failure of ballot propositions is clearly needed, but will likely prove somewhat difficult. We can, for example, measure the role of spending on proposition election results (see chapter 5). If the professionals we interviewed are correct, however, their impact is more subtle than aggregate spending totals would reflect. Future studies might consider measuring not only spending effects, but the stage in the process that professionals were brought in and the discretion that groups granted them.

The initial distinction between narrow and broad (grassroots) groups discussed above suggested that initiative campaigns often pit special interests against broad, grassroots groups, with narrow groups having a structural advantage due to the assistance they receive from campaign professionals. This sort of distinction is seen in many of the common criticisms of the initiative process. For example, politicians such as Jerry Brown suggest that initiative politics is a process whereby special interests push forward their legislative agenda at the expense of the common good. "Genuine grassroots" initiative attempts are said to be undercut by the high-priced opposition campaigns of "special interests." Discussions with campaign professionals suggest that this perspective might be too simplistic, as it is increasingly difficult to determine who the genuine grassroots groups are.

In the next chapter, we pose two counterarguments to the general notion of initiative campaigns as a series of one-sided battles between grassroots groups and special interests. The first is that this is only a partial view of the range of disputes and groups that fight each other through the initiative process. "Narrowly based" special interests can fight each other just as they may fight some "grass-roots" citizen effort to advance a "general public good." A second counterargument is that a more meaningful way of looking at campaigns is to distinguish between proponents and opponents in terms of each group's size and financial resources, and also in terms of when the group plays its hand in a campaign. Although the professional campaign industry might grant substantial advantages to certain groups in the initiative process, these advantages lie more with opponents than proponents.

## Conclusion: The New Professionalism in Direct Legislation

Professional campaign consultants have become meaningful actors in California's political environment. Directing which proposals are put to the voters, designing campaign strategies, and guiding the direct democracy process, California's "mercenaries of the political wars" have become intimate cousins behind the scenes of the state's politics (Green 1992, 413). Some contend that the initiative process has become a haven for special interests who are checked by a legislature doing its job well. One legislative leader has remarked, "Usually [a surge in initiatives] means we're doing our jobs and turning down ill-advised proposals that are little more than special interest efforts" (Scott 1996, 17).

California's political environment requires professional assistance in qualifying and operating a successful ballot measure campaign, but this is not something that is unique to California. In the fall of 1996, all but one of the statewide ballot measures that reached the ballots in Washington (four measures), Oregon (seventeen measures), and California (twelve measures) made some use of professional signature-gathering firms. It is hard to find volunteer efforts anymore in any of these states. But the costs are particularly high in California. As one interviewee relates, "In California, it takes money and lots of it. In order to win, you need to start early, have direction and fund-raising . . . this is our role" (Interview, 13 September 1996).

In California, groups who typically have a "capitol presence," such as trade associations, unions, major public-interest organizations, and the like, have all developed a degree of sophistication about statewide initiative campaigns. They play in the legislative arena and the direct legislation arena with equal professionalism. Consultants who gather signatures, conduct voter surveys, and formulate media messages serve this constituency and provide them a service. The days of party bosses controlling access to legislation disappeared long ago. Campaign professionals working on direct democracy reflect a newer form of access to legislation. They reflect a subtle, circuitous level of access to the (direct) legislative processes. These personnel, engaged in the art of modern campaigns, offer the tools of mass political communications to groups willing to pay for the services. From their perspective winning in California requires not only money, but money coupled with a team of skilled advisors who know how to craft a successful strategy. One consultant spoke of the skill he believes is required to conduct these campaigns: "You are trying to get inside the head of the voter. . . . [Y]ou are trying to figure out what they're thinking so you can communicate to them in language that they understand. . . . It goes past that bullshit, though. What really matters is you called up 400 people and you asked them a series of relatively objective questions, and they gave it back to you. And you want to look at their language, almost the texture of the way that they see the world so that you can figure out who you are talking to and why" (Interview, 19 January 1995).

Initiatives and ballot measure campaigns are an important nexus in the battle over California's politics. These ballot measures, the associated campaign themes, and the methods of campaigning often portend future trends in electoral politics nationwide. Much is known about the national diffusion of issues from California's ballots. In 1978, Proposition 13 ushered in a new era of antitax politics. The battle over adoption of a California lottery preceded campaigns to legalize gaming establishments in states throughout the country. In the 1990s, California ballot measures on term limits, tougher sentences on criminals, services for illegal immigrants, affirmative action, and medical marijuana stirred debate throughout the country, affecting the discourse of presidential elections. Direct democracy's campaign professionals have also been exported from the Golden

State, setting up shop in Florida, Washington, Oregon, and many other states. The diffusion of their techniques and campaign tools might have as much impact on politics in these states as the issues on the ballot.

## APPENDIX

### Composition of the Industry

Estimates of the size of the professional campaign industry in California were compiled from several sources. This method was used in order to fully capture the consulting universe and to account for redundancy in estimating the number of professionals engaged in direct democracy. Our estimate of roughly ninety regular, full-time professionals includes individual firms who assist initiative campaigns in the following areas: ballot signature gathering/petition management services, database and list management, direct mail, field operations, fund-raising, general consulting, legal services (including drafting of ballot language and compliance measures), media consulting and production, and polling.

We arrived at our estimate of the size of the industry by tracing its development through three sources. First, we culled through the listings of the trade publication, *Campaigns and Elections,* in their annual collection of sources of information for more than 300 firms. This publication lists political professionals nationwide and segments these individual firms into areas of specialization. Second, we utilized the annual listing of political consultants for California published in the newsletter *The Political Pulse.* This trade journal, published by Bud Lemke, is billed as an insiders guide to California government and politics. Third, we referred to the work of journalists who have given political consultants greater attention in coverage of California politics. Two publications serve this purpose, *California Journal* and the *California Political Almanac.* Annual selections from this later work on state lobbyists and political "insiders" proved invaluable in providing a framework with which to conduct our interviews.

### Conduct of the Interviews

Much of the material in this chapter is based on impressions of the industry we received from campaign professionals. These professionals were surveyed in open-ended interviews. A copy of the survey is available from the editors of this book upon request. Each interview was tape-recorded and notes transcribed immediately after each interview. Recordings were also transcribed. Interviews lasted, on average, 55 minutes.

## NOTES

1. In the California Assembly's 1972 Public Hearings on the Initiative Process (still one of the few detailed sources of information on the initiative campaign industry), the head of the Whitaker & Baxter firm noted that Whitaker Sr. had began freelance campaigning on initiatives as early as the 1920s.

2. Indeed, they seem to have exercised enormous influence over every aspect of the campaign, from planning the basic message to writing checks (Kelley 1956)—a situation modern managers might find quite enviable.

3. One consultant who specializes in local ballot measures relies more heavily on grassroots organizing than using technological means to get out the vote. He adds, "You've got to get people who are potential 'no' votes to vote 'yes.' And the only way I know to do that is persuasion" (Lindsay 1996). While sometimes retaining pollsters, most of the campaigns handled by this consultant are "in-house" operations.

4. See also California Assembly 1972 for an extensive, albeit dated, discussion of this industry and the techniques it used in order to get people to sign up. Also see Cronin 1989.

5. This is the son of the original husband-and-wife team who founded Whitaker & Baxter.

# 4

## Contending Players and Strategies: Opposition Advantages in Initiative Campaigns

TODD DONOVAN, SHAUN BOWLER,
DAVID MCCUAN, AND KEN FERNANDEZ

The last chapter illustrated that the all-volunteer statewide initiative, or "grassroots" effort, is largely a thing of the past. We demonstrated that a highly specialized industry has developed to contest ballot measures, and that few contemporary statewide initiative campaigns, if any, are conducted without some assistance from this political marketing industry. At first glance this conclusion might seem to lend support to those who see the direct legislation process as having been completely taken over by the wealthy, narrowly based interests that the process was ostensibly designed to counterbalance.

This is not necessarily the case. Although it is becoming increasingly costly to gain ballot access and run initiative campaigns in general, and although some initiatives generate tremendous amounts of spending pro and con, our evidence suggests that wealthy interests are rarely able to use campaign professionals to promote policies favorable to their interests. Their success lies in defeating initiatives, but this success should not be overestimated. However, in terms of marginal returns per dollar, money spent by narrow interests is probably better used defending than advancing their interests. We will examine the role of campaign spending pro and con in greater detail in chapter 5.

80

Despite the escalating costs of direct democracy, we find that organized groups with modest resources[1]—groups who represent fairly broad, diffuse constituencies—continue to place measures on the ballot that do pass. In California, in fact, measures that are promoted by representatives of broad constituencies are more likely to pass than other initiatives, and the groups backing these policies are by no means the best-financed players in the direct democracy arena. A respectable proportion of these measures pass in spite of the fact that they threaten well-organized, wealthy interests who wage expensive opposition campaigns.

This chapter examines how efforts to pass policies affecting either broad or narrow constituencies might succeed or fail. We argue that the policy content of each initiative presents a certain type of political conflict. Different policies mobilize and affect different types of groups, causing unique intergroup conflicts in any individual initiative campaign. The nature of this intergroup conflict, and of which group "moves first" in proposing an initiative, affects the extent to which money and the initiative industry might shape outcomes.

## Types of Players

We illustrate intergroup conflict between proponents and opponents by developing a simple typology of initiative campaigns that represents the different groups (or potential beneficiaries) that might contest a specific measure. The typology draws from the "policy determines politics" theme found in much of the public policy literature (Lowi 1972). For the purpose of simplifying the discussion, we borrow heavily from Wilson's (1980) method of classifying the politics surrounding different policy issues (for very similar policy typologies, see Meier 1987; Ripley and Franklin 1987; Gormley 1983). Where Wilson focused on the perceived distribution of costs and benefits surrounding a policy, we focus on the types of groups that organize to advance or defeat certain public policies. Campbell (1997) has also used Wilson's typology to classify Colorado's ballot initiatives, but in a manner somewhat different than we employ here.

We assume that there are two types of groups (or players) that engage in using the initiative: (1) Those who represent a broad, diffuse constituency who might benefit or be harmed by a measure, and (2) those who represent narrower interests who might benefit or be harmed by a measure. These players can propose or oppose a measure. Initiatives are classified in our typology on the basis of the "breadth" of the constituency of these proponent or opponent groups. We recognize, however, that as with nearly all political efforts, relatively small groups bear the burden of organizing almost all "yes" and "no" initiative campaigns (Michels 1915). Group "breadth" is thus defined also to include the groups who stand to be affected by the policy, and by the constituencies represented by the groups contesting the initiative. The concept of a group's breadth goes beyond mere size by considering how unified or diffuse the constituency affected by an initiative might be.

First, there are narrow-based, well-organized groups who seek to protect clearly identifiable interests and seek exclusive, divisible benefits for members (i.e., protection of profits, exemptions from regulations, tax breaks, etc.). They are likely to be smaller, more homogeneous, and have well-established political activities if not formal political action committees (PACs). Since the benefits they seek are exclusive and highly visible, they may have a small number of actors or firms shouldering the organizational burdens of maintaining the group's political efforts (i.e., the tobacco industry, beer and wine distributors, oil companies, trial lawyers, rice farmers, etc.; see Olson 1965). Business groups might also have advantages in organizing politically as a "by-product" of their preexisting business organizations (Downs 1957).

Compared to broad-based groups, these narrow groups should be most likely to have access to a legislature on a regular basis, and might often have some success in advancing their goals via the legislature (we will refer to these as type A players). Having well-maintained, enduring political organizations representing their interests, these groups can raise the money to hire professionals skilled at engaging in initiative politics. As noted in the previous chapter, these trade and industry groups typically employ campaign professionals early in the process of developing and promoting an initiative.

Second, there are other groups associated with diffuse constituencies that, as a result of having no clear threat to their interests or having no consensus about goals and threats, experience collective-action problems that cause them to be less well organized (we refer to these as type B players). We assume these groups often seek nondivisible benefits, collective goods, or both. As such, they lack an ability to maintain the sort of enduring, well-financed political organizations that might provide regular, enduring influence in a legislature (examples would included consumer groups, some environmental groups, antinuclear activists, homeowners, etc.). Some of these broad-based groups do have enduring political organizations that could promote or resist various ballot initiatives. However, they (or entrepreneurs trying to mobilize them) may engage in politics on a sporadic basis, thus leaving the group ill equipped at rapidly mobilizing financial resources to respond to proposals that threaten their interests.

We can think of campaigns in direct democracy as variants of simple games played between these actors. The first move of the game involves one actor proposing an initiative that changes some status-quo course of events. The second phase of the game involves response to the proposed change. The campaign, and the initiative industry's role in the campaign, are structured by the nature of the initial proposal, by the type of actor(s) threatened by the proposal, and by the ability of competing actors to mobilize financial resources pro or con. To simplify things quite a bit, we can conceive that four general types of initiative contests defined by these criteria are represented in figure 4.1. We suggest that the role of the initiative industry is most evident in one specific type of contest (type 1), and is somewhat important, though less so, in two others (types 2 and 3). In other initiative contests (type 4), campaigns are less likely to be dominated by political marketing professionals.

# Type 1. Interest Group Contests: Narrow Group Challenges Narrow Group(s)

On some rare (though increasingly common) occasions, initiative contests reflect a battle between two well-organized type A groups (or coalitions of such groups), each fighting to defend itself from perceived incursions by the other. Since proponents and opponents alike maintain long-standing political fund-raising, lobbying, and

**Figure 4.1** A Simple Classification of Initiative Contests

## Opposition or Affected Interests

|  | NARROW | BROAD, DIFFUSE |
|---|---|---|
| **NARROW** | **Type 1 Contest**<br>*Interest - Group Politics*<br><br>Trial attorneys v.<br>insurance companies<br><br>Rival fishing groups<br><br>Securities lawyers v.<br>corporations | **Type 3 Contest**<br>*"Client" Politics*<br><br>Repeal smoking regs.<br><br>Professional regs<br><br>Industry regulatory<br>proposals |
| **BROAD, DIFFUSE** | **Type 2 Contest**<br>*Entrepreneurial/<br>Populist Politics*<br><br>Bottle bills<br><br>Environmental regs.<br><br>Tax the rich<br><br>Insurance rebates<br><br>Minimum wage | **Type 4 Contest**<br>*Majoritarian Politics*<br><br>Criminal justice<br><br>Social issues/<br>moral issues<br><br>Political reform<br>(governance policy)<br><br>Broad tax &<br>spending issues |

campaign organizations, these intra-interest-group conflicts can be characterized by extremely high levels of spending. Given the resources available to each side, the players can end up engaging in a qualification-and-advertising arms race, since each player has the resources to match the other player's campaign moves. Given the narrow electoral base of these groups, the proponent's petition efforts are unlikely to benefit much from volunteer efforts, and will rely nearly exclusively on hired help.

These conflicts are often spillovers from legislatures unable to broker a compromise between interest group titans. By definition, type A groups are more likely than type B groups to enjoy access to legislatures and are more frequently successful in achieving legislative policy goals. By virtue of the access available to these type A groups, there are moments when they might come into conflict with each other within a legislature. On some occasions they reach a stalemate. The initiative industry and the direct legislation process provide them an alternative.

In California in the 1980s and 1990s, for example, the legislature had on repeated occasions been unable to broker deals between business, insurance interests, and trial lawyers regarding torts and automobile insurance. In November 1988 negotiations between trial lawyers, insurance firms, and consumer groups aimed at brokering a regulatory compromise failed. This led the insurance industry to qualify three rival auto insurance measures, with one (Proposition 106) specifically targeting trial lawyers. Lawyers responded by sponsoring their own initiative targeting insurers (Proposition 100). In the end, over $82 million was spent contesting five insurance-related measures—with nearly 98% spent by trial lawyers and insurance interests (Lupia 1994b).

In March of 1996 similar groups clashed again. Sensing they were victims of frivolous securities lawsuits, Silicon Valley business interests spent over $12 million promoting two tort-reform initiatives that would limit attorneys' contingency fees and bar certain lawsuits. The measures were awkwardly linked to a third initiative proposing no-fault auto insurance. Trial lawyers matched the proponent's $12 million in campaign spending and defeated all three measures (*California Journal*, May 1996, 9). But the conflict did not stop there. In addition to spending millions of dollars on media in March, lawyers opposing the Silicon Valley–backed initiatives employed a counterproposition strategy and drafted their own measures designed to protect contingency fees and securities lawsuits. Designed to weaken support for the March initiatives, the lawyers' countermeasures qualified late and appeared on the November 1996 ballot[2] (Borland 1996). By November, tort reformers had been placed in the same position in which they had once put trial lawyers. Business concerns spent another $40 million in the 1996 fall election against the lawyers' initiative in an attempt to maintain the status quo (*California Journal*, Dec. 1996).

These narrow-interest-group conflicts are not limited to California, or the modern era. In Oregon, some of the earliest initiatives were rival measures filed by distinct groups competing over the same fish stock. In 1908, after they were unable to reach a compromise in the legislature, rival regional groups qualified initiatives designed to block the other from fishing (Eaton 1912). Eighty-eight years latter, Oregon voters were presented with a tobacco industry-funded initiative relating to health care. The tobacco industry spent $750,000 to help qualify an initiative (Measure 39) to counter another initiative sponsored by health care interests and insurers that would increase taxes on tobacco in order to fund public antismoking programs. The tobacco-backed initiative would have required health plans to cover "alternative health providers," such as chiropractors, acupuncturists, and naturopaths. Tobacco interests hoped that the health care industry would be forced to spend resources defending themselves, rather than promoting "yes" voting on the tobacco tax. A second measure sponsored by an ophthalmologist (Measure 35) also diverted potential health care industry (or HMO) funds away from advocating the tax.

Given the resources that each type A group can bring to these contests, the utilization of the initiative campaign industry is most pronounced here. Each side can respond to proposals and campaign moves by the other—making use of law firms to draft and challenge measures, petition management firms for rapid qualification of counterproposals, and media consultants for production of ads and purchasing of airtime. Given the narrow electoral base of support for a type A group, and the tendency for negative spending to have greater impact than proponent spending (see chapter 5 in this volume), type A opponents should enjoy substantial advantages over type A proponents. The ability to qualify countermeasures can advantage opponents if it confuses voters, but it also advantages opponents by forcing the proponent to divert potential "yes" campaign spending into fighting other measures.

All of this suggests that interest group initiative-politics often leads to a stalemate (or continues an existing stalemate), where vast amounts of money are spent but few measures are passed. In the California "businesses v. lawyers" example noted above, all nine of the initiatives sponsored by these rival groups were defeated.[3] The only measure to pass from these battles was a consumer group's insurance proposal (Proposition 103, which we classify as a type 2 contest).[4] In the Oregon "health care v. tobacco" example, the tobacco industry-backed countermeasure and the ophthalmologist's measure both failed, though the tax on tobacco, a type 2 measure, passed easily despite a $4.8 million spending advantage by the "No on 44" side (see Woodward 1996).

Data in table 4.1 and appendix 4 from all California general election initiatives from 1986 to 1996 demonstrate that only one initiative passed that pitted narrow groups against each other—a measure proposed by sportfishers to regulate commercial fishers, which might also have appealed to environmentalists. These type 1 initiative contests include many that set campaign expenditure records in California (Propositions 100, 106, 207, and 211). Yet on average they received fewer votes than initiatives did overall (40.5% v. 44.6%). They are also far less likely to pass. We found that only 14% passed, compared to 41.5% for all initiatives in this sample. (This 41.5% passing rate compares to the 40% rate found by Magleby [1994, 229] for all statutory initiatives between 1898 and 1992.)

# Type 2. Entrepreneurial Contests:
# Broad Groups Challenge Narrow Interests

Many other ballot initiative contests involve a loosely organized, broad-based type B player initiating a proposal that threatens a narrow type A actor. These contests are perhaps some of the most critically analyzed initiative campaigns in the modern era in terms of the effects of campaign spending. When critics of the professionalization of direct democracy cite examples where popular support for an initiative was "reversed" due to heavy opposition spending, they are often referring to contests in this category. This is the arena of entrepreneurial politics, where nonprofit organizations, volunteer groups, and policy entrepreneurs claiming to represent broad public interests promote initiatives that threaten wealthy, narrow, well-organized interests.

Examples of policies from this arena include environmental regulations applied to industry, provisions for public access to coastal areas, minimum wage, implementation of bottle recycling bills, forest preservation, taxes directed at specific industries, and taxes directed at the rich. In each case the benefits are fairly nondivisible and are directed to a large public, while costs are borne by a fairly narrow group. The groups threatened by one of these proposals are likely to have full-time paid staff and experience with campaigns and legislative politics, and are able to mobilize financial resources to respond to the threat—perhaps even before the type B group's initiative actually qualifies.

In some of these cases, the proponent can use a large base of volunteer labor to lower the costs of circulating petitions (often using volunteers augmented by some paid help). Lacking the cash reserves of an established interest, advertising and direct-mail use might be limited for such groups. These groups often have access to numerous small contributions, but this makes it difficult to raise funds rapidly.[5] In contrast, groups threatened by their proposal are often quite small, homogeneous, well organized politically, and well funded. Opponents should thus be able to raise money quickly and make use of broadcast media. In terms of the examples above, a group qualifying an initiative that enacts environmental regulations might easily exhaust its financial resources paying the lawyers, consultants, and petition firms needed to draft and qualify the measure, leaving the group scrambling for small contributions once the campaign begins. In contrast, the threat of an initiative can mobilize affected industry groups having substantial financial resources, and as noted in chapter 2, there are no limits on what they can contribute to an opposition campaign.

This ability to raise money rapidly and without limits produces a double advantage for well-organized opponents, since, as we demonstrate in chapter 5, opposition spending has a far greater impact on the vote than proponent spending. Risk-aversive voters might simply be more responsive to opposition information than proponent information (see Bowler and Donovan n.d. for a review). Type A opponents in these situations can also use spending advantages to further complicate the type B proponent's efforts by rapidly qualifying countermeasures designed to confuse voters or kill the intent of the original initiative—just as they would use similar methods to counter proposals by rival type A groups.

Contests involving type A groups responding to type B proposals thus involve substantial advantages for opponents. In these contests, the "initiative industry" weighs in heavily as a force hired by threatened (opposition) interests acting to maintain the status quo. If spending advantages in these contests often lead to defeat of proposals advanced by "popular" (or populist/grassroots) actors, then we might conclude that the "industry" has partly subverted the Progressive ideals of direct democracy (if only in these contests). We should stress, however, that in these entrepreneurial contests, the industry and media campaigns should typically play a more substantial role for opponents than proponents. As such, if the campaign industry has any structural influence in affecting policy and public agendas, its influence is largely conservative and lies in its use as a tool for narrow interests to defeat proposals.

But opposition advantages should not be overstated. Broad, diffuse constituencies and interests, represented by policy entrepreneurs and other advocates who assume the organizational burdens of contesting a ballot measure, do have success passing initiatives. The evidence from California presented in table 4.1 illustrates that initiatives proposed by a group with a diffuse constituency and opposed by narrow interests are no more likely to pass or fail than initiatives overall.

We identified fourteen initiatives on general election ballots from 1986 to 1996 that would benefit a broad constituency and threaten narrow interests. Of these, 35% passed, a rate lower than the overall approval rate of initiatives during this period (41.5%), and only slightly higher than the historic initiative passage rate of 40% that Magleby (1994) calculated. We also found that these measures receive the same amount of voter support on average as all initiatives (44.4% for type 2 v. 44.5% overall). Campbell's (1997) study of Colorado initiatives from 1966 to 1994 found an even greater success rate (48%) in entrepreneurial contests, a rate that exceeded Colorado's overall passage rate for the period of 37%. Thus, as the initiative process has been professionalized, it has not excluded policy entrepreneurs and organizations from passing measures that benefit broad, diffuse (or "public") interests by systematically giving narrow groups the ability to defeat such measures.

## Type 3. "Client Contests": Narrow Group Challenges Broad, Diffuse (or Latent) Group

On some occasions when narrow groups resort to the initiative, they propose measures that have consequences for a broad, diffuse

**Table 4.1** Success of California General Election Initiatives by Nature of Intergroup Conflict, 1986–1996

| Type of Contest | Mean Yes Vote (%) | % Passed | N |
|---|---|---|---|
| Narrow Proponent, Narrow Opposition (1) | 40.5 | 14 | 7 |
| Diffuse Proponent, Narrow Opposition (2) | 44.4 | 35 | 14 |
| Narrow Proponent, Diffuse Opposition (3) | 28.1 | 14 | 7 |
| Diffuse Proponent, Diffuse Opposition (4) | 51.7 | 58 | 25 |
| Total | 44.5 | 41.5 | 53 |

*Note:* See appendix for classification schema.

public. These proposals differ from the interest group politics of type 1 contests in that the proposal advanced by a well-organized group involves costs that are to be borne by the general public, or some unorganized constituency. When these measures arise in a legislative context, Wilson (1980) labels them "client group" politics, since the beneficiary of the policy is often the client of the government (i.e., a subsidized industry, a firm seeking regulations restricting competition, a firm receiving a tax break). Client politics are possible in the legislative arena, if not prominent, due to the low visibility of these policies. The mass public simply cannot know the policies that are being proposed in a legislature, and once policies are passed, the public is unlikely to detect costs that are widely diffused. This gives legislators the ability to support these policies without fear of much electoral retribution.

Given that direct democracy publicizes such policies by placing them on the ballot for voters to evaluate, it is unlikely that narrow interests would frequently go this route. Although they can use their financial resources to hire consultants and to pay petition management firms to gain ballot access, they face a much "harder sell" to the general public than in a legislature, where logs can be rolled and deals can be cut. Still, there are occasional initiatives that fit into this cell. Unlike the type 1 "arms race" initiatives, in these contests proponents of client-like policies do have the resources to dominate the paid broadcast media with "yes"-side messages. Narrow interest groups might find this route necessary when their efforts inside the state legislature are going nowhere.

Some examples include attempts by the gaming industry to implement gambling and state lotteries, attempts by landlords to repeal rent controls on their properties, tobacco industry attempts at repealing local smoking ordinances, a railroad company's effort to pass a tax to build railroads, insurers' efforts to write rules about insurance regulations, and possibly, professional groups seeking to alter regulatory structures that affect them (e.g., denturists in Washington, chiropractors in California).[6]

California's Proposition 188 of 1994 is perhaps a defining example of this sort of contest where proponents have huge advantages in campaign resources. In this case, Philip Morris and associated parties interested in rolling back local smoking regulations wrote Proposition 188 and spent nearly $20 million in favor of it, much of it on direct mail (Scott 1996, 24). Other initiative contests in this cell set spending records: the insurance industry spent over $40 million promoting Proposition 104 of 1988, which would have protected the industry's profits from consumers (in tandem with an intra-interest-group, type 1 initiative targeting lawyers, Proposition 106).

In all of these cases, the potential opposition (renters, taxpayers, those morally opposed to gambling, people offended by secondhand smoke) is far less cohesive than the proponent, which can be as cohesive as a single firm. If there is an organized opposition, it could be advantaged by any "when in doubt, vote no" phenomena that might affect voting. However, the opposition can have a difficult time raising money needed to air advertising designed to raise doubts about the proposal, since these diffuse opponents can suffer from collective-action problems that limit the amount of money they will be able to raise in a short period (Olson 1965).

Again, if the initiative industry provides advantages that somehow corrupt the original ideal of the process, we might see that narrow groups such as these would be able to spend heavily and pass their policies. These are the sort of contests that some of the original critics of direct democracy feared most: relatively wealthy interests using the initiative to advance their goals, free from the organized opposition that might exist in partisan legislatures (Eaton 1912). If the opposition to an initiative remains latent, or is poorly organized, there might be no opposition campaign at all beyond press releases issued by concerned groups. Unlike the type 1 and type 2 contests discussed above, opponent advantages are rather muted here. For poorly financed or poorly organized opponents, the initiative industry might simply not be an option. Their campaigns can be limited to the efforts of voluntary groups gathering elite and group endorsements and by attempts to influence free media.

One problem that wealthy proponents like Philip Morris (or insurance companies, industrial firms, etc.) have in these contests is that by spending vast sums of money, they publicize their role in drafting initiatives, as well as publicizing the clientele politics of their effort. In other words, as they make themselves visible, they risk revealing themselves as the primary beneficiary of their self-drafted policy. By doing this, they might aid any limited opposition that exists. Citizens, it turns out, often use information about who backs an initiative as a cue when deciding how to vote (Lupia 1994; Bowler and Donovan n.d.; see also chapter 7 in this book). High levels of spending can eventually lead to media stories revealing, for example, that the group backing a measure advertised as promoting smoking regulations is a tobacco firm. Voters favoring regulations might, once they know who backs the measure, come to doubt that the measure would do anything to effectively regulate smoking.

Campbell (1997) found a very low rate of passage (1 out of 12) in Colorado for these initiatives between 1966 and 1994. Our data reveal that these are indeed the hardest initiatives to market in California, and that money spent by proponents in this arena is largely wasted. Of the seven client-politics initiatives we identify in California (see appendix) and include in table 4.1, only one (14%) passed—a measure that fits into this category fairly awkwardly (Proposition 162, promoted by public employee unions to protect their Public Employees Retirement System (PERS) from augmenting the state's general fund). Even with this measure included, the average vote for initiatives backed by narrow interests and affecting a diffuse opposition was only 28% in favor.

## Type 4. Majoritarian Contests: Broad Group Challenges Broad (or Unorganized) Group(s)

The final cell in our matrix includes majoritarian contests. The success or failure of these initiatives affects such large constituencies that they are some of the most visible, and controversial, measures on the ballot. Since the groups affected by (or concerned about) the proposals are fairly large and diffuse, the "campaigns" promoting and opposing these initiatives often extend far beyond the actions of groups that might have initially proposed the measure. With majoritarian initiatives, we often see candidates and political parties dominating the campaign discourse.

Unlike entrepreneurial contests where representatives of a broad group challenge an established interest, these proposals primarily affect another diffuse group. The opponent might also be loosely organized, or likely to suffer collective-action problems that make it difficult to stage much of a campaign (the same type B opponent from client-politics contests). The proponent's initial efforts might be driven by a policy entrepreneur or volunteer group similar to those in type 2 contests. Poorly financed groups with a dedicated volunteer base—or more likely, with assistance from policy entrepreneurs or candidates for office—frequently do qualify measures for the ballot. Following qualification, however, the formal activities of these "yes" campaigns might be completed. Furthermore, with some of these initiatives the interests affected by the proposal are so diffuse that no opposition campaign, or opposition discourse, will ever materialize.

The absence of high-end spending or professional campaigns, however, does not mean that these ballot measures are always invisible. As the scope and diversity of interests affected by the proposal widen, and as the political stakes get higher, so too does the chance that the measure will be discussed publicly and in the free media by candidates, parties, and pundits.

Indeed, one of the most celebrated initiatives in California history falls in this category, the anti-illegal immigrant Proposition 187. Total campaign spending by proponents of 187 was only $800,000, and opponents spent only $1.6 million. Similarly, proponents of California's famous "three-strikes" crime measure spent only $1.2 million total, and opponents spent less than $50,000, while opponents of California's medical marijuana initiative raised only $30,000 by the final week of the campaign. To put this spending in perspective, by the mid-1990s the average *qualification* costs in California were about $1 million (Scott 1994, 18). Despite low spending beyond the costs of qualification, each of these initiatives came to capture the attention of the national media and national political elites, including presidential candidates.

In some of these contests, proponent groups that might begin as amateur, "grassroots" activists eventually welcome the adoption of their issue by other groups, political parties, or politicians. For example, California's anti-affirmative action initiative (Proposition 209) was drafted by two university professors having little previous involvement in state politics. Yet the issue quickly became important to major political elites. Their campaign later benefited from fund-raising and appeals by Republicans Newt Gingrich and Pete Wilson, who saw Proposition 209 as a clear "wedge" issue to be used against the Democratic Party (King 1996; see also chapter 3 in this volume). There are other similar examples. Amateur activists promoting three-strikes criminal-sentencing proposals received financial assistance for the petition drive from the National Rifle Association (NRA), while a liberal political outsider promoting Washington's term limits measure came to rely upon funds from a national conservative "congressional-reform" organization after early petition efforts stagnated (Olson 1992). Indeed, some of these initiatives are designed by parties or politicians seeking to expand their mass appeal (e.g., Pete Wilson and Proposition 165).

Initiatives in this cell also include many political reform proposals[7] that change the rules about how politics will be conducted (campaign finance reforms). We also include tax measures that, rather than affecting a narrow industry or narrow group (such as alcohol or tobacco), apply to large segments of the general public. Many social and moral questions (e.g., assisted suicide, medical marijuana) and crime issues also fall in this cell, since beneficiaries or potential opponents of these policies, while perhaps small, are typically quite diffuse (e.g., the terminally ill, people fearing crime, people hostile to pot use, crime victims, criminals). In many of these cases, neither proponents nor opponents will have the resources or organization to mount a big-budget campaign.

With many majoritarian initiatives, then, much of the information the public receives comes independent of the paid broadcasts and direct mail associated with professional "initiative industry" campaigns. With these measures, rival political elites and parties are often forced to take controversial positions on public policies. As groups and elites take positions and the free media grant attention to the measures, citizens are offered alternative sources of information and elite cues that can be used in making decisions. It is important to note that much of the criticism directed against direct democracy emphasizes the possible corrupting influence of campaign professionals. Yet, by our classification, a plurality of California initiatives (47%) from 1986 to 1996 fall into this category. Thus, we suggest that many of the most prominent choices that voters make about initiatives are cast in an environment where the effects of campaign spending—by proponents or opponents—are fairly muted. Majoritarian contests thus possibly reflect some of the Progressive Era aspirations about how direct democracy would be contested (as well as the sort of "reform" issues to place before voters: term limits, open primaries, and constraints on government's tax and spending).

Type 4 contests, conversely, can also provide the clearest examples of things feared by direct democracy's critics (anti-immigrant measures, antigay measures, civil rights issues, etc.). This can be the arena where contests might reflect the demagoguery that critics of direct democracy have long feared, as these initiatives often ask voters to cast judgments about racial and social groups, or about moral and social issues. Lacking resources to campaign through paid media, opponents and proponents can resort to targeting unpopular minorities in attempts to gain public support and attention.

Most (58%) of the majoritarian initiatives we identify in California from 1986 to 1996 were approved. Campbell (1997) also found a relatively high approval rate (50%) for majoritarian initiatives in

Colorado. This should not be entirely surprising, since by definition these are contests where the opposition is diffuse and possibly unorganized. Thus, when diffuse groups propose measures that fail to threaten a well-organized interest, they have a good chance of victory. The 50-58% passage rates are impressive, considering that most initiatives fail.

When all the data in table 4.1 are considered, we suggest they illustrate that direct democracy primarily serves broad constituencies, but that broad groups face an uphill fight if they challenge a well-organized interest. Half of all measures we identify as benefiting or being promoted by someone representing a diffuse constituency (type 2 and type 4 contests) were approved (19 of 38). Narrow constituencies do have success in blocking over 65% (14 of 21) of the proposals that threaten them (type 1 and type 2 contests), but only 14% of the policies they proposed have passed.

## The Advantages of Moving Second

The role of political marketing, or possible "manipulative" initiative campaigns, varies greatly across each type of contest. While professional campaigners do interact differently with "grassroots" groups as opposed to narrow groups, their services to a certain extent are available to all players. The campaign process in direct democracy as a whole is not so much a continuing game of gentlemen-versus-the-players (or amateurs-versus-the-pros), but more of a mixed "pro-am" tournament. The sporting metaphors may be strained, but the simple distinctions of figure 4.1 allow more complex sets of group competition. Campaign techniques, and the relative weight of the initiative industry v. the "grassroots" in each matchup, are to some extent determined by the context of intergroup competition.

In addition to intergroup competition and utilization of campaign professionals, there is another structural factor associated with initiative campaigns that can affect who wins or loses. One of the biggest advantages for players in the process lies not so much in the resources available to a group, but in who moves second in the campaign. As we have seen so far, the existence of a professional campaign industry does not always give an automatic edge to one group over another when it comes to passing initiatives. Indeed, as illustrated in the previous section, it is something of an oversimplification to see all ballot proposition campaigns as involving conflict between groups buying access to campaign professionals and groups who do not. To the extent that one set of players in this process is given an edge over another, it might lie with those who oppose and move second, rather than those who propose legislation. This advantage, we argue, offers a partial explanation of why most initiatives fail. Opponents have structural advantages in the process.

Perhaps the major disadvantage faced by proponents is the asymmetry of resource deployment before the election campaign. Petition costs can range between $500,000 and $1 million per ballot proposition. From 1978 to 1986, these petition costs accounted for an average of 72% of qualification expenditures for all California propositions (Berg and Holman 1989).[8] Signature gathering has now become the single-largest expense for many proponents' campaigns—particularly if proponents use little broadcast media. Charles Price's data indicate that from 1980 through June 1988, for 65% of all initiatives qualifying in California, proponents spent more during the qualification phase than during the actual election period.[9] In many instances, including efforts by grassroots groups that mobilize volunteers to help gather signatures, proponents spend nearly all their resources during the qualification phase (Price 1988, 484). Evidence of the growing professional nature of the qualification stage is apparent from the comments of one consultant: "I think [Proposition] 187 is a great example. I'll note for you that almost all the money spent on the initiative in favor of it, was spent to qualify it for the ballot. Maybe $300,000 was finally spent to get it approved" (Interview, 19 January 1995).

Costs of petition efforts are further escalated if initiative proponents must rely upon direct mail for soliciting signatures—although these costly efforts can also yield campaign contributions in return (Price 1988). When the market is crowded and many petitions are circulating simultaneously, proponents' costs can also escalate as crews concentrate on advancing petitions offering the highest per-signature price. Lesser-paying efforts can thus be forced to pay more, or see their returns decline.

Despite its cost, however, paid signature gathering is a necessary expense for large- or small-membership groups. Most volunteer or grassroots organizations simply cannot mobilize sufficient volunteers to collect signatures within the time limits imposed. Very few if any initiatives reach the ballot in California, Oregon, or Washington without professional assistance with qualification (Scott 1996, 17; Price 1988; see also chapter 3). Generally, paid signature gatherers are used by trade associations and interest groups in California without fail. As another consultant working on initiatives noted: "You hire one of two or three major companies to circulate the petition. There are variants on that. . . . Some grassroots organizations take some percentage of the petitions and attempt to get signatures through volunteers. A couple of the anti-tax groups have perfected direct mail strategies for getting signatures. But *everybody* relies completely or to a substantial extent on paid signature gatherers throughout the state. You usually figure it costs $500,000, plus or minus $100,000, to get the measure qualified" (Interview, 18 January 1995).

Clearly, proponents of the initiative process must devote substantial resources simply to getting a proposal on the ballot, and then they may not even succeed. Once the proposal is on the ballot, fund-raising, organizing, and campaigning must begin all over again to convince voters that they should support it. Once proponents do qualify, groups who object to the proposal have a number of ways in which they may exert their opposition. Opponents, moreover, do not have to spend any resources on petitioning.[10] If two contesting groups or coalitions had the same amount of resources going into a contest, opponents would have more to spend on campaigning once the qualification period was over.

One of the most direct ways of opposing an initiative is to broadcast advertisements that question the validity of some element of the proposal. The fact that the wording of the proposal is fixed means that opponents are able to find loopholes, rebuttals, and counterarguments that apply to even the most minor provisions in the text of the initiative. Drafting "errors" or strategic miscalculations in proposing a policy, exposed through advertising, can thus become a major source of embarrassment for any "yes" campaign. While candidates may change their positions or statements, subtly or not so subtly, over the course of a campaign, the wording of propositions remains fixed through the qualification stage to the election. Opponents thus have the advantage of shooting at a target that cannot move or take cover.

Opponents with ample resources can also take a more proactive stance by fostering rival propositions (see chapter 5), including measures containing "kill clauses." A kill clause means that the specified counterproposal will supersede the initial proposal if it receives more votes. The industry or group threatened by an initiative might divert attention from its own initiative containing the kill clause by including a softer version of the original initiative in their proposal; examples include industry responses to California's "Big Green" and "Forests Forever," Proposition 128 and 135, respectively.

Opponents with legislative access have additional advantages. Some opposition countermeasures may come directly from the legislature—particularly at the local level—in the form of a referendum that can include kill clauses and/or modified proposals. A state-level example of this is California's Proposition 126 (1990), the legislature's industry-sponsored alternative to an initiative tax proposed on alcohol. Finally, opponents can resort to legal action to invalidate some or all of a given proposition if it passes. Opponents of California's immigration, affirmative action, and term limits measures, for example, each waged campaigns only to lose on election day, later filing suit to delay implementation of the measures.

## Conclusion

By "moving first" in direct democracy, type A or type B proponents are both in a difficult position: they must often spend more than opponents, must overcome voter tendencies to "just vote no" when in doubt (Bowler, Donovan, and Happ 1992), and must defend a proposal that cannot be modified over the course of the campaign as it is publicly critiqued. Furthermore, campaign professionals provide services that might be most effective when applied to opposition campaigns. Many of these "initiative industry" tools and strategies are defensive, aimed at preserving the status quo in response to a threatening initiative.

If we think in terms of the discussion in the first section of this chapter, opponent advantages could be most pronounced for those narrow groups who make full use of the initiative industry. To be sure, proponents can try to protect themselves from some of the advantages that opponents possess. Care in drafting, for example, can reduce the scope for opposition exploitation of embarrassing loopholes and unpopular provisions. But the larger point is that opponents of a given proposal have a wider range of strategies open to them than do proponents. Little wonder, then, that approximately more than 60% of ballot propositions fail.

Combining the findings from the first section with the discussion above, we find that direct democracy is a rather conservative process: it is difficult to pass things, and even more difficult to pass something that threatens the well-established interests. By this measure, it might be said that the initiative process—at least outside of the arena of majoritarian policies—has not met the Progressive reformers' expectations that public policy would better reflect the demands of broad, "public" interests. The contemporary process does not make it easy for advocates of large, diffuse, public benefits to take on "the interests."

There are, nevertheless, successful campaigns in this area. Indeed, there are far more examples from California of broad public groups (or entrepreneurs representing broad groups) using the initiative to defeat narrow interests than there are examples of narrow interests being advanced at the expense of a diffuse constituency. In the period covered by these data, voters approved rebates from the insurance industry, health advocates raised cigarette taxes, the minimum wage was increased, and worker safety regulations were reinvigorated, all through direct citizen legislation that threatened fairly wealthy, narrow interests. The public also came within a hair (1%) of voting to increase the income tax on the rich. "Clientele" politics, something that characterizes much of the politics of legislative policy making, is largely absent here. Although state-level direct democracy does not resemble "grassroots" populism, those policies that do come out of the process typically serve a broad constituency.

# APPENDIX

Classification of All California General Election Initiative Contests, 1986–1996

| Proposition Number | Issue | Proponent v. Opponent[a] | Type of Contest | Yes Vote (%) |
|---|---|---|---|---|
| 61 | Public employee pay | Taxpayers v. public employee unions | 2 | 34 |
| 62 | Taxes | Taxpayers v. general fund[b] | 4 | 58 |
| 63 | English only | Volunteers v. citizens | 4 | 73 |
| 64 | AIDS | Larouche | 4 | 29 |
| 65 | Toxics regulations | Volunteers v. citizens | 4 | 63 |
| 95 | Homeless funds | Volunteers v. business | 2 | 45 |
| 96 | AIDS tests | Law enforcement | 4 | 62 |
| 97 | Calif. OSHA | Labor v. business | 2 | 54 |
| 98 | School funding | Public education v. taxpayers | 4 | 51 |
| 99 | Cigarette tax/ health education | Education & health v. industry | 2 | 58 |
| 100 | Auto insurance | Lawyers v. insurers | 1 | 41 |
| 101 | Auto insurance | One firm v. consumers | 3 | 13 |
| 102 | AIDS tests | Dannemeyer | 4 | 34 |
| 103 | Auto insurance | Consumers v. insurers | 2 | 51 |
| 104 | Auto insurance | Insurers v. consumers | 3 | 25 |
| 105 | Public disclosure | Consumers v. business | 2 | 54 |
| 106 | Auto insurance | Insurers v. lawyers | 1 | 46 |
| 128 | Environmental regulations | Greens v. industry | 2 | 36 |
| 129 | Crime prevention | Candidate v. taxpayers | 4 | 28 |
| 130 | Forest regulations | Greens v. industry | 2 | 47 |
| 131 | Term limits | Voters v. legislature | 4 | 38 |
| 132 | Gill nets | Sport v. commercial fishers | 1 | 56 |
| 133 | Drug enforcement | Candidate v. taxpayers | 4 | 32 |
| 134 | Drink tax | Public health v. liquor industry | 2 | 31 |
| 135 | Pesticides | Industry v. greens | 3 | 30 |

*continued*

Classification of All California General Election Initiative Contests, 1986–1996 (continued)

| Proposition Number | Issue | Proponent v. Opponent[a] | Type of Contest | Yes Vote (%) |
|---|---|---|---|---|
| 136 | Tax increase reforms | Taxpayers v. general fund[b] | 4 | 48 |
| 137 | Initiative reforms | Voters v. legislature | 4 | 45 |
| 138 | Forest regulations | Industry v. greens | 3 | 29 |
| 139 | Prison labor | Government v. labor | 4 | 54 |
| 140 | Term limits | Voters v. legislature | 4 | 52 |
| 161 | Suicide | Hemlock v. CMA/ church | 4 | 46 |
| 162 | PERS funds | Unions v. general fund | 3 | 51 |
| 163 | Repeal snack tax | Industry/Taxpayers v. general fund | 4 or 3 | 66 |
| 164 | Term limits | Voters v. legislature | 4 | 62 |
| 165 | Welfare | Welfare v. general fund | 4 | 46 |
| 166 | Health care | Uninsured v. insurers | 2 | 32 |
| 167 | Tax the rich | Unions, etc. v. business | 2 | 42 |
| 184 | Strikes/crime | No opponent | 4 | 72 |
| 185 | Gas tax | SP RR v. taxpayers | 3 | 19 |
| 186 | Health care | Uninsured v. insurers | 2 | 29 |
| 187 | Illegal immigrants | Taxpayers v. immigrants | 4 | 59 |
| 188 | Smoking regulations | Philip Morris v. volunteer groups | 3 | 30 |
| 207 | Lawsuits | Lawyers v. corporations | 1 | 34 |
| 208 | Campaign reform | Public interest group v. parties | 4 | 61 |
| 209 | Affirmative action | Party v. party | 4 | 54 |
| 210 | Minimum wage | Labor v. business | 2 | 62 |
| 211 | Securities | One lawyer v. corporations | 1 | 26 |
| 212 | Campaign reform | Public interest group v. parties | 4 | 49 |
| 213 | Limit drunk driver rights | Quackenbush | 4 (?) | 77 |
| 214 | HMO regulations | CA Chamber of Commerce v. SEIU | 1 | 42 |

Classification of All California General Election Initiative Contests, 1986–1996 *(continued)*

| Proposition Number | Issue | Proponent v. Opponent[a] | Type of Contest | Yes Vote (%) |
|---|---|---|---|---|
| 215 | Medical marijuana | Volunteers v. government/law enforcement | 4 | 56 |
| 216 | HMO regulations | CA Chamber of Commerce v. nurses | 1 | 39 |
| 217 | Top tax bracket | Populists v. business | 2 | 49 |
| 218 | Property tax limits | Taxpayers v. general fund | 4 | 56 |

[a]This classification is based primarily on the organized groups contesting the campaign. It also relies on evaluations of the unorganized groups who will benefit or lose from the policy. The groups benefiting might not necessarily be actively associated with the proposing groups.

[b]If a proposal affects public spending by allocating existing funds to new programs, or changes rules about revenue used in the general fund, the individuals affected include those benefiting from other programs supported by general funds.

## NOTES

1. "Modest" relative to the wealthier industry and trade groups that contest initiatives.

2. California moved its primary from June to March in 1996. This affected the timing of qualification for the counterproposition.

3. These include Proposition 100, Proposition 101, Proposition 104, and Proposition 106 of November 1988; Proposition 200, Proposition 201, and Proposition 202 of March 1996; and Proposition 207 and Proposition 211 of November 1996.

4. We would categorize the proponents of Proposition 103 (Harvey Rosenfield and Ralph Nader) as reflecting a broad-based group traditionally suffering from collective-action problems that inhibit mobilization (consumers groups). As noted by professional campaigners in the previous chapter, Rosenfield's efforts, while representing a broad constituency, are not necessarily amateur politics.

5. However, the CCCF report (1992, 265) indicates that there are some wealthy individuals who now single-handedly bankroll the campaigns and qualification of a few consumer-oriented and environmental initiatives.

6. Sometimes these type 3 initiative contests can trigger opposition from well-organized groups. Gambling initiatives often establish a state lottery where none existed previously and generate little opposition from existing gaming interests. In some states, however, gambling initiatives will divide an existing industry over issues concerning what forms of betting (horses, video, slots, table games, etc.) may be located where (Arkansas, Washington). Likewise, if dentists viewed denturists as a grave economic threat, or if orthopedists perceived chiropractors this way, and each group mobilized substantial resources for media campaigns, some type 3 professional regulation initiatives could be classified as type 1 contests.

7. It may seem odd to consider choices about institutional reform policies (e.g., term limits) in terms of a conflict between diffuse groups, rather than a battle between a group and the state or between diffused supporters and a narrow opposition. However, the "state" itself cannot directly engage in campaigns; instead, the state's "interest" is furthered by a set of private actors. Parties, furthermore, are very broad coalitions of diffuse interests.

8. One reason for high costs is that only the signatures of registered voters count, which requires signature gatherers to collect more than the bare minimum required by law. Other qualification costs can include legal expenses, consulting fees, exploratory polling, and fund-raising.

9. Propositions must qualify several months before the actual election.

10. We should note that opposition groups occasionally become active in the qualification stage. Examples include the California Teachers Association's (CTA) organized efforts to discourage people from signing petitions for a school choice initiative. CTA members tracked paid signature gatherers and asked people not to sign. They claimed to have succeeded in delaying qualification until a higher-turnout general election. Other examples include "decline to sign" campaigns organized to counter antigay initiative petitions.

# Part II

## Elections and Voters

The rise of the initiative industry, the use of initiatives as vehicles for individual candidates, and the renewed use of initiatives by issue groups since the 1970s mean that more issues are reaching the ballot in many direct democracy states. In Oregon, California, Arizona, and North Dakota, a single ballot might have a dozen or more state propositions. With the diffusion of the California-based petition management industry and initiative consultants to other states, we might anticipate that even more state ballots will eventually resemble Oregon and California. In chapter 5, we examine when these initiatives are most likely to be used, and assess factors that explain why they pass or fail.

As illustrated in part 1, a broad-based group might occasionally qualify an environmental-regulation initiative or a proconsumer initiative that threatens some narrow, well-organized interests (a type 2 contest). Using the tools of paid signature gathering and the modern initiative industry, opponents can rapidly qualify a counterproposal to be placed on the same ballot as the initiative that threatens some well-organized interest. Little is known about how voters respond to the strategies employed by the modern initiative industry. As Susan Banducci illustrates in chapter 5, these counterinitiatives do appear to be associated with increased negative voting.

Crowded ballots and competing initiatives can be expected to place substantial demands on the individual voter. To some, finding that voters say "no" to competing initiatives might suggest that confused voters simply say "no," and are thus easily manipulated by the initiative industry's tactics and campaigns. Yet other chapters in this section demonstrate that individual voter behavior and attitudes under direct democracy need not be viewed as confused, capricious, or random. Rather, voters appear to respond predictably to information about initiatives and appear to show some consistency in attitude across numerous propositions.

In chapter 6, Banducci assesses how voters reason under the difficult decision context associated with competing initiatives. She studies voted ballots from Oregon to examine if voters are consistent in their attitudes across multiple initiatives, and she determines that choices on propositions do reflect some degree of ideological consistency.

In chapter 7, Jeff Karp builds on work by Lupia (1994b) and Zaller (1992) and examines voter decision making on a term limit initiative. He illustrates that many voters take cues from party elites when deciding how to vote, and that they can obtain these cues from easily accessible media sources. This is an important finding, given the discussion of majoritarian initiative politics in the previous section. For many majoritarian policies like term limit initiatives, voters have ample opportunity to learn where politicians stand on ballot issues. Karp's chapter illustrates how voters get this information, and how they might use it to figure out if they are for or against an initiative.

# 5

## Direct Legislation: When Is It Used and When Does It Pass?

SUSAN A. BANDUCCI

After a decline in popularity in the 1950s, there was a resurgence of interest in direct legislation in the late 1970s and early 1980s. In a 10-year period beginning with 1983, 291 initiatives appeared on statewide ballots, whereas only 97 initiatives appeared from 1962 to 1972. The increase in initiative use has continued into the 1990s. In 1994, the number of initiatives appearing on ballots increased to 73.[1] The latest growth of interest mirrors the decline of political parties, the rise of single-issue interest groups, an increase in the public's dissatisfaction with legislative effectiveness (California Commission on Campaign Financing [CCCF] 1992), and the growth of a direct legislation industry that makes qualifying initiatives for the ballot easier (Magleby 1984; see also chapters 3 and 4 in this book). During this latest growth in use, the initiative has had profound effects on the institutions of representative democracy (Magleby 1990). In its report on the initiative industry in California, the CCCF (1992) argued that there had been a shift of power between the state legislature and the electorate and that increasingly, most important policy decisions are made in initiative elections.

Accompanying this trend of increased initiative use by citizens and state legislators (Magleby 1988) is a trend of increasing use of counterproposals in direct legislation elections (Holman and Stodder 1991; McKenna 1990; Stodder 1992) as well as in local ballot measure elections (Glickfeld, Graymer, and Morrison 1987). Competing measures may appear on a ballot for three reasons. First, a legislature may place an alternative measure on the ballot either because it does not approve of an initiative proposed through the indirect initiative process or because it feels the initiative is too extreme. Likewise, interest groups or political activists may also qualify an initiative to counter another initiative that might threaten them. They might propose a countermeasure that is more moderate in the hope that the public can be persuaded to select the most moderate change in the status quo.

More likely, however, interest groups can propose a competing measure in an effort to prevent any policy contrary to their interests from passing. In these cases, the more moderate alternative measure might simply be meant to confuse voters so that they vote "no" on both initiatives, maintaining the status quo. Most of the increase in initiative and counterinitiative use has occurred in western states, and tremendous variation exists in how frequently citizen-initiated legislation is used in direct legislation states. In this chapter, I examine several explanations for the cross-state variation in use of initiatives and counterinitiatives, and I assess the effectiveness of the countermeasure strategy at maintaining the status quo.

## Interstate Variation in Direct Legislation Use

In chapter 2, table 2.1 shows the total number of initiatives qualifying for ballots from the period of state adoption to 1994. Although the use of legislatively referred measures and referenda also vary across states, table 2.1 only examines propositions initiated by citizen petition, since the increase in direct legislation is most pronounced among initiatives (Magleby 1988). Direct and indirect initiatives[2] have been included, while constitutional amendments and statutes are listed separately for the purpose of illustration.

In order to count counterpropositions, I examined the content of ballot propositions occurring on statewide ballots in each initiative state. Initiatives were coded as "competing" if they contained conflicting provisions. Provisions are conflicting when one initiative is designed with language that addresses a subject differently than language contained in a rival measure on the same subject. Initiatives with similar subjects will often appear on ballots; however, they do not always contain conflicting provisions. For example, two abortion initiatives appeared on the Oregon ballot in the 1990 general election. One initiative banned all abortions except in cases of rape or incest or to preserve the life of the mother. The other initiative required parental consent for a minor wishing to obtain an abortion. In these cases, the initiatives were not coded as "counter," since provisions did not conflict.

From table 2.1 it is readily apparent that there is a great disparity in the use of initiatives between states and between regions. The citizens of Oregon have placed the most initiatives on the ballot, while the citizens of Wyoming have placed the least. Wyoming adopted the statutory initiative in 1968, but 1992 was the first election in which citizen-initiated measures appeared on the ballot. California and Oregon led in the total number of initiatives as well as in the total number of counterpropositions. Most of the high-use states, where the average use of initiatives is three or more per two-year election cycle, are in the West (with the exception of North Dakota). Price (1975) explains that the initiative was adopted in these states when they were relatively new to the union and their political institutions were not yet firmly established; therefore, the citizen-initiated petition may have become a more routine process. Although Oregon has had more initiatives qualify for the ballot since the states began using initiatives in 1902, California has exceeded all others states in initiative use in recent years, leading the CCCF (1992) to call direct democracy California's "fourth branch" of government.

## The California Experience

There have been several instances of counterpropositions in California on issues ranging from auto insurance to property taxes. Looking at California ballot propositions from the 1968 until the 1990 general elections, there have been 37 originating initiatives listed on the same ballot with a competing countermeasure. Figure 5.1 shows the number of counterinitiatives since the general election of 1968. I have coded all similar-subject propositions with conflicting

**Figure 5.1** California Ballot Propositions: November 1968–1990

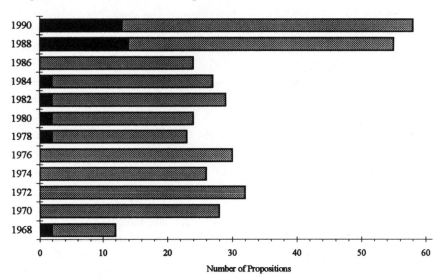

■ Counter Propositions ⊠ Total Propositions (General and Primary except 1968 - General Only)

provisions as counterpropositions. Because ballots do not distinguish between originating initiatives and counterinitiatives, I refer to both the originating proposition and the counterproposal as "competing propositions." Although 1988 and 1990 have many more competing propositions than do the other years, the figure demonstrates that it is not a new strategy. In fact, a counterproposition appeared on the 1922 ballot against a legislative proposal setting new requirements for judges.[3]

## Explaining Variations in Use of Initiatives and Counterpropositions

Except for Price's earlier work (1975), the causes of variation in initiative use have not been systematically examined. Price (1975) summarizes several explanations for variations in use of initiatives. States with strong interest groups and weak parties are expected to have a higher rate of initiatives. An ineffective legislature and voter frustration may also cause an increase in initiative use. Generally, reasons for variations in use can be grouped into structural, political, and cultural explanations. The structural explanations focus on the rules governing access to the initiative process and structural features of the state legislature that may affect legislative effectiveness (the number of legislators, divided government, and legislative professionalization). The political explanations focus on actors such as interest groups and political parties. The cultural explanation considers the states' prevailing attitude toward the place of the individual in political society (Elazar 1972). These factors should also contribute to explaining variation in the use of counterproposals.

Structural factors have been divided into two categories: first, factors related to legislative structure or function, and second, factors related to ballot access. Indicators of legislative structure and function are proxy variables for legislative gridlock and inaction. The argument proposed here is that certain legislative structures and functions are ultimately related to legislative gridlock and inaction, which in turn are related to frustration with the legislative process. Two examples of competing proposals from California, property tax and insurance initiatives (see chapters 3 and 4), were the result of the legislature's inability to resolve a conflict between powerful interests. Divided government is one possible source of this legislative inaction. Studies at the national level argue that the consequences of divided government are gridlock and stalemate (Brady 1993; Sundquist 1988). This view has been challenged by Mayhew (1991), who finds no effect on policy outputs or the policy process. However, divided government may heighten institutional conflict and, at the state level, force the governor to exercise veto power more often. In terms of initiative use, issue activists may be disappointed by the inability of the parties to reach a compromise, and may find it easier to seek the approval of voters than the legislative supermajorities necessary to override a veto. The CCCF found that during periods of divided government in California, initiative use increased (1992, 61). Likewise, an increased use of counterpropositions is expected as battles between competing interests, rather than being resolved by the legislature, are instead carried into the popular initiative arena.

The level of professionalism in state legislatures may also affect variation in initiative use. Membership in professional state legislatures is more attractive than in amateur legislatures. Therefore, elections for these seats are more competitive and more costly. The CCCF (1992, 62) suggests that because candidates must raise large amounts of money from the interest groups, they will be reluctant to favor one interest over another. The resulting inaction on some key legislation may lead interest groups to turn to the initiative process—as the insurance industry and trial lawyers did in the case of auto insurance reform. The California legislature was unwilling to take sides, so both groups brought their cases directly to the voters through the initiative process (Reich 1988).

Another link between professionalism and initiative use is through public opinion. Professionalization has a negative effect on evaluations of state legislatures. Jewell (1982) suggests that the more a legislature is in session, the more aware the public is of conflicts. Squire (1993) explains that professional legislatures may have larger agendas with more complex issues due to the economic and social diversity of the states. The larger the agenda, the more failures—and the more likely people are to be dissatisfied. The links between professionalism, legislative conflict or agenda complexity, and public support for the legislature are speculative, because the relationship has never been empirically tested.

Ballot qualification procedures, the second structural explanation, differ by states (see chapter 2). All states require that a certain percentage of signatures be gathered, but the percentage and the base used to calculate the number of signatures differ. For example, Alaska requires that the number of signatures gathered be at least 10% of the turnout in the last general election, while California requires only 5% of the turnout in the last gubernatorial election. It would appear as if California has much easier qualifying provisions. However, 5% of the turnout in a California gubernatorial election (7,699,467 in 1990) is much greater than 10% of the turnout in Alaska (200,000 in 1990). Initiative studies note that states with lower thresholds of signatures do have more initiatives on the ballot (Magleby 1988; Price 1975). Other regulations, such as time limits and geographical distribution requirements, will also affect the ease of qualifying a measure for the ballot.

Political factors such as party competition and strength and interest group strength may also affect initiative use. Strong interest groups and weak parties are often associated with greater initiative use (Price 1975; Dwyer et al. 1994). Because they have the resources to gather the signatures to qualify the measure for the ballot as well as the resources to run expensive campaigns, organized interests are frequent submitters of initiatives. Many observers of direct legislation suggest that interest groups have come to dominate the initiative process (CCCF 1992; Cronin 1989; Magleby 1984, 1988). Therefore, I hypothesize that states with strong interest group systems will more frequently use initiatives and counterpropositions. Interest group strength is also associated with weak parties (Morehouse 1982), a relationship suggesting that weak parties will be related to initiative use. Interest group strength may also reflect the number of "issue activists" that are organized to use the process. As Magleby (1994) notes, the rise of issue activists might also explain growth in initiative use.

Arguments about interparty competition suggest that in states with competitive party systems, parties will adopt more-liberal welfare policies in order to gain votes.[4] If this logic is applied to initiative use, states with competitive parties could have lower initiative use because the legislature will be more representative of the median voter.[5]

Regardless of political and structural factors, some states may have a cultural predisposition toward citizen-initiated legislation. Elazar's (1972) conception of political culture within the United States as individualistic, moralistic, or traditionalist reflects migration patterns of religious and ethnic groups and relates to the way individuals view government activity. Most initiative states tend to fall along the moralistic–individualistic continuum (Price 1975). We might expect the most initiative activity in moralistic states, as they "embrace the notion that politics is ideally a matter of concern for every citizen" (Elazar 1972, 91).

## Results: Predicting Initiative Use in the States

In order to empirically test the hypothesized relationship between structural and political variables and initiative use, cross-sectional data from the 23 states employing the initiative process have been collected from 1962 to 1990. Initiative use is measured using the number of initiatives occurring on the ballot during a two-year period. The data were collected at two-year intervals to reflect the electoral cycles and legislative sessions. Therefore, the unit of analysis is a two-year period in state time. Each state contributes equally to the total sample size of 327.[6] There are two advantages to using a pooled cross-section: (1) this design allows for analysis over time as well as across cases, which is theoretically desirable; and (2) pooling cross-sections over time increases the number of observations and increases statistical power (Berk 1979; Sayrs 1989; Stimson 1986). Results of the analysis are displayed in table 5.1.

Considering the structural explanation related to legislative capability, there is some support for the hypothesis that individuals or groups may try to circumvent an unresponsive or ineffective legislature by turning to the initiative process. Of the hypothesized structural factors related to initiative use, divided government, constituency size, and legislative professionalization are all significantly related to the number of initiatives appearing on the ballot in 23 states (see table 5.1, equation 1). When divided government exists between the governorship and the legislature, a state's initiative use is predicted to increase by approximately one-half of an initiative (.54) per election cycle. Although the effect is significant, it is substantively small. However, the effects of legislative professionalization and qualification difficulty are much larger. The number of initiatives is predicted to increase by almost 3 (2.95) as the professionalization of the state legislature increases by 1 unit (see appendix for codings).

The other structural explanation, access to the ballot, is also significantly related to initiative use. As the difficulty of qualifying an initiative for the ballot increases, the number of initiatives actually on the ballot is predicted to decrease. For every increase of 2,000 signatures required per day, the number of initiatives on the ballot is predicted to decline by over 3.

Of the political factors, only the indicator of interest group strength is related to initiative use. As with divided government, the effect of interest group strength, while significant, is small. A strong state interest-group system is expected to increase the number of initiatives by less than 1 initiative (.66) per two-year election cycle. Party competition and party strength appear to be unrelated to initiative use.

**Table 5.1** Initiative Use in the American States, 1962–1990 (Pooled GLS Estimates with a Single AR(1) Model)

| | Initiatives (1) | Counter-initiatives (2) | Counter-initiatives (3) |
|---|---|---|---|
| No. of initiatives | | | 0.12* |
| | | | (.02) |
| Divided government | .54** | 0.15* | .11 |
| (governor) | (.25) | (.09) | (.08) |
| Divided government | -.31 | .10 | .15 |
| (legislature) | (.31) | (.11) | (.10) |
| Enacted/introduced | .01 | -.01 | -.01 |
| | (.21) | (.07) | (.07) |
| Constituency size (1,000) | .06** | 0.03** | 0.02* |
| | (.01) | (.005) | (.004) |
| Professionalization | 2.95* | -2.24** | -2.51** |
| | (1.72) | (.66) | (.62) |
| Qualification difficulty | -1.59** | -0.53** | -.25 |
| | (.56) | (.27) | (.24) |
| Party competition | -1.64 | -.10 | .32 |
| | (1.38) | (.59) | (.54) |
| Party strength | .21 | .06 | .06 |
| | (.31) | (.16) | (.14) |
| Interest group strength | .66** | .05 | -.04 |
| | (.31) | (.15) | (.14) |
| Moralistic state politics | .85** | -.07 | -.16 |
| | (.32) | (.17) | (.14) |
| Population (×100,000) | -0.03** | -0.01** | -0.01** |
| | (0.1) | (.005) | (.005) |
| Constant | .03 | -.15 | -.16 |
| | (.43) | (.20) | (.18) |
| Adj $R^2$ | .25 | .21 | .30 |
| $N = 327$ | | | |

*Note:* For the dependent variable, one case equals the number of initiatives in a state, per two-year election cycle.

Standard errors are in parentheses.

$*p < .05$ (one-tailed), $**p < .025$.

A moralistic state political culture seems to contribute to initiative use. Moralistic states tend to be in the western region, where high-use initiative states also tend to be. The effects of region and culture, however, are difficult to distinguish, as migratory patterns (westward) are part of Elazar's (1972) measure of political culture.

Turning to counterinitiative use, the results demonstrate that the same conditions that lead to initiative use are most likely also the causes of counterproposal use, except for qualification difficulty and interest group strength (see table 5.1, equations 2 and 3). Results shown in equation 3 in table 5.1 control for total initiative use, and thus provide the most conservative test of hypotheses about counterinitiative use. While qualification difficulty is negatively related overall to initiative use, it appears to have no effect on counterproposal use (see equation 3). Likewise, interest group strength has no effect on counterinitiatives but significant effect on initiative use. Both of these results suggest that counterproposals are no more or less likely to occur in states with weak or strong interest group systems or with easy or difficult qualification requirements. This null finding is surprising, as interest groups are the primary initiators of counterproposals (CCCF 1992).

States that are more likely to use the initiative process are also more likely to use counterproposals. The coefficient for total initiatives (table 5.1, column 3) illustrates that an increase of 10 initiatives is likely to increase counterproposal use by over 1 ($.12 \times 10 = 1.2$). When controlling for the total number of initiatives, the effects of divided government (governor and legislature controlled by different parties) on counterproposal use are shown by equation 2. Divided government does not increase the use of counterproposals. Once the effects of initiative use are held constant (equation 3), divided government no longer has any impact on counterinitiative use. The lack of a relationship between divided government and counterproposals when controlling for the number of overall initiatives indicates that interest groups or even legislators may turn to the initiative process to address issues when the state government cannot reach a compromise.

In high-initiative-use states there appears to be greater use of counterpropositions regardless of whether or not there is divided government. Therefore, divided government has an indirect effect on counterinitiative use. If interest groups are likely to turn to the initiative process because the state government is unresponsive due to divided government, this leads to a greater likelihood of their fighting proposed ballot initiatives by proposing countermeasures. Another structural factor, qualification difficulty, also has an indirect effect on counterinitiative use; as qualification difficulty increases, both initiative and counterinitiative use decreases. As with divided government, the effect on counterinitiative use disappears when controlling for overall initiative use.

Professional state legislatures tend to have higher numbers of initiatives and counterproposals qualifying for the ballot. The direction of the relationship, though, differs between the two dependent variables. As expected, as the professionalism of the state legislature increases, the number of total initiatives also increases. Unexpectedly, as professionalism decreases, counterproposals increase. There are at least two reasons that states with professional legislatures would have higher initiative use. First, expensive campaigns mean that legislators rely more on interest groups for contributions; therefore, legislators are unwilling to favor one in the legislative process, leading interest groups to turn to the initiative process. Second, professional state legislatures have larger agendas, raising public expectations but also making it more difficult to achieve objectives, and ultimately leading to a dissatisfied public that might then turn to the direct legislation process. This positive link between professional legislatures and initiative use is supported in the first equation. However, there is a negative, and statistically significant, relationship between professionalism and counterinitiative use. California, a state with a highly professionalized state legislature since the 1960s, had the highest use of counterproposals. However, Oregon, with the second highest number of counterproposals, has a relatively amateur state legislature with small staffs and only biennial sessions.

Overall, the structural, political, and cultural factors account for only 25% of the variation in initiative use over time and between states and for 21% of the variation in counterinitiative use. When the number of initiatives is added to the equation predicting counterinitiative use, the model explains 30% of the variation in counterinitiative use.

## Maintaining the Status Quo: Initiatives, Campaign Spending, and Direct Legislation Outcomes

In the previous section, I examined the factors contributing to initiative and counterinitiative use, finding that structural factors were the most successful in explaining variation in use across the states. In this section, I develop a model for direct democracy outcomes in order to test the effectiveness of the counterinitiative strategy. Have political elites hit upon a successful strategy for defeating ballot measures? I propose to answer this question by testing whether or not competing initiatives are more likely to fail. At first glance the counterinitiative strategy appears successful. For example, in 1990 there were 13 measures on the ballot in California related to the environment, alcohol taxes, and term limits that competed with other measures on the same topic. All of the alcohol tax and environment measures failed. The only counterinitiative to pass was the more extreme term limit initiative, sponsored by a retiring Los Angeles County supervisor, Pete Schabarum. The failure of the environmental propositions was especially disconcerting to environmentalists because opinion polls showed concern about the environment to be higher than in any previous year.

One reason that the counterproposition strategy might facilitate defeat is that these contests typically involve heavy negative spending. Yet observers offer several explanations for the failure of competing initiatives. Some have argued that, although polls showed growing concern about the environment, the public was not willing to pay the price during a recession. Bowler and Donovan (1993) show that adverse economic conditions increase the likelihood of negative voting on ballot measures; and California was suffering the effects of a recession in 1990. Others explained that the sheer number of propositions on the November ballot turned voters off, leading them to stay home or vote "no." Another explanation was that the complexity of the initiatives led voters to reject rather than adopt. The latter two explanations fit the conventional wisdom about initiative voting that says confused voters will vote "no." In fact, 22 out of the 28 initiatives on the November 1990 California ballot failed.

This negative voting on counterinitiatives is illustrated in table 5.2. The average percentage of individuals voting "no" on ballot propositions and average expenditures on each type of proposition for California and Oregon are also listed.[7] Looking at the totals for competing and noncompeting propositions, the average percentage of "no" votes is significantly higher for the competing than the noncompeting propositions ($p < .01$). In California, counterpropositions received an average "no" vote of 52.3%, whereas noncompeting propositions received an average "no" vote of only 44.3%. The difference between the average percentage voting "no" on competing and noncompeting propositions in Oregon is slightly less than in California (10%).

Overall, these competing propositions are less likely to receive a majority vote when compared to other measures. The one exception is legislatively proposed measures in California, where there is no significant difference between competing legislative ballot amendments (average "no" vote = 42.5%) and legislative amendments that do not compete with similar propositions (average "no" vote = 42.3%). Indeed, the average "no" vote on legislative amendments is lower than on all other types of ballot measures. This result is consistent with other findings. Propositions put on the ballot by the legislature for citizen approval (bond acts and constitutional and statutory amendments) are less likely to fail than propositions put on the ballot by citizen petition (Magleby 1984; Bowler, Donovan, and Happ 1992).

Counterinitiatives also involve far more money than other measures. In California, significantly more money is spent by the pro side on measures that end up in competition with another initiative on the same topic (avg. = $5,127,754) than is spent by the pro side when an initiative is not competing with another measure on the same subject (avg. = $1,446,217). These differences in spending are not surprising if we consider that the "yes" side promoting a counterinitiative is typically well organized and well financed, and in a position where they must pay top-dollar to get signatures. What is surprising is that the most expensive "yes" campaigns in California coincide with the largest "no" vote. If initiatives are separated from legislative amendments, the gap still exists. Legislative amendments that are competing proposals have, on average, $886,081 spent by the "yes" side, while "yes" spending on noncompeting legislative amendments averages only $134,607.

Differences in spending also exist in Oregon; however, overall spending there is much lower than in California. In both states, more is spent on initiatives than on legislative amendments. The obvious conclusion about spending in both states is that the most expensive measures, for both pro and negative spending, are competing initiative campaigns. At first glance, the counterproposal strategy appears to be effective at maintaining the status quo; counterinitiative campaigns are more expensive *and* counterinitiatives

**Table 5.2** Spending and Outcomes on Ballot Propositions

|  | Competing | | | Non-Competing | | | |
|---|---|---|---|---|---|---|---|
|  | Total | Initiative | Legislative Amendment | Total | Initiative | Legislative Amendment | All |
| **California** | | | | | | | |
| Average % voting no. | 52.3 | 57.2 | 42.5 | 44.3 | 49.6 | 42.3 | 45.1 |
| Average expend. per prop. (1988 $) | | | | | | | |
| For | $3,831,687 | 5,127,754 | 886,081 | 444,013 | 1,446,217 | 134,607 | 969,973 |
| Against | 2,607,387 | 3,754,637 | 0 | 611,101 | 2,514,042 | 23,615 | 925,599 |
| N | 36 | 25 | 11 | 195 | 46 | 149 | |
| **Oregon** | | | | | | | |
| Average % voting no. | 57.3 | 58.5 | 51.2 | 47.4 | 48.4 | 47.0 | 48.0 |
| Average expend. per prop. (1988 $) | | | | | | | |
| For | 134,034 | 160,840 | 0 | 56,116 | 141,451 | 18,103 | 61,585 |
| Against | 598,465 | 718,158 | 0 | 131,516 | 422,702 | 1,806 | 164,284 |
| N | 12 | 10 | 2 | 159 | 49 | 110 | |

*Sources:* California Fair Political Practices Committee (1988); California Secretary of State (1988, 1990); Oregon Office of the Secretary of State (1970–1990).

are more likely to fail. But these data also suggest that "yes" spend-ing might be associated with "no" voting.

To better understand the relationship between initiatives, coun-terinitiatives, spending, and election outcomes, table 5.3 presents the results from a model that examines the impact of each spending variable while controlling for others factors. The multivariate model is based on other models that predict aggregate direct legisla-tion outcomes (see Bowler, Donovan, and Happ 1992; Hadwiger 1992; and Magleby 1984, 1994b). The estimated equations for Cali-fornia and Oregon are in table 5.3.

The nature of the relationship between spending and election outcomes is not well defined and raises questions about the specifi-cation of spending effects. Campaign spending is expected to be a powerful indicator of who wins in direct democracy elections (Cronin 1989). However, the relationship between spending and outcomes is not just a matter of one side outspending the other, with each having equal impact. Negative spending can be expected to have a large effect on initiative voting behavior if voters are somehow more responsive to "vote no" appeals in general. Magleby (1984, 1994b) shows that, at certain levels, negative spending has more of an impact on election outcomes than proponent spending. Others have cited a similar relationship between spending and di-rect legislation outcomes (Bowler, Donovan, and Happ 1992; Cronin 1989; Lee 1979; Shockley 1980; Zisk 1987). By focusing on any triv-ial implications of the targeted measure, high-end negative spend-ing can shape voters' perceptions by confusing or frightening them (Lowenstein 1982). However, Thomas (1991) found a relationship between spending and outcomes regardless of whether the spending was one-sided. In one analysis of the relationship between spending and direct legislation outcomes, Magleby (1994b) finds that oppo-nent spending will increase the "no" vote, and that *proponent* spending, at high levels, also increases the "no" vote.

To account for this counterintuitive finding, Magleby (1994b) points to Gary Jacobson's work and draws an analogy between spend-ing in congressional elections and spending in direct legislation elec-tions. Jacobson (1980, 1990) suggests that when an incumbent antic-ipates a close race due to a strong challenge, he or she will spend more money. Because the incumbent spends a lot of money promot-ing herself in the anticipation of a close race, incumbent spending

**Table 5.3** Campaign Spending, Counter Proposals, and Direct Democracy Outcomes: Explaining "No" Votes in Direct Legislation Elections (Two-Stage Least Squares Estimates)

| | California (1976–90) | | Oregon (1970–90) | |
|---|---|---|---|---|
| | *Coefficient* | *SE* | *Coefficient* | *SE* |
| First Stage (Proponent Spending') | | | | |
| Counter proposal | 1.69* | .95 | -1.29 | 1.33 |
| Initiative | 3.81** | 1.16 | 2.85** | .88 |
| Business regulation | 1.99* | 1.18 | .23 | .94 |
| Opponent spending | 0.42** | .08 | .50** | .08 |
| Constant | 3.59** | .40 | 2.2** | .41 |
| Adj $R^2$ | .46 | | .42 | |
| Second Stage (% "No" Vote) | | | | |
| Counter proposal | 6.25** | 2.54 | 7.78 | 5.32 |
| Proponent spending' (log) | -.43 | .16 | -.47[a] | .30 |
| Opponent spending (log) | .97** | .18 | 1.09** | .32 |
| Presidential election year | -6.35** | 2.25 | -.16 | 3.01 |
| Primary | -5.24** | 2.09 | 4.36 | 2.98 |
| Constitutional amendment | .20 | 1.70 | -2.64 | 3.26 |
| Ballot placement | .53** | .15 | -.18 | .47 |
| Turnout (in 100,000s) | -0.13** | .04 | -.08 | .10 |
| Constant | 67.40** | 8.25 | 55.04** | 11.17 |
| Adj $R^2$ | .29 | | .13 | |
| N | 231 | | 170 | |

[a]$p = .12$, *$p < .05$ (one-tailed), **$p = .025$ (one-tailed).

appears to negatively affect vote share in some analyses of congressional spending; but proponent spending does not directly cause the vote share to be lower.

If this analysis is applied to direct legislation campaigns, ballot measure proponents sensing a hard sell or a close race will spend more while getting only limited returns per dollar. Because it is a response to the appearance of a strong challenge, the level of proponent spending, like incumbent spending in congressional elections, is not a variable that is completely external to any model that predicts initiative voting. Strong opposition is likely to occur on more controversial measures. As with congressional elections, proponent and opponent spending are wrapped up in each other—in other words, they are endogenous variables. Furthermore, if there is some decline in returns per dollar for very high amounts of spending, the relationship between spending and outcomes is not necessarily linear.

If spending is endogenous, it is necessary to use a two-stage model and some indicator of the controversy or competitiveness of each proposition to correctly specify how spending affects outcomes. This allows us to account first for the effect of opponent spending on proponent spending, and then to see its effect on votes.

The first stage of the model predicts the proposition proponent's spending while controlling for opponent spending. I use three indicators that tap how competitive or controversial each measure is: whether or not there is a competing proposition; whether or not the proposition is an initiative (v. a legislative amendment); and whether or not it contains provisions regulating or taxing an industry.[8] Because most industries already have organizations or lobbyists to represent their interests (in the language of the previous chapter, these are type A narrow interests), any attempt to regulate or tax an industry can be met with quickly organized and well-funded opposition.

These four variables are regressed on proponent spending to predict how much proponent spending is driven by the threat of opposition. Proponent spending *predicted* from this first stage is used in the second stage, along with opponent spending, to predict vote outcomes. This allows us to see the independent effects of each type of spending, while isolating and eliminating the effects of proponent spending that is driven by the anticipated closeness or competitiveness of the contest. Since spending might have diminishing returns at very high levels, I use the natural log of proponent and opponent expenditures in the models (Magleby 1994b). This helps model the potential nonlinear effects of spending on outcomes.

Besides spending, the model controls for other variables in the second-stage equation that may affect direct legislation outcomes. The success or failure of an initiative depends on several factors:

whether the proposal is a constitutional amendment; placement on the ballot; and the type of election (general or primary) and turnout (see Bowler, Donovan, and Happ 1992; Hadwiger 1992; Magleby 1984). Because constitutional amendments tend to be more "remote and obscure" than statutory initiatives, a higher "no" vote is expected (Bowler, Donovan, and Happ 1992). Primary elections can produce different outcomes from general elections, since the composition of the electorate may affect voting. Primary voters tend to be more interested and thus better informed than general election voters. Because confusion and lack of information can lead voters to reject proposals, propositions on the ballot in primaries might be more likely to pass or have a lower percentage of "no" votes than those on the ballot in the general election. Furthermore, presidential election years may bring out a larger share of the population; research on turnout and outcomes at the local level suggest that higher turnout increases the likelihood that the measure will not pass (Coleman 1957; Knox, Landry, and Payne 1984). To control for the effects of primaries and election years I have created two dummy variables: (1) ballot measures appearing on the ballot during primary elections have been coded "1"; all others have been coded "0"; (2) ballot measures appearing on the ballot during presidential election years have been coded "1"; all others have been coded "0." Turnout during the election is also included in the multivariate model.

## Results: The Disproportionate Effects of Negative Spending

Table 5.3 reports the results of this analysis with data from California (left columns) and Oregon (right columns). Examining the results from the first stage predicting proponent spending (logged) shows that for both Oregon and California, if a measure had been placed on the ballot by citizen petition, proponent spending is significantly increased. Counterproposals and business regulations also significantly increase proponent spending in California. As expected, there is a significant relationship between opponent and proponent spending, suggesting that proponent spending is a function of opponent spending. Overall, both equations explain over 40% of the variation in proponent spending on all of these propositions, largely due to the inclusion of opponent spending in the model.

The second stage estimates the percentage of "no" votes on each measure with values of proponent spending (the predicted value of logged proponent spending from the first stage). It shows that, once proponent spending has been "purged" of effects shared with opponent spending, proponent spending does have a significant, inverse effect on the proportion of people voting "no" on a ballot measure in both states. In other words, as proponents spend more, "yes" voting increases. Remember that this analysis accounts for the declining marginal returns on high levels of spending (by logging the data) and for the fact that proponent and opponent spending are often "wrapped up" in each other (or, in the jargon of statistics, multicolinear). By using a two-stage estimation, this analysis may have accounted for Magleby's counterintuitive findings that high "yes" spending was associated with more "no" voting. At least with these data, "yes" spending appears to buy more "yes" votes.

However, the effect of opponent spending on "no" votes is still much larger than the effect of proponent spending. This finding supports the conclusions of previous research that negative campaigns are much more effective at decreasing support than proponent campaigns are at increasing support. Using the natural log of proponent and opponent spending also appears to produce a model that fits the data fairly well. This suggests that modest levels of spending have larger returns (per dollar) than spending at the higher end. Both proponents and opponents appear to get a diminishing marginal return on their spending.

The data in table 5.3 also tell us something else about opponent advantages, confirming something discussed in the previous chapter. In California, the countermeasure strategy seems to be effective in reducing support for a measure, and the effect is above and beyond the impact of negative spending. The first stage of the estimation shows that counterproposals (in California) are significantly more costly—as the existence of a counterproposal already indicates a well-formed opposition. In the second stage, the coefficient indicates that counterproposals, holding spending constant, are still more likely to fail. Whether an originating or subsequent conflicting measure, counterpropositions receive 6% more "no" votes, other things being equal. Therefore, not only are counterproposal campaigns more expensive, but counterproposals are also more likely to fail when proponent and opponent spending are equivalent. This finding provides some evidence that targeting an unwanted proposition with a counterproposition is an effective strategy for defeating measures. Competing measures may add confusion (if not negative advertising information) to direct legislation elections; voters may be confused about which alternative to support or fatigued from more choices on the ballot and may vote "no" on both the originating and countermeasure. The estimates in table 5.3 suggest that this does have an effect on direct legislation outcomes in the aggregate.

As for the other variables in the equations, contrary to expectations, the different composition of the electorate in presidential elections decreases the negative vote in both Oregon and California. Also, the negative vote is significantly higher in Oregon primary elections. These findings differ somewhat from those of Bowler, Donovan, and Happ (1992). They also find a negative relationship between presidential elections and negative voting, but it was not significant. They also found a positive and significant relationship between primary elections and the proportion of negative votes when they hypothesized a negative relationship. Perhaps the hypothesis that a more informed primary electorate is more likely to support initiatives is flawed.

## Conclusion

In this chapter I have examined two questions about initiative and counterinitiative use. First, I examined the factors that explain variation in use of initiatives and counterinitiatives across time and between states. The analysis demonstrated that initiative use is more frequent where interest groups are strong, where states have divided government, in states with professional legislatures, and where qualification burdens are low. The same conditions largely determine use of counterinitiatives, although these are less constrained by qualification requirements and divided government.

Next, the chapter examined the effects of spending and counterinitiatives on direct legislation outcomes. Counterproposals lead to more "no" voting. Results further demonstrate that proponent spending increases support and opponent spending decreases support. More interestingly, opponent spending, dollar for dollar, has a much greater impact on votes than proponent spending. Given the discussion in chapter 4, this furthers our understanding of why narrow interests have a difficult time using money to advance their interests, but are well positioned to defend themselves when threatened. Well-financed opponents have two major defensive advantages in the process: using countermeasures to defeat an original proposal, and receiving higher returns on each dollar of campaign spending.

Stodder (1992) suggests that industry groups created the counterinitiative strategy as a response to the weakening effect of negative spending. The second part of my analysis on elections outcomes suggests that although this may have been the perception, negative spending is still a significant factor affecting vote margins. The results show that negative spending is much more effective in defeating a measure than affirmative spending is at promoting a measure. Although the success of counterproposals at maintaining the status quo relies partly on the large amounts of money spent on the campaigns, my findings in this chapter suggest that counterproposals also have an independent effect on direct legislation outcomes.

## APPENDIX

INITIATIVE USE

> *Initiatives* Number of initiatives appearing on the ballot in a two-year election cycle.
>
> *Counterinitiatives* Number of counterinitiatives appearing on the ballot in a two-year election cycle.

STRUCTURAL VARIABLES

### Legislative Capability

> *Divided Government 1* Governor of different party than legislature (1); otherwise (0).

*Divided Government* 2 Chambers of legislature controlled by different parties (1); otherwise (0).

*Legislative Functionality* Proportion of bills enacted of bills that have been introduced in state legislature.

*Professionalization* Compares legislative compensation, session length, and staff size to that of the U.S. Congress. The closer the state legislature is to the Congress, the more professional it is. The three proportions are averaged for each state (Squire 1992). Information on compensation and session length is from the Council on State Government's *The Book of the States.* Staff size is from Weberg (1988).

*Constituency Size* Population per district of lower chamber member.

**Ballot Access**

*Qualification Difficulty* Number of signatures required per day of circulation = number of signatures required/number of days allowed to circulate petitions.

POLITICAL VARIABLES

**Party Competition:** Party competition is the moving average over three gubernatorial elections: |%Dem - %Rep|, where %Dem and %Rep are the Democratic and Republican votes for governor (Morehouse 1982, 66).

**Party and Interest Group Strength:** I use Morehouse's (1982) categorization of states into weak, medium, and strong for the appropriate year. For the analysis, the weak and moderate rankings of interest group and party strength have been collapsed into one category. Although collapsing these indicators gives up some variability in the measures, using the full scales did not yield different results, and the dichotomous measures performed better.

## NOTES

1. Personal correspondence with the Public Affairs Research Institute, 22 May 1995.

2. See chapter 1 for a discussion of direct versus indirect initiatives.

3. Since this chapter was written, a new phenomenon has emerged, in which allied groups, after failing to agree on a plan for a policy, place competing measures on the same ballot.

4. The literature testing V. O. Key's (1949) suggestion that more-competitive state party systems will result in more-liberal welfare policies is too vast to review here. For reviews of the literature see Lewis-Beck (1977) or Carmines (1974). The arguments rest on the assumption that both parties will appeal to the larger disadvantaged group in order to gain an electoral advantage when there are competitive elections. This interpretation is closely related to Downs's (1957) argument in *Economic Theory of Democracy*.

5. If the legislature is more responsive to opinion, there would be fewer initiatives in response to "sins of omission," although Weingast (1988) and Matsusaka (1996) show that logrolling within legislatures could cause policy to depart from median voter preferences if logrolling is common.

6. The starting sample size was 345 cases. Four cases are missing from Nebraska because data were not available on eligible voters from 1962 to 1968. Four cases are missing from Illinois, 8 from Florida, and 3 from Wyoming because the initiative was not adopted until after 1962. Therefore, the sample size is reduced to 326.

7. I focus on California and Oregon here because these states have the highest occurrences of counterpropositions.

8. These are not the best indicators of the controversial nature of a proposition. Certainly, propositions occur on the ballot that are neither counterpropositions nor regulatory measures that are nonetheless very controversial. For example, 1988's Proposition 102 in California was a highly controversial antigay initiative that called for reporting anyone believed to have been exposed to the AIDS virus. Good indicators of whether or not a measure is controversial would be spending and the margin of victory or defeat. However, these variables do not predict controversy; they are after-the-fact indicators of controversy.

# 6

# Searching for Ideological Consistency in Direct Legislation Voting

## SUSAN A. BANDUCCI

Central to the debate over direct legislation is the question of voter competence—whether voters can make meaningful choices that reflect underlying preferences. While some argue that voter choice in direct legislation elections is capricious (Mueller 1969), other evidence suggests that ideological self-placement is a strong predictor of choice. Using measures developed to test attitude consistency, I examine the structure of electoral choices for ballot measures. Although there is not one underlying attitude dimension, choices are structured within particular issue areas.

The individual voter faces an information vacuum in direct legislation elections. If a proposed ballot measure is noncontroversial, a voter is not likely to be exposed to any information about the measure before entering the voting booth. Even the usual decision-making shortcuts that make up for the lack of information in candidate elections—party cues, candidate evaluations, and retrospective judgments—are absent in direct legislation elections. Even if the measure is controversial and information is available, the complexity of the measure may make it difficult for voters to translate preferences into electoral choice. Given this lack of information, some researchers claim that there is little to structure electoral choices in direct legislation elections, and therefore choices appear to be nothing more than "snap judgments" made in the voting place (Magleby 1984, 179). However, the one factor that does seem to be consistently related to choice is self-identified ideology (Magleby 1984; Bowler and Donovan n.d.). In this chapter, I examine the extent to which voting decisions in direct legislation elections are structured by some underlying predispositions or whether they are random marks on a ballot.

## The Structure of Electoral Choice in Direct Legislation Elections

Voting-behavior studies of direct legislation elections often focus on a single issue such as auto insurance reform (Lupia 1994b), nuclear power (Kuklinksi, Metlay, and Kay 1982), property taxes (Lowery and Sigelman 1981), open housing (Wolfinger and Greenstein 1968), and term limits (Karp 1995). These studies model outcomes as a binary choice between the status quo and the proposed alternative, with votes ("yes" or "no") regressed on a series of predictor variables. On economic issues, social class is a strong explanatory factor; parental status is a strong predictor of support for school bond measures; and religion affects support for a casino-gambling measure (Magleby 1984). Because of the focus on a single issue at a time, the results are not applicable to initiatives generally. However, political ideology is one factor that is consistently related to voting on many individual ballot measures (Gerber and Lupia 1992; Magleby 1984). Yet with a focus often directed at a single issue or types of issues, the underlying coherence of multiple electoral choices from a single given ballot is rarely assessed.

It is important that we understand how voters behave when casting decisions across several policy measures in any particular election. Given our democratic ideals, we expect a coherent outcome to an election after the votes have been counted. Outcomes should "make sense" to observers who are interested in gauging how votes on specific policies might express mass preferences in general. Consider two abortion measures on Oregon's 1990 ballot. Measure 8 proposed prohibiting all abortions except in cases of rape or incest or to save the mother's life, while Measure 10 would have required parental notification for a minor to obtain an abortion. Had neither passed, representatives might infer that the public was decidedly pro-abortion rights. Had both passed, they might infer that the public was decidedly anti-abortion rights. If only parental notification passed (the more moderate departure from the status quo), they might infer the public was somewhere in the middle. However, given that the near prohibition was an extreme departure from the status quo, it would be much more difficult to infer voter intent if near prohibition passed while parental notification failed.[1]

Studying the relationship between policy choices in a single election is important, since it can illustrate how election outcomes might come to be structured by some underlying policy preferences that constrain how voters think. If there is evidence of structure, choices across multiple issues should be more logically constrained, and election results should be more likely to "make sense."

For the past 35 years the subject of attitude structure has been central to public opinion research. The more politically sophisticated voters are expected to have attitudes on issues that are consistent with one another and that reflect some underlying ideological predisposition. Testing for attitude consistency, or testing the extent to which attitudes on a wide variety of issues are structured along a single dimension, is one way to approach studying the relationship among choices on ballot measures. Can voters organize their preferences on a list of ballot measures in a coherent way that reflects some underlying principle to the organization such as ideology? Because attitude consistency is related to behavior in candidate elections (Levitin and Miller 1979; Stimson 1975), we might also expect a relationship in direct legislation elections.

Research on political belief systems, although not without significant debate, has generally concluded that very few people attain a high level of abstract ideological thinking, and that many individuals hold inconsistent attitudes. The authors of *The American Voter* concluded that only about 10 % of the electorate came close to approximating the ideal of a sophisticated or ideologically thinking voter; they suggest that "the concepts important to ideological analysis are useful only for that small segment of the population that is equipped to approach political decisions at a rarefied level" (Campbell et al. 1960, 250). From this perspective, few voters have attitudes across several policy issues that are constrained by ideology in a manner producing logical consistency. While the debate over the distribution of sophistication may have been settled (Kinder

1983; Luskin 1987), questions still remain about measurement (E. Smith 1989; Luskin 1987) and about how the use of abstract ideological reasoning varies by cognitive ability (Sniderman et al. 1991).

## Ideological Consistency on Ballot Propositions— Should We Expect It?

In terms of issue attitudes we might expect consistency in responses for at least two reasons—one psychological, the other sociological. If one understands the connections among different policies, their implications, and consequences, then opinions will be logically tailored on these policies so that they do not conflict. This notion of constraint is drawn from the psychological theory of cognitive consistency, or balance theory. If you are aware that two beliefs are inconsistent, this produces tension, and you are likely to change beliefs to be consistent. On the other hand, if you do not associate the two beliefs or connect them in any way, there is no need to change them, because there is no tension (Osgood and Tannenbaum 1955). We would expect, therefore, greater constraint among those more aware of politics, because they are more likely to recognize when positions conflict. The other reason for attitude constraint is social. People might learn from elites how beliefs about policies "fit together" into nice little packages. For example, liberal elites typically favor spending more on social services and less on defense; some voters can pick up on these ideological packages.[2] Evidence does suggest that elites have more constrained belief systems than do non-elites (see Jennings 1992).

There can also be many dimensions along which people organize their political beliefs. Converse (1964) argues that, since political elites in the U.S. structure their beliefs along the left-right ideological dimension, the same dimension should be used as the yardstick for mass belief systems as well. Hence, the politically "involved" should exhibit belief systems constrained by some underlying dimension of liberal–conservative ideals. Controversy about the dimensionality of sophisticated belief systems has raised some questions, however. What, for example, really suggests greater complexity: having fewer or more numerous dimensions structuring attitudes?

Stimson (1975) presents evidence suggesting that more-educated voters have fewer dimensions underlying attitudes, while Marcus, Tabb, and Sullivan (1974) support the opposite position. Many scholars have pointed out that beliefs can be structured along several "ideological" domains—domestic policy, foreign policy, economic matters, racial affairs, and social policy. Conover and Feldman (1984) argue that each domain should be considered in political belief systems, yet they still interpret results in terms of a single underlying left-right ideology (Luskin 1987). Using exploratory factor analysis, Stimson (1975) finds two distinct dimensions among policy positions for the more highly educated individuals (elite), while four dimensions emerged for the least educated. The difference in the number of factors between the least- and most-educated could indicate that the more highly educated have more constrained belief systems, since variation in attitudes about many policies could be explained (or constrained) by only two underlying dimensions. Importantly, there was not a single underlying dimension for the best-educated; rather, there were two. Stimson interpreted these as a dimension of reasoning involving social issues, and another involving traditional left-right issues. The social dimension structured attitudes about issues such as women's rights and legalization of marijuana, while the traditional left-right dimension structured attitudes about guaranteed jobs and inflation.

In addition, self-placement on a left-right ideological spectrum has been shown to be highly correlated with issue positions and electoral choices, and the left-right placement continuum fits a broad range of attitudes (Sniderman, Brody, and Tetlock 1991). Because ideology is one factor consistently related to preferences on ballot measures for many voters, we might expect choices on ballot propositions to be structured along ideological lines, even for fairly complex issues. Kuklinski, Metlay, and Kay (1982), for example, find that "core values"—defined as political ideology and attitudes about technological advances—played a significant role in voters' decisions on a nuclear energy initiative (619). The most knowledgeable voters were found to be more likely to rely on political ideology in decision making, while the least knowledgeable relied on general feelings about technology. Furthermore, out of the three models of decision making tested (cost-benefit, core values, and reference group cues), core values had the most pervasive influence on the policy choices of individuals: "Core values . . . are the key to understanding how citizens decide" (Kuklinski, Metlay, and Kay 1982, 633). This conclusion is particularly notable given that nuclear energy was a relatively new and highly technical issue not easily defined in terms of a left-right continuum. Lowery and Sigelman (1981) also claim that ideology played a much larger role than economic self-interest in explaining support for California's Proposition 13.

Even beyond these two examples, ideological self-placement is consistently related to voting preferences regardless of ballot measure content. Magleby (1984) regressed vote choice for ten California ballot measures on a series of six predictor variables, including party and ideology; ideology was statistically significant in seven of the equations (176). No other predictor variables worked as well. In an analysis of voting in direct legislation elections, Gerber and Lupia (1992) regressed vote preference for 42 California initiatives on party identification, age, education, union membership, gender, race, home ownership, and awareness. Party identification was significant in over two-thirds of the equations. Because ideological self-identification was not used in these models, party identification was most likely picking up some of its effects.

All of this demonstrates that there is a solid basis for assuming that preferences on ballot measures are structured by ideological predispositions. If this is true, and ideology constrains and structures attitudes across numerous policy issues, we can also expect decisions across multiple propositions on one ballot to be somewhat consistent.

## Searching for Consistency

Using surveys to test attitude consistency in a single election is problematic, because most preelection surveys only include questions on controversial ballot measures. Preelection samples also include many individuals who have not made up their minds on ballot measures. Using exit polls would solve this latter problem, but the number of questions about ballot measures is still limited by the financial considerations of polling organizations. Instead of relying on survey data, I use the actual voted ballots from the 1990 general election in Oregon's Marion County,[3] thus avoiding some problems associated with surveys. First, because the voted ballot records actual votes rather than reported votes, I avoid some of the unreliability of survey questions. Second, during the campaign, voters are more likely to have been exposed to some information about the ballot measures and are therefore more likely to have opinions, which also reduces unreliability. However, this does not mean voters may not be confused by the description of the measures on the ballot. Another advantage to using voted ballots is that we are measuring actual behavior rather than reported behavior or reported attitudes. Of course, the drawbacks of using voted ballots is that we do not have access to questions that directly measure factors related to consistency, such as education, political knowledge, awareness, and interest in politics.

On the 1990 Oregon ballot, there were 11 measures addressing several issues. Because the dynamics of choice for legislative referrals and referenda are different from those for initiatives (Magleby 1984; Bowler, Donovan, and Happ 1992), I limit my analysis to the 8 citizen-initiated measures on the ballot, thereby eliminating a referendum and two legislatively referred constitutional amendments. These policies are listed in table 6.1. Briefly, the policies voters evaluated included Measure 4, which proposed closing a nuclear power plant until safety measures had been met; Measure 5, which proposed cutting property taxes; Measure 6, which called for all product packaging to be recyclable; Measure 7, which proposed that welfare recipients be required to work for benefits; Measure 8, which proposed prohibiting abortions except in a few cases; Measure 9, a proposal to require the use of safety belts; Measure 10, which proposed that parental notification be required for a minor seeking an abortion; and Measure 11, a school voucher measure.

## Measuring Consistency

I use two methods of assessing consistency here. First, I use principal components analysis to test the number of underlying factors that structure voting on the eight initiatives, with the expectation that votes can be reduced to a smaller number of common dimen-

**Table 6.1** Ballot Measure Titles, Oregon 1990

| Measure No. | Summary |
| --- | --- |
| 4 | Prohibits Trojan operation until nuclear waste, cost, earthquake standards met |
| 5 | State constitutional limit on property taxes for schools government operations |
| 6 | Product packaging must meet recycling standards or receive hardship waiver |
| 7 | Six-country work in lieu of welfare benefits pilot program |
| 8 | Amends Oregon constitution to prohibit abortion with three exceptions |
| 9 | Requires use of safety belts |
| 10 | Doctor must give parent notice before minor's abortion |
| 11 | School choice system, tax credit for education outside public schools |

sions if there is some underlying ideology or principle that guides voters making choices across many issues. I have also constructed a measure of consistent partisan voting in order to test whether partisan voters have more constrained attitudes. Partisan consistency serves as a rough indicator of one form of ideological reasoning. The scale identifies those who are consistent in partisan voting in candidate races. High scores are given to individuals who vote consistently with one party on five candidate races (U.S. Senate, U.S. House, governor, state senator, and state representative). These scores are used to divide the sample into subgroups so I can test if there is more structure to ballot proposition voting among highly consistent partisan voters.

Second, I measure consistency on ballot measures using Guttman scales. If votes on the ballot propositions have some underlying structure, approval of the propositions should scale like a Guttman scale. The special feature of a Guttman scale is that items will be related in such a way that an individual with a particular attitude will agree with less extreme items on one side of that position and disagree with the other items. Each value is a function of the underlying continuum and from the respondent's score on a Guttman scale we should be able to predict the responses to all the individual items on the scale (McIver and Carmines 1981). Errors in the scale occur when an individual gives a negative response to an item lower than the individual's scale score. The test of whether to reject or accept the unidimensionality of the scale is based on the number of errors.

## Factor Analysis

Principal components analysis illustrates how a large number of variables might share a smaller number of underlying traits. It allows us to find the underlying structure—or factors—among a large number of things, like votes on several initiatives. With this method, the number of factors found is nearly always a function of the number and type of issues chosen. In my analysis the issues are limited to the initiatives that appeared on the 1990 Oregon ballot. The analysis resulted in three unique factors (each with eigenvalues[4] greater than 1) that explain variance in votes across the 8 initiatives. At the top of table 6.2, I present the factor structure derived from the analysis of all voters in the sample, as well as the factors for highly consistent party voters and for the least-consistent party voters.

Although the factor analysis does not support the existence of a single underlying dimension, the measures load onto three factors in coherent fashion. The three underlying dimensions seem to reflect established social, economic, and regulatory domains of a left–right ideology (Asher 1980; Weisberg and Rusk 1970). Votes on the two abortion-restriction measures (Measures 8 and 10) are explained by one factor (social), the school voucher and workfare initiatives (Measures 7 and 11) by another single factor (economic), while voting on two regulatory questions (Measures 6 and 9) is explained by a third factor (regulatory). We can thus say that support for both of the abortion initiatives is structured by some common source (which we assume is underlying social attitudes), and that support for initiatives dealing with workfare policies and school choice (or tax credits for private schools) is structured by another, distinct dimension of attitudes about economic issues. Similarly, voting on requirements for product packaging and safety belts is structured by a separate dimension of attitudes about regulation. When all voters are considered, these three factors explain over 58%

**Table 6.2** Principal Components Analysis of Voted Ballots by Level of Partisan Consistency

| Group | Factor | Explained Variance (%) | Interpretation of Factor | Ballot Measures |
|---|---|---|---|---|
| All | 1 | 25.5 | Social | 8, 10 |
| | 2 | 17.5 | Economic | 7, 11 |
| | 3 | 15.1 | Regulatory | 6, 9 |
| Total variance | | 58.1 | | |
| Low partisan constituency in candidate voting | 1 | 23.8 | Social | 10 |
| | 2 | 17.1 | Economic | 5 |
| | 3 | 13.8 | Mixed | 9 |
| | 4 | 13.0 | Regulatory | 6 |
| Total variance | | 67.7 | | |
| High partisan constituency in candidate voting | 1 | 28.4 | Social | 8, 10 |
| | 2 | 17.6 | Economic | 7, 11 |
| | 3 | 14.4 | Regulatory | 6, 9 |
| Total variance | | 60.3 | | |

of the variance in votes across all 8 initiatives, with the two largest explaining 43% of the variance.

Support for the final two ballot measures (closing a nuclear power plant and a tax limitation initiative) fails to load on any of these factors, illustrating that these three underlying dimensions do not structure votes on all measures, including two that might have been expected to be affected by whatever underlying attitudes the economic and regulatory factors represent. For example, if attitudes were perfectly structured or constrained by a small number of underlying factors, we might expect that voting on the tax limitation initiative (Measure 5) would be affected by the same attitudes that structure voting on the school choice and workfare initiatives (the economic factor). Similarly, we might except support or opposition to the nuclear power question to be explained by the same underlying dimension that structures voting on product packaging and safety belt requirements (the regulatory factor). But as table 6.2 illustrates, these measures fail to load on these factors.

Table 6.2 also shows the factor structure for each level of partisan consistency. For individuals with a low level of partisan constraint, the 8 ballot measures loaded onto four rather than three factors, with each failing to structure opinions on multiple initiatives. The two largest factors for the least partisan explain 40.9% of the variance in voting on all initiatives. However, for those with high partisan constraint, the 8 ballot measures reduced to three factors, with each structuring opinions on multiple initiatives. The first two factors from highly partisan voters explain 46% of variance in votes, while all three explain over 60% of variance in votes on all 8 initiatives. The increase in the number of factors for the least partisan, and the failure of any of these factors to constrain votes across multiple initiatives, suggest that those who vote without partisan consistency in candidate races also have a less coherent structure to their votes on ballot measures. Thus, whatever it is that causes voters to behave in terms of a straight partisan lens in candidate races (i.e., ideological reasoning, cognitive ability, education) might also cause them to structure their decisions on the basis of underlying principles when evaluating numerous ballot measures.

## Guttman Scales

Guttman scaling assumes the underlying pattern to responses are "triangular," such that people who answer "yes" to the first item in an ordered scale should consistently answer "yes" to other items. If a person answers "no" to items early in the scale, once they answer "yes" to any item they should agree with the remaining items.[5] I use this method to test how voted ballots might be structured by left-right scales of policy choices. The people's responses are ordered as a scale, so there should be few errors in predicting actual votes with the scale.

Creating and interpreting a Guttman scale using all 8 ballot measures can prove difficult, especially when we have no a priori reasons for placing the ballot measures on a left-right scale. It is difficult, for example, to know whether support for closing the Trojan nuclear power plant (Measure 4) is further to the left than rejecting the measure to prohibit abortions. Therefore, I have used the principal components solution from table 6.2 to separate the measures and build Guttman scales for each of the three issue dimensions. The two propositions that failed to load on any factor (Measures 4 and 5) are placed on what are assumed to be the most appropriate issue dimensions. Measure 5, the property tax limit, is placed on the economic dimension and the nuclear initiative on the regulatory dimension. Within one of these dimensions, the placement of the measures on the left-right continuum is based on newspaper endorsements. In using elite (newspaper) endorsements to construct a Guttman scale, I am assuming that editorial staffs reflect highly constrained reasoning about ballot measures. These elite endorsements from newspaper editorial boards are given in table 6.3.

A clear Guttman scale for the regulatory dimension can be illustrated by newspaper endorsements. Assume the conservative, status-quo position would be to oppose all measures. All papers endorsed the more moderate regulation (safety belts). One paper (*The Willamette Weekly*) has taken the position farthest to the left of the status quo by endorsing each measure. Two papers endorsed the safety belt measure and also endorsed the product packaging measure, while one paper endorsed the safety belt measure only (*The Oregonian*). *The Oregonian*'s position is thus closest to the status quo, and the *Willamette Weekly*'s the farthest from it. The endorsements

**Table 6.3** Newspaper Endorsements on Oregon Measures

| Scale | Ballot Measure | Willamette Weekly | Statesman-Journal | Oregonian |
|---|---|---|---|---|
| Social | 8 | No | No | No |
| | 10 | No | No | No |
| Regulatory | 9 | Yes | Yes | Yes |
| | 6 | Yes | Yes | No |
| | 6 | Yes | No | No |
| Economic | 5 | Yes | No | No |
| | 7 | No | No | No |
| | 11 | No | No | No |

*Source: Oregonian*, 6 November 1994; *Salem Statesman-Journal*, November 1994; *Willamette Weekly*, 1 November 1994.

illustrate that elites (editorial boards) who favor the more extreme regulatory intervention (of nuclear plants) should also favor safety belt regulations. If voters have a similar structure to their reasoning, we might expect that voters who support Measure 4 (nuclear plants) would also support Measures 6 (packaging) and 9 (safety belts). Likewise, a voter who supports Measure 6 and not Measure 4 would also support Measure 9.

A Guttman pattern is as clearly evident for the economic issues. One endorsement for Measure 5, the property tax measure, places it closest to the status quo and places the other two measures (7 and 11) to the right of Measure 5. However, because none of the papers supported Measure 7 or 11, it is difficult to distinguish whether Measure 7 or Measure 11 is closer to Measure 5. I tested the scale with both Measure 7, the welfare benefits measure, as the most extreme and then Measure 11, school vouchers, as the most extreme. The placement of these measures did not make any difference to the number of errors. Figure 6.1 shows the placement of the measures on a left-right dimension according to the newspaper endorsements.

For the other two issue dimensions (social and economic, respectively), creation of the underlying scales was more subjective. No paper endorsed either of the abortion restrictions measures. Measure 8, which prohibits abortion, has been placed to the right of Measure 10, the parental notification requirement. Therefore, we would expect that voters who supported Measure 8 would also support Measure 10, whereas voters who favored some restrictions but not a ban would also support parental notification only.

The distribution of actual votes is presented in table 6.4. Individuals whose responses did not fit the anticipated Guttman scale pattern are listed in the last row as errors. The standard used for identifying if the response pattern is logically consistent (or unidimensional) is to have fewer than 10% errors. Thus, for the social dimension, high constraint is evident. On these abortion measures, fewer than 2% of the voters can be classified as casting a set of choices that depart from the scale (i.e., voting for a ban, but not for parental notification). This finding complements the factor analysis, which found that the dimension of underlying social attitudes explained the largest proportion of variance in initiative votes.

The distribution of votes on the economic and regulatory dimensions does not appear to be as consistently ordered as votes on the

**Figure 6.1** Placement of 1990 Oregon Ballot Measures on Left-Right Continuum

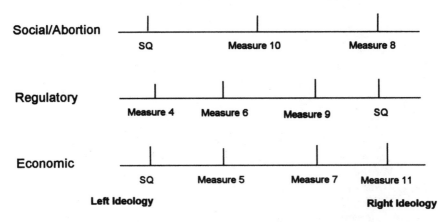

social issues. On the regulatory scale, approximately 30% of voters cast a set of choices that did not fit the left-right patterns derived from the newspaper endorsements. A similar rate of errors is found for the economic scale. While the number of errors exceeds the acceptable standard for a unidimensional Guttman scale, that an overwhelming majority of voters fit the pattern is exceptional given the number and complexity of the issues.

## Conclusion

Electoral choice on ballot propositions does appear to be constrained by some underlying attitudinal dimensions. For the ballot measures I have analyzed, the structure of choices appears to be fairly consistent with common ideological dimensions. While the principal components analysis does not reveal a single underlying dimension, the factor loadings coincide with clear social, economic, and regulatory ideological dimensions that have been proposed as alternatives to the single left-right ideological dimension. Furthermore, the Guttman scale analysis suggests ideological consistency in decisions within the three specific issue areas.

There is also some evidence that the underlying structure of electoral choices varies in the population. Admittedly, my measure of

**Table 6.4** Guttman Scale: Patterns of Responses
on Ballot Measures

| Ballot Measure | Response | | | | Errors |
|---|---|---|---|---|---|
| Social Issues | | | | | |
| Vote on | | | | | |
| Measure 10 | no | yes | yes | | no |
| Vote on | | | | | |
| Measure 8 | no | no | yes | | yes |
| % with | | | | | |
| response | | | | | |
| pattern | 43.0 | 16.7 | 38.7 | | 1.6 |
| Economic Issues | | | | | |
| Vote on | | | | | |
| Measure 5 | no | yes | yes | yes | |
| Vote on | | | | | |
| Measure 7 | no | no | yes | yes | |
| Vote on | | | | | |
| Measure 11 | no | no | no | yes | |
| % with | | | | | |
| response | | | | | |
| pattern | 24.7 | 18.8 | 8.9 | 13.4 | 30.1 |
| Environmental Issues | | | | | |
| Vote on | | | | | |
| Measure 9 | no | yes | yes | yes | |
| Vote on | | | | | |
| Measure 6 | no | no | yes | yes | |
| Vote on | | | | | |
| Measure 4 | no | no | no | yes | |
| % with | | | | | |
| response | | | | | |
| pattern | 18.7 | 11.4 | 21.5 | 19.7 | 28.7 |

partisan consistency is a poor substitute for cognitive ability, political involvement, or ideological reasoning, factors that have been acknowledged as causing variation in the structuring of attitudes. My analysis is limited by the lack of explanatory variables. However, I do find higher attitudinal consistency on ballot measure voting for the groups that also vote consistently with the same party in candidate races. My evidence does not establish that the structure of attitudes is markedly different when highly partisan and less partisan voters are compared, but rather that there is less structure to ballot measure voting among those whose candidate voting is not structured by party.

The factor analysis and the Guttman scale analysis reveal patterns that should not exist if numerous choices on ballot measures were merely random marks on a ballot. Thus, when voters make choices on a large number of initiatives, it is reasonable to expect that outcomes "make sense" after all the votes are counted. That is, it might be relatively unlikely that a majority of voters would approve two policies that are logically incompatible with each other, given the sort of structure demonstrated here. This is not to say that inconsistent outcomes could not happen on occasion, but we should not expect it to be common.

Finally, I should note that I have not directly tested what leads to consistency or to ideological structuring of choices, but have only found some evidence of consistency and structure. Comparisons with newspaper endorsements suggest that some structure may be learned from elites. However, it is difficult to establish a causal link between the endorsements and choices with these data from Oregon. The next chapter examines how knowledge of another form of elite endorsements (elected officials' positions) structures choices on a term limit initiative in Washington.

## NOTES

1. Or, for another (hypothetical) example, consider how one would interpret the results of a single election where voters approved tougher criminal-sentencing for drug crimes in one initiative, while approving decriminalization of marijuana use in another.

2. For a summary of the research on ideological consistency, see Smith 1989.

3. The sample of approximately 1,200 voted ballots was systematically drawn from all voted ballots in Marion County, Oregon. An examination of the representatives of the sample is presented below ($N = 1,198$).

|                             | Sample (%) | Actual Outcome (%) |
|-----------------------------|------------|--------------------|
| Governor—vote for Roberts   | 39.51      | 39.59              |
| Measure 10—yes              | 55.68      | 54.94              |
| Measure 11—yes              | 34.79      | 34.74              |
| Measure 5—yes vote          | 59.11      | 55.47              |

4. An eigenvalue of 1 is the most common criterion used for determining the number of components in a principal components analysis (Kaiser 1958). Any component that a number of variables have in common with an eigenvalue greater than 1 indicates that the component explains more variance in the responses than a single variable. Therefore, if a component is explaining more variance than a single variable, it is explaining a meaningful amount of variance.

5. The scale is said to be triangular, since it assumes an underlying pattern of ordered responses such as the following:

| Choice       | Voter 1 | Voter 2 | Voter 3 |
|--------------|---------|---------|---------|
| Initiative A | yes     | no      | no      |
| Initiative B | yes     | yes     | no      |
| Initiative C | yes     | yes     | yes     |

# 7

# The Influence of Elite Endorsements in Initiative Campaigns

JEFFREY A. KARP

In November of 1991, voters in Washington State rejected an initiative that would have placed limits on the number of terms elected officials could serve. The term limits initiative would have forced the state's entire congressional delegation, including Speaker of the House Tom Foley, to leave office after serving just one more term in office. The 1991 term limits defeat in Washington State was unique and unexpected. Just one year before, the term limits movement appeared to have strong momentum when voters approved term limits initiatives in California, Colorado, and Oklahoma. Initially the Washington measure enjoyed widespread support; however, after an expensive and hotly contested campaign, the measure failed with 46% of the vote. A year after the defeat, voters in Washington and 13 other states passed similar term limits measures. Most of these measures passed easily, with little or no opposition. By the end of 1995, voters in more than 20 states approved ballot measures limiting the number of terms of either or both state legislators and members of Congress.

Washington was one of the few states to experience organized opposition to term limits. Moreover, the nature of opposition was unique in that well-known elites, like Speaker Tom Foley, actively campaigned against the initiative. Foley and the other members of the congressional delegation warned that passage of the term limits initiative would result in Washington State unilaterally disarming its clout in Congress. Pundits as well as the campaign strategists themselves attributed the defeat of the initiative to the crafting of this message (see Robinson and Dixon 1992).

This chapter focuses on the term limits campaign in Washington State in 1991, examining how citizens use cues and other information from political elites to help them decide whether or not to vote for a ballot measure. While the chapter provides insight into the nature of public support for legislative term limits, its broader objective is to explain the influence of elites in direct democracy elections.

## Opinion Formation

Studies of mass opinion change contend that the attitudes of the electorate are shaped by the political rhetoric of elites, that "[t]he voice of the people is but an echo" (Key 1966, 2). V. O. Key believed that public opinion is part of a dynamic system in which activists, organized groups, and elected officials influence mass opinion: "Mass opinion is not self-generating; in the main, it is a response to cues, the proposals, and the visions propagated by the political activists" (1966, 557). Similarly, Converse (1964) believed that individuals rely on information or messages from political elites to help organize political issues and ideas. For an individual's political reasoning about an issue to be influenced by elite opinion, he or she must have knowledge of these issues and opinions. Exposure to messages from political elites depends in part on the individual's level of political involvement as well as the intensity of the message. Individuals who pay attention to current political events and understand them are more likely to develop stable attitudes on major political issues (Feldman 1989) and to think in ideological terms (Converse 1964; Stimson 1975). Because high political awareness is associated with stable attitudes and probability of exposure, those individuals who are more likely to be exposed to cues from political elites are also likely to have knowledge about the sources of the cues and whether or not they are consistent with prior attitudes. The least-informed individuals, while in theory being more susceptible to campaign messages, are likely not to respond to cues from elites because they are less likely to be exposed to the persuasive messages, especially when the flow of information is low (Con-

verse 1962). Those who are moderately informed are most susceptible to campaign messages because they have a higher probability of
being exposed to the message than the least aware and are more
likely to be persuaded by the message than the highly aware.

Following on Converse's work, Zaller (1992) outlines scenarios
for mass opinion change in two cases: first, when there is consensus
among elites; and second, when there is elite polarization. Zaller defines these elites as persons who devote themselves full-time to
some aspect of politics or public affairs (1992, 6). These would include politicians, journalists, and policy experts, as well as some activists. The model treats opinion formation as a two-step process
wherein individuals must first be exposed to new political information, and then decide whether to accept or reject the information
based on their own political predispositions. If there are no ideological or partisan cues in the messages—meaning there is a consensus
in elite opinion—then support for the elite position should increase
among the politically aware. However, if there are partisan or ideological cues in the messages, the politically aware liberal will resist
the conservative message and accept the more consistent liberal
messages. Likewise, politically aware conservatives will be exposed
to persuasive messages but reject the inconsistent liberal ones.
While Zaller is not necessarily referring to direct legislation campaigns (for an exception, see Zaller 1987, 826, on gay rights), the
model is applicable, as these campaigns present information to voters in attempts to persuade them with messages from political elites.

Elite endorsements may be a source of information about the ideological or partisan nature of ballot propositions. In candidate elections, party labels serve as a critical reference point for voters by
helping to reduce the costs of information (Downs 1957). Without
partisan cues, information costs are substantially higher, and as a
result, few voters will be informed about propositions. As a substitute for party, elite endorsements may serve as a cost-cutting decision-making strategy in direct legislation elections. Research on the
effects of elite endorsements in direct democracy elections indicates that they do play an important role in voters' decision making
(Bowler and Donovan 1993; Lupia 1994; Magleby 1984) and that
these effects may be greater when there are high levels of consensus
among elites (Magleby 1984, 152–53). The influence of elite endorsements may also depend on who the endorser is. The positions

of elected officials who are better known to voters than part-time activists may receive a disproportionate amount of coverage during a campaign. As a result, persons who are equally attentive might be more aware of the politician's position than that of the activist.

To summarize, elite endorsements are a source of information for voters in ballot proposition campaigns. How voters respond to this information will depend on the extent of elite involvement, the individual's level of political awareness, and the nature of elite messages in the campaigns, whether it is contentious or unanimous. The next section examines the nature of elite messages in the Washington term limits campaign.

## The 1991 Washington Term Limits Campaign

The term limits initiative that qualified for the ballot in 1991 in Washington followed three successful term limits initiatives in Oklahoma, Colorado, and California. Unlike its predecessors in Oklahoma and California, Washington's term limits initiative proposed limiting the terms of both state *and* federal lawmakers and was more severe. The limits varied from 6 to 12 years, depending on the office. The measure would also limit the terms of the governor and lieutenant governor to 8 years. Unlike the term limits measures in other states, the limits were retroactive; all incumbents who had reached their limit, with the exception of the governor, would be allowed one more election for office. Officials could run again for office after a 6-year break. Passage of the measure would have prevented incumbent Governor Booth Gardner from running for a third term in 1992. Additionally, House Speaker Tom Foley and all seven of his House colleagues, and 109 of the 147 state legislators, could seek and serve just one additional term before leaving office in 1994 if the measure passed (Olson 1992, 69).

Proponents for the initiative came from both sides of the political spectrum. The term limits initiative was authored by a group of liberal activists calling themselves LIMIT (Legislative Mandating Incumbent Terms) but funded primarily by antitax conservatives and Libertarians. Sherry Bockwinkel, who led the campaign for LIMIT, had worked in the previous year as a staff member for a congressional candidate who attempted to unseat a veteran incumbent in the Democratic primary, and later for a Democratic candidate running for the state assembly. The failure of these candidates to win election convinced Bockwinkel and several other LIMIT organizers that incumbent advantages in fund-raising, franking privileges, and media access made them invulnerable. Passage of term limits measures in Oklahoma, California, and Colorado led them to believe that term limits would provide a solution to the problem. The primary source of funding for the signature drive and the campaign came from a national term limits group controlled by conservative Republicans and Libertarians. The coalition between left-wing Democrats and right-wing conservatives was rather tenuous. Bockwinkel accepted the money, saying, "Wring 'em dry. Let 'em spend it on this one instead of spending it on taking people's civil liberties away. Then we'll save the left's money to fight the war machine" (Olson 1992, 75).

The opposition campaign was spearheaded by the state employees union and joined by good-government and environmental groups. Initially, members of the state's congressional delegation, including Speaker Tom Foley, stayed out of the term limits battle. Foley and the other members of the congressional delegation were reluctant to voice an opinion against an issue that appeared to be popular with voters. Moreover, they believed that the measure was unconstitutional at least as it applied to members of Congress (Olson 1992, 76). In an effort to forestall passage of the initiative, Washington's top elected officials, including Governor Gardner and Speaker Foley, joined other good government groups, such as Common Cause and the League of Women Voters, in a lawsuit to declare the initiative unconstitutional before it was placed on the ballot. The Washington Supreme Court, however, refused to hear the case before the election.

With seven weeks to go before the election, opponents of the measure were running out of money. Proponents enjoyed a 7.5 to 1 advantage in fund-raising. Almost all of the money that LIMIT had received came from Citizens for Congressional Reform (CCR), a national, Washington, D.C.-based term limits group funded primarily by the Koch brothers, two billionaires from Kansas who were active in the Libertarian Party. Given the funding advantage, it appeared as if the measure would easily pass. Six weeks before the election, Foley and all of the other members of the state's congressional delegation, which included three Republicans, began to raise money to defeat the initiative and began to speak out against the measure. A month later, the opposition campaign had received $300,000 in campaign contributions. These contributions came from the nation's most well-financed lobbying interests: tobacco giants Philip Morris and RJR Nabisco, defense contractors Northrop and General Electric, and the National Rifle Association (Young 1993).

In the final month of the campaign, the dialogue shifted from term limits and government's unresponsiveness to one that focused on the loss of clout. The opposition argued that losing the Washington congressional delegation could cost voters their jobs, threaten their low electric rates, and jeopardize their environment (Robinson and Dixon 1992, 18). In the final three and a half weeks, the opposition aired radio and television commercials, focusing on Washington's losing its powerful delegation and unilaterally disarming itself while other states retained their entrenched representatives. Proponents relied primarily on radio advertisements, emphasizing anti-incumbent and abuse-of-office themes. The vast majority of newspaper editorials were against the initiative and focused on the costs to the state of losing Foley. In the last two weeks of the campaign, Governor Gardner announced that he would not run for a third term in 1992, and U.S. Representative Al Swift, a seven-term Democrat, made a pledge to seek just one additional term. Foley, who had tried to remain on the sidelines, entered the fray in the last week of the campaign and crisscrossed the state in a major media blitz from Seattle to Spokane (Olson 1992, 81). He emphasized how the loss of clout would affect the state.

In the end, proponents outspent the opponents by a 2 to 1 margin, spending $705,403 compared to $316,250. However, about one-third of the money spent by proponents was just to obtain access to the ballot. On November 5, 1991, voters in Washington rejected the measure by a 54% to 46% margin.

## Explaining Opinion Change on Initiative 553

Before the onset of the campaign, public opinion polls in Washington, like surveys elsewhere, indicated strong support for legislative term limits. Support for term limits appears to be the result of widespread dissatisfaction with the political process, manifested in an increasingly cynical electorate (Karp 1995). In an exit poll taken during the 1990 midterm election, 72% of Washington voters favored unspecified limits on members of Congress.[1] National surveys conducted at that time revealed similar levels of support.[2] When respondents are presented with a hypothetical term limit of twelve years, a majority still expresses support for the idea.[3] In August, three months before the election, about two-thirds of likely voters expressed support for the term limits initiative, compared to 28% opposed and 4% undecided.[4] Comparing these data with surveys conducted later in the campaign and after the election reveals a dramatic change in opinion, though care must be used in interpreting these results, as the surveys were based on different samples.[5] As figure 7.1 reveals, initial support for term limits was high, but declined rapidly for both Democrats and Republicans as election day neared. After a strong and visible campaign, aggregate support fell off by almost 30 points, leading to an opinion reversal. Preelection polls of registered voters taken the Sunday and Monday before the election showed 39% in favor and 49% opposed, with 13% undecided.[6] Splitting the undecided voters almost evenly results in the eventual 46% to 54% margin of defeat. Republicans were more supportive than Democrats or independents, though these differences are not statistically significant. Nor are there significant partisan differences in the exit poll as support drops off equally over the course of the campaign for Republicans, Democrats, and independents.

Changes in public opinion over the course of a campaign are not unusual. Most ballot measures appear to have a great deal of support, only to have that support erode by election day (see Magleby 1984). But changes in support for term limits measures are unexpected if one considers the nature of the issue. Unlike the typical ballot question, which is technically worded, the ballot language of most term limits initiatives is rather straightforward. Moreover, most surveys indicate that only a small minority of voters remain undecided, indicating that the issue is not one of great complexity for voters. For these reasons, voters may be more sure of their opinions. Data from other states where term limits initiatives later appeared on the ballot indicate very little change in aggregate opinions

**Figure 7.1** Changes in Partisan Support for Initiative 553

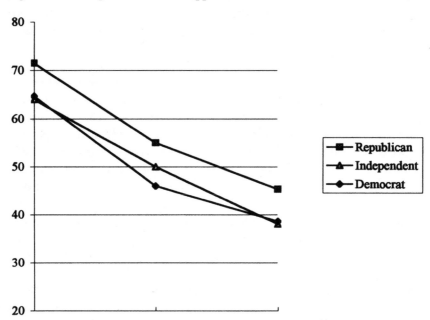

*Sources:* Greenburg-Lake: The Analysis Group (Aug. 20, n = 648; Nov. 14, n = 489); Fairbank, Maullin, Associates (Oct. 8–9, n = 400).

before the election, despite differences in both population and question wording. An Arizona poll, for example, taken over six months before the election, showed 73% in favor of term limits. The initiative received 74% of the vote. In Florida, surveys in the fall of 1991 and July 1992 showed roughly three-fourths of the respondents supporting such measures.[7] The initiative passed with 77% of the vote. In Montana and Wyoming, polls taken a month before the election were virtually identical to the final results.[8] In Missouri, polls in June 1992 showed that 80% of the respondents supported term limitations for both state legislators and members of Congress. By November, support had eroded by only 5%. Similar polls in Ohio and Nebraska reveal that support eroded only by 5 to 7 percentage points.[9]

Why the erosion of support in Washington and not in most other states? We cannot be certain, given the nature of the data, which factors account for changes in individual voting intentions over the course of the campaign. Nevertheless, we can draw some general conclusions based on the pattern of aggregate support. The Washington case was relatively rare in that well-known elites actively campaigned against the measure. In other states where term limit measures appeared on the ballot, many elites chose not to oppose an idea that was extremely popular with the voters, because they were convinced that the initiatives, at least as they applied to members of Congress, would never go into effect. They believed, correctly as it turned out, that term limits for members of Congress were unconstitutional.[10] These initiatives also did not impose the immediate threat that they had in Washington State. Many initiatives contained a "trigger clause" that delayed the implementation of term limits until a given number of states enacted similar provisions.

In some cases, as in Missouri, term limits for members of Congress would begin only after similar limits were adopted by one-half of the states. This requires at least one state without the initiative process to pass term limits, which is a hard trigger to pull. Other elites chose not to risk the political capital by opposing a popular issue. In Ohio, for example, the Democratic political leadership was convinced that the term limit initiative would pass if it got on the ballot, and they could do nothing much to stop it (Jewell 1993, 13). And in Missouri, the opposition spent all of its money, $7,380, on legal fees to have the initiative removed from the ballot. None of the members of the Missouri congressional delegation publicly opposed the measure, most likely because it would never apply to them. Thus, Washington was one of the few states where there was organized opposition and elites were outspoken.[11] While proponents spent a great deal of money responding to the criticism, the campaign was led by previously unknown activists and funded by individuals who would have preferred to remain anonymous.

If we assume most voters were paying attention to the campaign and were aware of elite discourse, it appears from the aggregate data displayed in figure 7.1 that some voters accepted the information carried by Foley and other elected officials. The preelection poll taken just before the election shows that Democratic support for the initiative plummeted by nearly 39 points after August. Aggregate Republican support also dropped by 23 points, indicating that some Republicans were also likely to accept the messages conveyed by elites.

## Estimating the Influence of Elite Endorsements

Since aggregate data can only be suggestive, we must turn to individual-level data to examine the influence of elite endorsements. Given that Speaker Tom Foley was a central figure in the campaign to defeat the term limits initiative, the analysis that follows focuses on his involvement. Foley was a well-known figure in Washington politics who symbolized the political establishment and whose tenure in Congress demonstrated the value of seniority. He was thus in an excellent position to define the issue.

To examine Foley's influence, a model is specified that takes into account both the voters' awareness and the extent to which voters found Foley credible. Based on the theory of opinion formation discussed earlier, it is hypothesized that persons supportive of Foley are likely to accept his message and vote "no" on the initiative, whereas those persons who are not supportive of Foley are likely to reject his appeals and vote "yes." The effect of these attitudes toward Foley will depend on whether a voter is aware that Foley opposed the measure. Thus, the model presupposes a two-stage process wherein voters must first be exposed to the cue and then must decide whether or not to accept or reject. The first stage in the model estimates the likelihood that individuals are aware of Foley's position. The second stage estimates the impact of awareness on the likelihood of voting for the initiative, using an indicator of awareness predicted from an equation estimating awareness as a function of media exposure.[12]

Those most likely to know Foley's position are those who were exposed to information about the campaign through radio and television advertisements as well as editorials in various newspapers. According to Magleby (1984, 130–39) these are the primary sources of information about ballot propositions, although information about politics comes from other sources, such as friends and family, work associates, fellow members of groups or organizations, and the voter's pamphlet. The variables used here are based on questions asking respondents if they remembered reading or hearing the advertisements.[13] To measure awareness, the dependent variable in the first stage of the model, the following question is used: "Do you remember seeing or hearing during the campaign that Speaker of the

House Tom Foley was against Initiative 553?" A sizable majority of those who voted on the initiative, 64%, were aware of Foley's position, compared to only 30% who knew that their own member of Congress was against the term limits measure. Former California Governor Jerry Brown also came to Washington to campaign in support of the initiative, but only 27% of the voters knew about that. Thus, the influence of elites depends not only on their prominence but also on the extent of their involvement.

The final stage in the model estimates the likelihood of voting for the initiative. To estimate Foley's influence, an interaction is specified between those who are aware of Foley's position and their feelings toward Foley. A "feeling thermometer" is used to measure feelings toward the Speaker, ranging from cold (0) to very warm (100). Partisanship is measured on a seven-point scale ranging from strong Democrat (1) to strong Republican (7), with independents coded in the middle (4). Another included variable measures respondent's feelings toward LIMIT, the organization that placed the initiative on the ballot. Finally, a measure of responsiveness is included in the model, based on the hypothesis that individuals who think government is out of touch are more likely to support term limits. The measure is based on the question, "Do you agree or disagree that Congress is out of touch and elected officials do not care about the people they represent?"[14]

## Results

The results in table 7.1 demonstrate how mass opinion is shaped in part by elites when their positions are known. The first-stage results illustrate that persons who were exposed to radio and television advertisements, both for and against the initiative, were more likely to know Foley's position. The second-stage results demonstrate that knowing Foley's position (predicted as a function of media exposure) in turn influenced their vote. Newspaper editorials against the initiative were also an important determinant of knowing Foley's position. These results coincide with those of Magleby, who found that a popular source of information on Proposition 13 in California was the newspaper (1984, 131). Those who knew that Foley opposed the

**Table 7.1** Vote on the 1991 Washington Term Limits Initiative
(Two-Stage Logit Estimates)

| Variables | First Stage Know Foley's Against | Effect | Second Stage Vote on Initiative | Effect |
|---|---|---|---|---|
| Radio/TV | .615** | .141 | .127 | .031 |
| ads (pro) | (.284) | | (.324) | |
| Radio/TV | .589** | .136 | .094 | .023 |
| ads (con) | (.282) | | (.319) | |
| Editorials (con) | .814*** | .187 | .413 | .100 |
| | (.213) | | (.219) | |
| Female | -.334 | -.077 | | |
| | (.208) | | | |
| Age | .067 | .015 | | |
| | (.050) | | | |
| Education | .028 | .006 | | |
| | (.075) | | | |
| Income | -.013 | -.003 | | |
| | (.062) | | | |
| Union member | -.025 | -.006 | | |
| | (.244) | | | |
| Party ID | — | | .025 | .006 |
| | | | (.051) | |
| Know Foley against | — | | 1.606*** | .389 |
| I553 | | | (.441) | |
| Foley (x) temperature | — | | -.038*** | -.009 |
| | | | (.006) | |
| LIMIT temperature | — | | .039*** | .009 |
| | | | (.005) | |
| Responsiveness | — | | .458*** | .111 |
| | | | (.186) | |
| Constant | -.762 | | -2.178*** | |
| | (.471) | | (.443) | |
| N | 489 | | 489 | |
| -2 Log Likelihood | 570.771 | | 535.127 | |
| % correctly classified | 70.50 | | 70.66 | |

*Sources:* Stan Greenberg and Celinda Lake, "1991 Survey of Washington
Initiative 553." Survey commissioned by the Washington State Federation
of Employees and conducted by Greenburg-Lake: The Analysis Group.

initiative were more likely to vote for the measure, but their feelings toward him also conditioned this relationship. The significance of the interaction term in the second-stage results indicates that those with favorable feelings toward Foley were least likely to support the initiative, while those with unfavorable feelings toward Foley were most likely to vote for the initiative. These effects are illustrated in figure 7.2, which reveals that Foley's position has a dramatic effect on the probability of supporting the initiative, depending on feelings toward Foley. Those with negative feelings toward Foley are almost twice as likely to vote for the initiative as those who are unaware of Foley's position.[15] Support for the initiative drops off sharply among those who are aware of Foley's position, as feelings toward Foley become more positive. On average, feelings toward Foley are generally favorable, which translates into a net advantage in persuading persons to vote "no" on the initiative. The differences at the extremes are rather large. Individuals who are the most positive toward Foley are three times as likely to vote against the measure as those at the other extreme.

Empirically, there is little evidence to suggest that simply hearing or seeing advertisements or reading editorials is enough to directly persuade voters. On average, about two-thirds of those who voted on the measure had heard radio commercials or seen television advertisements for and against the initiative. Less than 10% had heard only one side of the debate. These advertisements appear not to have influenced voters one way or another. Just under half of the voters (46%) had read newspaper editorials against the initiative. These too did not appear to directly influence voters to vote "no" on the initiative. These findings do not, however, disregard ad-

---

Thanks to the Washington State Federation of Employees for providing me access to their data.

*Note:* Standard errors are in parentheses.

Dependent variables: $Eq^1$, 1 = Aware of Foley's Position; O = otherwise; $Eq^2$, 1 = voted for I553; O = voted against.

*Effect:* Net effect on probability of a one-unit change in the independent variable evaluated at the mean. $Eq^1$ = .64; $Eq^2$ = 41.

$**p < .05$, $***p < .01$.

**Figure 7.1** Estimated Support for Initiative 553 by Feelings toward Foley and Awareness

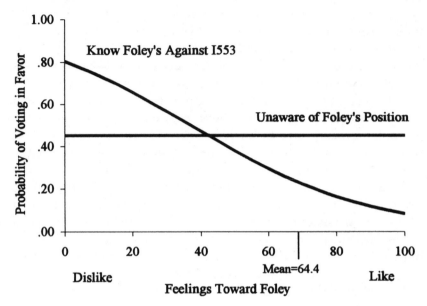

vertisements as an important source of information. The information carried in these ads was probably more effective in providing cues to voters about elite positions than they were in directly persuading voters. Foley's role in the debate was effective as a means of providing cues to voters who, in turn, chose to accept or reject arguments depending on feelings toward him.


## Conclusion

Most commentary after the election concluded that the fear of losing clout was the principal factor for the defeat of Initiative 553. In an article in *Campaign Magazine,* the campaign strategists against Initiative 553 claimed that the crafting of a persuasive message was critical to their success (Robinson and Dixon 1992). Proponents also believed that the message was the major factor for the loss (Struble 1993, 6). Indeed, in their second attempt at passing term limitations in Washington, LIMIT tried to diffuse the clout issue by making term limits nonretroactive. The findings in this paper suggest that the message was probably not quite as important as the messenger. While 20% of those who voted for term limits mentioned the loss of clout as a reason for voting against the measure, the analysis presented here suggests that without Foley, the message would probably not have had the impact it did. These findings are consistent with a large body of research that suggests that citizens who are well informed react to political ideas on the basis of cues provided by elites.

This model may also explain why term limits eventually passed in Washington in 1992 as well as in other states across the country. Unlike the Washington campaign in 1991, elites in the vast majority of states where term limits initiatives appeared on the ballot chose not to become involved in the debate. California was one exception, where prominent Democratic elites such as California Assembly Speaker Willie Brown led a campaign to defeat two term limits measures for state legislators that appeared simultaneously on the ballot in 1990 (see Donovan and Snipp 1994; Price 1994). One of these measures had the backing of the state's Republican leadership, while the other measure—which did not have as severe limits and also included campaign finance reform—was sponsored by a group of liberal reformers. Brown, who was joined by gubernatorial nominee Dianne Feinstein and other prominent Democrats, was successful in defeating one of these measures, largely because both Democratic *and* Republican elites, such as Republican gubernatorial candidate Pete Wilson, also opposed the measure (see Banducci and Karp 1994). On the other measure, however, elites were divided along partisan lines, and the measure passed with 52% of the vote.

A year later in Washington, term limits supporters qualified another measure for the ballot. A coalition of interest groups, similar to the one in the previous year, opposed the measure. Foley, however, was preoccupied with his own reelection bid, and as a result was less active in fighting term limits. The other members of the congressional delegation were also much less active in opposing term limitations in 1992 than in 1991. Not only were they all running for reelection, but the term limits restrictions were not retroactive and were less severe, giving them less of an incentive to oppose the measure. Although the opposing campaign relied on the same rhetoric, elites were not as active, and the initiative passed with 52% of the vote.

## NOTES

1. Voter Research and Surveys General Election Exit Poll, 1990, National File, Interuniversity Consortium for Political and Social Research (ICPSR) 9604.

2. CBS/*New York Times* Poll, October 1990.

3. CBS/*New York Times* Poll, October 1990.

4. Greenburg-Lake, 20 August 1991. Based on a sample of 648 likely voters.

5. The August poll sampled likely voters, whereas the two polls taken in October and November sampled registered voters.

6. Fairbank, Maullin & Associates. Based on a sample of 400 registered voters.

7. Hill Research, July 1992. Based on a sample of 485 likely voters.

8. University of Montana, October 1992; based on a sample of 389 likely voters. University of Wyoming, October 1992; based on a sample of 521 residents.

9. University of Akron, October 1992; based on a sample of 577 residents. University of Nebraska, 1992; based on a sample of 491 residents.

10. In a 5–4 decision in *U.S. Term Limits, Inc. v. Thornton*, 514 U.S. 779 (1995), the U.S. Supreme Court ruled that state-imposed term limits were unconstitutional, thereby overturning term limits laws in 23 states. According to the majority opinion, the qualifications for congressional service listed in the Constitution—age, citizenship, and state residency—are exclusive, and neither the states nor Congress could add additional qualifications.

11. Utah and California are other examples where partisan elite opposition could have driven an opinion reversal. For Utah, see Magleby and Patterson (1996); for California, Banducci and Karp (1994) and Donovan and Snipp (1994). None of these studies were able to directly account for the effects of media exposure and knowledge of elite positions in their analyses.

12. This two-stage estimation process thus tests if exposure to media has a direct impact on voting, or if the effects of media on vote operate indirectly, by structuring voter awareness of elite positions.

13. "Do you remember reading any newspaper editorials against Initiative 553?" "Did you hear any radio commercials or see any television ads for Initiative 553?" "Did you hear any radio commercials or see any television ads for Initiative 553?" Coded "1" for Yes; "0" otherwise.

14. Coded "1" for Agree, "0" for Don't Know, "-1" for Disagree.

15. Figure 7.2 plots the probability of supporting I553 predicted by feelings toward Foley when all other variables in the second-stage model are set at their mean values.

Part **III**

# State Public Policies
# and Direct Democracy

After examining how initiatives originate (part 1) and how voters respond to some initiative campaigns (part 2), in part 3 we examine the policy outcomes associated with direct legislation. The chapters in this section emphasize how politics in direct democracy states are, to a certain extent, fundamentally different from politics in states with traditional representative legislative institutions. These chapters explore three dimensions that distinguish direct democracy states from other states, one being popular "governance" reform policies adopted in direct democracy states. These policies differ from some of our standard classifications of public policies (i.e., distributive, redistributive, regulatory; see Lowi 1969) in that the agent being acted upon by policy is the government rather than the public. Chapter 8 demonstrates how governmental procedures and legislative operations in initiative states are systematically different from those in other states, since citizens are prone to pass governance policies that legislatures would not. Of immediate concern are reformist policies initiated by "citizens" (or groups outside the legislature) to constrain the operation of legislatures: term limits, tax and expenditure limits, and supermajority requirements. These governance policies change the way that legislatures can function in direct democracy states.

A second distinction of politics and policy outcomes in initiative states relates to the threat that the initiative (or potential initiative) places on legislatures. Proponents of direct democracy argued that the initiative would provide direct effects on policy by allowing citizens to propose and pass policies that legislators might not consider (as illustrated in chapter 8). The proponents also argued that the initiative would provide indirect influence by affecting the behavior of officials once they are sent to the legislature (see Cronin 1989). Chapter 9 demonstrates how the *threat* of direct legislation can affect legislative policies in direct democracy states.

169

The initiative can force legislators to consider voter preferences when drafting new laws. Legislators in these states might antici- pate initiatives and thus produce policy more in line with public opinion than legislative policy produced in noninitiative states.

A third way that initiatives might alter policies in direct democ- racy states is by facilitating an arena for what Meier (1994) and Haider-Markel and Meier (1996; see also Gusfield 1963) call *morality politics.* In the arena of morality politics (as opposed to interest group politics), issues are highly salient and are framed as moral issues that challenge the acceptability of a group or of some behavior. Those op- posed to a group or a behavior (i.e., drinking, homosexuality, abor- tion, etc.) seek to expand the scope of conflict beyond legislatures, where interest group politics might structure policy, to the mass pub- lic, where morality-based arguments can have greater effect. For pol- icy entrepreneurs or issue activists critical of homosexuality, moral- ity-based appeals in the context of the mass politics of direct democracy can be effective for overturning civil rights protections that gays and lesbians might win in legislatures (Haider-Markel and Meier 1996; see Cain 1992b for a similar argument about legislative gains, direct democracy losses, and racial minorities).

By allowing for an expanded scope of public conflict based on morality, or feelings toward a minority group, direct democracy might thus provide an environment where minority groups can be targeted by critics in a manner distinctly different from a legislative setting's. The classic criticism of direct democracy—that it might en- gender a tyranny of the majority—is addressed, at least in part, in chapters 10 and 11. Minorities who might find civil rights protec- tions or sympathetic policies (or ambivalence) from legislatures can become the targets of hostile statewide campaigns in direct democ- racy states. Chapter 10 examines the racial and ethnic context that spawned two policies that might be seen as targeting minorities: Cal- ifornia's anti-immigration Proposition 187 and its "Official English" measure. The consequences of these policies are noteworthy when these measures pass (e.g., Proposition 187 and Colorado's antigay ini- tiative); yet as chapter 11 illustrates, there are also consequences, though less obvious ones, in placing these initiatives on the ballot, even when they fail. Chapter 11 demonstrates that mass opinion about groups targeted by initiatives is more likely to shift toward in- tolerant attitudes in areas holding initiatives that target the groups.

# 8

# Changing Rules for State Legislatures: Direct Democracy and Governance Policies

CAROLINE J. TOLBERT

This chapter examines the adoption of state governance policies, such as legislative term limits and tax and expenditure limitations. Governance policies are procedural reforms that constrain the autonomy of state legislatures, change the "rules" that state and elected officials must follow, and restructure political institutions. A reemergence of populism is developed as critical in the adoption and linkage between governance policies. Constitutional provisions for the initiative and a history of using the process are developed as indicators of state populism. Analysis indicates that states with a history of direct democracy usage are more likely to adopt governance policies than nonpopulist states; states with high usage of the initiative process are the first to adopt governance policies. Research also suggests that the current political climate (1980–90s) can be compared to the late nineteenth and early twentieth century, an era that produced a range of political reforms. Both periods have strikingly similar characteristics, as each era is marked by a rise in the use of direct democracy, the adoption of a significant number of reforms, preference for procedural over substantive policies, and the pervasive distrust of representative government's institutions.

# Growing Public Disenchantment with Government

A distinguishing feature of politics in the 1990s is a pervasive sense of public distrust of, frustration with, and alienation from government—from Washington to the state capitols. Public dissatisfaction with government and elected officials is documented in the print media and public opinion polls. A recent Gallup Poll showed that only 20% of respondents said they can trust the federal government all or some of the time—half the percentage during the Watergate scandal of 1974 (Shogan 1994). Rather than following circular swings, public discontent with government has intensified over the past 20 years.

In 1976, for example, 60% of the public said that the government was run for "a few big interests" rather than for the "benefit of all the people"; in 1992, 75% felt this way. Over the same period, the proportion of the public believing that the government in Washington could be trusted "to do what is right" only some of the time rose from 63% to 73% (Citrin 1996, 269). Before the Vietnam War and Watergate, 8 out of 10 people said they could trust the government in Washington to do what was right all or most of the time. In 1994, only 3 out of 10 people share that confidence in government (Broder 1994).

The factors driving the public's discontent are complex and may reflect a deep-rooted dissatisfaction with representative institutions of government (Dodd 1995). Phillips argues that public discontent is rooted in growing public awareness that representative government has failed to address voters' most pressing concerns—violent crime, national health care, K–12 education, a clean environment, and economic security (1993). Revelations of governmental corruption and scandal fuel the public's negative assessment of their elected officials. For example, after the 1994 indictment of Congressman Dan Rostenkowski (D-Ill.) for misuse of public funds, a Gallup Poll found that 49% of the public believed that Congress was more corrupt than it had been 20 years before; only 7% felt Congress was less corrupt. Also, 51% said that most House members were corrupt, and 29% expressed this view about their own representative (Citrin 1996, 270). It is often through revelations of governmental corruption and scandal that the public understands the actions of their elected officials (Merida 1994).

This chapter defines governance policies, a set of political reforms that arise from a context of popular distrust of government. I argue that the 1990s can be characterized by a reemergence of populism. Use of the initiative process is conceptualized as an indicator of state populism. I model the impact of this explanatory/independent variable on the adoption of three state governance policies: term limits, tax and expenditure limits, and supermajority tax rules—dependent variables.

## Public Support for Political Reform

Public discontent with lawmakers coincides with increased support for political reforms, such as legislative term limits, tax cuts, and restrictions on governmental spending. Support for these reforms may lie in the fact that the average citizen feels left out of the political process and distrustful of political elites. In the media, it is increasingly argued that a sense of powerlessness in the face of a growing "governmental bureaucracy" is what drives the anger and frustration so common in discussions of politics in the 1990s. For these individuals, the institutions of representative government have failed in their fundamental goal to represent the public. Political reforms are promoted as giving the public more control over their elected officials and the operation of government.

Public support for political reforms that give the public a more direct role in government decision making is widespread. An April 1994 poll of 900 individuals found broad support for "direct democracy" measures that would allow the public to make policy decisions without intermediaries. Sixty-four percent of those interviewed favored conducting national referenda on major issues and giving votes on national referenda equal weight with legislation passed by Congress. Also, 66% favored submitting all tax increases approved by Congress to a vote in the next national election.[1] Even when respondents were presented with arguments that term limitations would lead to a loss of expertise, penalize lawmakers who are doing a good job, and increase the power of career staff members and savvy lobbyists, 74% of those surveyed still favored term limitations for Congress and state lawmakers (Merida 1994).[2]

# Governance Policy

During the 1980s and early 1990s, a number of U.S. states enacted reform policies concerned with governance, several through ballot initiative. Although the passage of political reforms was common-place in the 1990s, academic research and the media often character-ize the passage of individual reforms as isolated phenomena. A grow-ing body of literature has addressed legislative term limits (Banducci and Karp 1994; Benjamin and Malbin 1992; Cain 1992a; Capell 1993; Clucas 1993; Copeland 1992, 1993; Copeland and Rausch 1991; Dodd 1995; Donovan and Snipp 1994; Jewell 1993; Lunch 1993; Thompson and Moncrief 1993; Moncrief et al. 1992; Mondak 1995; Noah 1995, 1996; Petracca 1992–1994; Polsby 1993; Pound 1993; Reed and Schansberg 1995a, 1995b; Rausch 1994; Sussman et al. 1994; Struble 1993). But little effort has been made to understand how diverse political reforms are related—whether they are re-sponses to a similar force, or combine to make a similar impact on politics and policy. I suggest that the adoption of legislative term limits and tax and expenditure limitations are not isolated, unique phenomena, but are part of a body of linked reforms that are sweep-ing local, state, and even national government. These political re-forms are part of a growing category of new policies that are restruc-turing state political institutions in the 1990s. I argue they can be construed as "governance policies."

Governance policy is an aspect of public policy that has received less attention than traditional substantive policies, such as health, welfare, education, or other expenditure policies. The definition of governance policy includes policies (1) that constrain the autonomy (or discretion) of the legislature in governing, and (2) have a promi-nent procedural component. Examples of governance policies include tax and expenditure limitations, supermajority rules for tax in-creases, and legislative term limits. Governance policies reform the institutions of representative government at the local, state, and na-tional level. Governance policies modify not only the actions of elected officials but also the very fabric of representative government.

Governance policies reform state governments by constraining their autonomy in areas including taxation, social policy, and leg-islative procedures (cf. Rausch 1994) by amending state constitu-tions and statutory law. Legislative term limits, for example, re-strict the tenure of elected officials in the state legislature and often reduce the size of the legislative staff. Tax and expenditure limita-tions regulate the tax take and expenditures available to the state legislature, and decrease its autonomy over fiscal policy. Supermajority rules for tax increases require a two-thirds vote of the legislature to raise taxes or enact a new tax. In each case, a defining feature of governance policy is a prominent procedural component.

Other examples that might qualify as governance policies include affirmative action, campaign finance reform, and criminal sentencing. Anti-affirmative action initiatives have qualified for the 1996 ballot in over ten states, including California. These measures would prohibit state governments and universities from considering race, ethnicity, or gender in awarding employment, contracts, or college admissions. Public regulation of the courts and judiciary via direct democracy is also evident in the adoption of "three-strikes-you're-out" measures that require the legal system to sentence repeat convicted felons to life in prison. These measures have been adopted in over 30 states nationwide. Other policies that attempt to govern the actions of the state and/or elected officials include campaign spending limits and disclosure laws. Although these diverse policies reform fiscal policy, legislative procedures, and even the court system, each attempts to *regulate* how the state should proceed to govern. Each policy is a procedural reform that changed the rules under which public officials can operate.

## "Governance Policy" and "Public Policy"

Governance policies can be distinguished from traditional public policies—policies that aim to distribute, redistribute, or regulate for the commonwealth—by the agent of action. The term "public policy" implies that the *public* is the subject being acted on by "governmental trustees" or elected officials. Public policies are justified as necessary for the public good and betterment of society. "Governance policies" aim to increase accountability, and imply that the *government* is the object being acted on by the public. Governance policies are justified by advocates as necessary for the efficiency and effectiveness of democratic rule. Traditional research on regulatory policy outcomes assumed that it is the behavior of the private sector that is modified by a governmental agency or congressional mandate. That is, the private sector is being told by government what it can and cannot do. In contrast, governance policies—term limitations, tax limitations, supermajority tax rules—modify the behavior of the public sector, or government officials.

Governance policy can be thought of as "procedural" policy. By definition, governance policies constitute "internal reforms" of state government, particularly state legislatures. Rather than constraining the actions of the private sector, governance policies constrain the way the public sector—state governments, legislatures, and bureaucratic agencies—can proceed to operate. Because governance policies place internal constraints on state governments, they may be as important as external constraints (partisan identification, economic conditions, etc.) for understanding state policy outcomes.[3]

Most empirical research on policy outcomes assumes a stable governing environment and primarily addresses external factors influencing policy outputs. This literature focuses on traditional institutional processes and assumes the primacy of a legislative or gubernatorial decision process. By assuming the centrality of the legislative process, this literature emphasizes a top-down process of policy formulation dominated by policy specialists, state government officials, and professional organizations. For example, Berkman (1993) focuses on networks of state elected officials in shaping the tax agenda in state legislatures and Congress. Dye focuses on economic determinants of state policies (1966), while Elazar (1984) emphasizes cultural and historical features shaping policy outcomes. In each case, political elites determine policy content, level of service provided, and which sector of society bears the costs and benefits. This literature, however, does not adequately explain governance policies, which are often adopted through alternative institutional contexts, such as direct democracy.

Governance policies are not unique in the history of U.S. politics, but rather are part of a series of policies that seek to change the institutional rules and operation of government. In recent decades, as in the late nineteenth century, there is an increasing interest in changing the rules of the political game. By institutionalizing rule changes for taxation, budgeting, and elections, governance policies potentially have a dramatic impact on substantive policy.[4] Changing the rules of the game can effectively determine who wins and who loses the game. And by changing the rules, governance policies can ultimately change the operation of representative governments.

## Governance Policy: State Incumbency and Fiscal Controls as Dependent Variables

This analysis examines the adoption of three governance policies: legislative term limits, state tax and expenditure limits, and legislative supermajority requirements for tax increases—all dependent variables in this analysis.[5] Each is a procedural policy that changes the internal "rules" elected officials must follow in campaigning for election, levying taxes, or allocating governmental resources.[6] This analysis includes state governance policies adopted as of November 1994. These policies were adopted in the states over nearly a 20-year period between 1978 and 1994.

### Legislative Term Limits

Since 1990, when legislative limits were first adopted in California, Colorado, and Oklahoma, term limits have been adopted in 22 states.[7] Each state measure varies in the length of terms in office, number of offices under limit, and method of restricting the terms of state and congressional lawmakers. Most measures apply to both state legislatures and congressional delegations, while some include limitations on other statewide officials, including the governor and secretary of state. Although there is some variation in the length of terms for state office-holders, strict limits allow only 6 years of service, while more lenient limits of 12 years offer more moderate incumbency controls. Of the governance policies examined here, none have had as direct an effect on legislative institutions as term limits.[8]

### State Tax and Expenditure Limitations (TELs)

State tax and expenditure limits create a fiscal control on state legislators that limits their taxing and spending authority. Beginning with the late 1970s tax revolt, state tax and expenditure limitations have been enacted in 21 states (ACIR 1994).[9] Eleven of these measures were adopted since 1980. Colorado voters approved a state tax and expenditure measure in 1992 that limits increases in state spending and taxes to population growth and the rate of inflation; no changes in taxes or tax policy are allowed without voter approval.

The Colorado legislature can no longer enact tax increases—tax hikes can only become law if approved by the voters in a referendum election. The general assembly can declare an emergency by a two-thirds vote and raise emergency taxes subject to voter approval. Measures like these institutionally weaken the ability of legislatures to collect revenue and provide services, a fundamental responsibility of government.

## Legislative Supermajority for Tax Increases

Eleven states have constitutional provisions requiring a "supermajority" or a two-thirds vote in the legislature to pass some or all tax increases. In the 1992 election, four states (Arizona, Colorado, Oklahoma, Washington) enacted constitutional amendments requiring tax increases to be approved by a margin larger than a simple majority of both houses. Arkansas was the first to adopt supermajority rules for tax increases in 1934. Arkansas voters approved a constitutional amendment that requires a two-thirds vote to increase "the rate for property, excise privilege, or personal taxes now levied" (Stansel 1994; Mackey 1993). Supermajority tax rules in seven states—Arizona, California, Colorado, Delaware, Oklahoma, South Dakota, and Washington—can be characterized as tax-revolt measures (Mackey 1993).

Supermajority rule changes are increasingly popular reforms for making policy changes immune from legislative modification. Supermajority rules, along with voter approval requirements to enact all tax increases, are examples of "second generation" state TELs (Tolbert 1994a, 1994b). In contrast to the 1970s tax revolt, which specifically targeted the property tax with tax rate limits, revenue limits, and caps on the increase in assessment ratios, the 1990s tax reforms limited the long-term growth in government and all tax types through procedural reforms of legislatures. Second-generation tax limitations consist of tax rule changes (supermajority rules or voter approval for all tax increases) that restrict the taxing and spending authority of elected officials and the long-term growth in government.

## Linkages between Adoption of Governance Policies

There is some overlap between the passage of state tax and expenditure controls, supermajority tax rules, and legislative term limits (see table 8.1). Thirteen states (Alaska, Arizona, California, Colorado, Idaho, Massachusetts, Michigan, Missouri, Montana, Oklahoma, Oregon, Utah, and Washington) have laws limiting legislative tenure in office and state taxation or spending. Eight states (Arizona, Arkansas, California, Colorado, Florida, Oklahoma, South Dakota, and Washington) place restrictions on both legislative terms and voting margins (a two-thirds vote required) for tax increases. Six states have both types of fiscal controls: state TELs and legislative supermajorities for tax increases. Stated another way, 73% of the states with term limits also have state taxation and spending limits. Only six states have term limits without also placing limits on the legislature's spending and taxation powers.

The lack of correlation between adoption of the three different governance policies suggests a distinct adoption pattern for each policy. The Pearson ($r$) correlation between legislative term limits and state tax limits (TELs) is .31. The correlation between term limits and supermajority tax rules is .31, and .14 between supermajority tax rules and state TELs. None of these correlations are statistically significant.

Fourteen of the 16 states with term limits and either state tax limits (TELs) or supermajority rules for tax increases have a tradition of moderate to high use of the initiative process. The exceptions are the states of Utah and Idaho, which have adopted governance policies but have low initiative use. The passage of governance policies is largely a western phenomenon, with 11 of the 13 most-reformist states located west of the Mississippi River. Some southern states, such as Arkansas, Florida, and Missouri, also appear more likely to adopt governance policies than their northeastern neighbors.

## State Populism/Initiative Use as a Determinant of Governance Policy Use

While public support for term limits and tax cuts appears to be fairly constant across individual states, there are significant variations in state institutional structures that might cause a state to adopt these polices—such as the initiative process. The argument developed here is that a New Populism is critical in the adoption of

**Table 8.1** State Governance Policies and Historical Use
of the Initiative

| State | Annual Use of Initiative | Term Limits | State TELs | Supermajority |
|---|---|---|---|---|
| Alabama | | | | |
| Alaska | Moderate | X* | X | |
| Arizona | High | X | X | X |
| Arkansas | High | X | | X |
| California | High | X | X | X |
| Colorado | High | X* | X | X |
| Connecticut | | | X | |
| Delaware | | | | X |
| Florida | Moderate | X | | X |
| Georgia | | | | |
| Hawaii | | | X | |
| Idaho | Low | X* | X | * * |
| Illinois | Low | | | |
| Indiana | | | | |
| Iowa | | | | |
| Kansas | | | | |
| Kentucky | | | | |
| Louisiana | | | X | X |
| Maine | Low | X* | | |
| Maryland | | | | |
| Mass. | Moderate | X* | X | |
| Michigan | Moderate | X | X | |
| Minnesota | | | | |
| Mississippi | Low | | | X |
| Missouri | Moderate | X | X | |
| Montana | Moderate | X | X | * * |
| Nebraska | Moderate | X | | |
| Nevada | Low | X* | | * * |
| New Hampshire | | | | |
| New Jersey | | | X | |
| New Mexico | | | | |
| New York | | | | |
| N. Carolina | | | X | |
| N. Dakota | High | X | | * * |
| Ohio | Moderate | X | | |
| Oklahoma | High | X* | X | X |
| Oregon | High | X | X | |
| Pennsylvania | | | | |

*continued*

**Table 8.1** State Governance Policies and Historical Use
of the Initiative *(continued)*

| State | Annual Use of Initiative | Term Limits | State TELs | Supermajority |
|---|---|---|---|---|
| Rhode Island | | | | |
| S. Carolina | | | X | |
| S. Dakota | Moderate | X | | X |
| Tennessee | | | X | |
| Texas | | | X | |
| Utah | Low | X* | X | |
| Vermont | | | | |
| Virginia | | | | |
| Washington | High | X | X | X |
| W. Virginia | | | | |
| Wisconsin | | | | |
| Wyoming | Low | X | | |
| Total | 24 | 22 | 21 | 11 |

state governance policies. One indicator of a populist climate is citizen usage of the initiative process. I argue that historical use of this process over the past century is a central component in understanding the adoption (and linkage between) governance policies.[10] Frequent use of the initiative is also associated with institutional provisions that regulate use of the initiative in each state (i.e., signature requirements; see chapter 5 in this volume).

State constitutional provisions for the initiative are an institutional mechanism that shapes state politics, public opinion, and policy. The importance of institutions is emphasized in the work of new institutionalist scholars who recognize that state political structures shape the strategic context in which political actors make policy choices (March and Olsen 1984, 1989; Steinmo 1989, 1992). These scholars argue that institutional contexts shape actors' strategic choices and thereby shape policy outcomes.

## Demands for Popular Rule: Initiative Use

One indicator of a populist climate is citizen demand and usage of popular-rule mechanisms, such as the initiative process. Over the past 100 years, certain states have tended to rely heavily on the initiative to formulate state law and policy. Usage of the initiative is measured by the average number of statewide initiatives appearing on state ballots per year from 1898 to 1992 (Neal 1993).[11] As the number of initiatives on the ballot increases, I predict the likelihood a state will adopt all three governance policies increases.

Over the past 100 years, citizen usage of the initiative process has varied substantially across the states. Table 2.1 (see chapter 2) ranks the states by the *total* number of initiatives on the ballot since adoption of the process. Oregon, California, North Dakota, Colorado, and Arizona have had over 100 initiatives on the ballot in the past century. Oregon tops the list, with 274 initiatives on the ballot since adoption of the process in 1902 (Neal 1993). In 1994 there were over 56 different petitions in circulation for the November 1994 ballot in Oregon, including one that legalized medically assisted suicides. Mississippi, on the other hand, the latest state to enact the initiative in 1992, had not qualified any measures for the ballot as of 1992.

While the majority of state initiative provisions were adopted between 1898 and 1919, in 1959 Alaska's electorate adopted the initiative, and in the 1960s and 1970s initiative provisions were approved in Florida, Illinois, and Wyoming. To control for the number of years that the initiative has been in place, I divide the total number of initiatives on the ballot by the number of years the initiative has been in place.[12] Based on this, the states are ranked low, medium, and high in Table 8.1, along with the governance policies adopted in each state. This standardized measure of historical use of the initiative can be used as a proxy for "state populism." States with a historical political tradition of lawmaking through the initiative have developed a distinct populist climate and are expected to be more likely to adopt governance policies.[13]

## Alternative Explanations for Governance Policies

The most common appeal for legislative term limits is the need to increase legislative rotation in office (Petracca 1992; Benjamin and Malbin 1992). States with highly professionalized legislatures and low member turnover are considered to be more susceptible to the adoption of term limits.[14] A distinguishing feature of the U.S. Congress and more professional legislatures is low membership turnover (Squire 1992; Fiorina 1994). Incumbents in professional legislatures have high electoral success rates. If internal features of state legislatures are important, states with low membership turnover should be the first to adopt term limits. State legislative turnover is measured by the average 10-year rate of turnover (1979–1989) in state legislatures (Benjamin and Malbin 1992).

If internal features of state legislatures are important, support for term limits should be strongest in states with the most-professional legislatures (Mondak 1995; Copeland and Rausch 1991; Jewell 1993). State legislative professionalism is measured by an index created by Squire (1992) that uses the U.S. Congress as a baseline against which to measure the salary, staff, and time-in-session of all 50 state legislatures. In states with less-professional legislatures composed of "amateurs," there may be less perceived need for term limits.

State TELs aim to reduce growth in levels of taxation and spending. If state fiscal features are important, states with high state and local taxes should be more susceptible to the adoption of tax and expenditure limits and supermajority rules for tax increases (Stansel 1994; Tolbert 1992a, 1992b). TELs and legislative supermajority rules are fiscal reforms to control high taxes and cap the growth in state and local spending. State and local tax burdens are measured by average total taxes (per $100 of income) over a 20-year period (National Conference of State Legislatures [NCSL] 1989).

## Empirical Model

This analysis utilizes a series of logistic regressions to analyze the adoption of governance policies. I present one bivariate model (series A) and one multivariate model (series B) for each of the three reforms. The bivariate models measure the strength of the simple relationship between annual use of the initiative and adoption of each procedural reform. The multivariate models analyze the strength of this relationship controlling for alternative explanations for adoption of governance policies.

In each equation, the dependent variable is a binary variable measuring whether the state has adopted the political reform: term limits, state TELs (ACIR 1994), and legislative supermajority for tax increases (Mackey 1993). If the state has adopted the procedural reform, it is coded 1; 0 if otherwise. Positive coefficients for the independent or explanatory variables indicate a greater likelihood the state will adopt that particular reform. The three models are estimated as follows.

As discussed above, use of the initiative (first explanatory variable in each equation) is measured by the average number of statewide initiatives appearing on the ballot per year from 1898 to 1992 (Neal 1993). As the number of initiatives on the ballot increases, I predict an increased likelihood that a state will adopt all three political reforms. The multivariate models control for alternative explanations for the passage of each governance policy.

## Discussion of Results

Maximum likelihood coefficient estimates are shown in tables 8.2 and 8.3. Table 8.2 displays three bivariate logistic regression models for the adoption of the three governance policies. In each case, citizen usage of the initiative is a powerful explanation for the adoption of legislative term limits and constraints on governmental taxation and spending. States with high initiative use are more likely to adopt all three governance policies.

Model 1A provides maximum likelihood estimates of initiative use on state adoption of legislative limits. Usage of the citizen initiative is positively associated with the adoption of term limits at the state level; the bivariate model predicts 96% of the cases correctly, and only two states are mispredicted (model 1A). Model 1B (from table 8.3) estimates state adoption of term limits controlling for legislative professionalism and the average turnover in state legislatures during the 1980s. Knowing the level of legislative professionalism or membership turnover in a state does not significantly improve our ability to predict the adoption of legislative limits. Rather than a response to legislative professionalism or low turnover, the adoption of term limits is associated with features of a populist climate (as reflected in the use of direct democracy).

Model 2A in table 8.2 estimates the impact of annual use of the initiative on the passage of state TELs. Again, citizen usage of the

**Table 8.2** Usage of the Initiative and Adoption of Governance Policies (State-Level Data) (Bivariate Models with Maximum Likelihood Estimates)

| | Term Limits Model 1A | TELS Model 2A | Supermajority Tax Rules Model 3A |
|---|---|---|---|
| Use of initiative | 35.77** | .62** | .94** |
| | (15.12) | (.27) | (.31) |
| Constant | 4.96*** | -.94** | -2.34*** |
| | (2.16) | (.27) | (.61) |
| N | 50 | 50 | 50 |
| Model $\chi^2$ | | | |
| (Improvement) | 62.34** | 5.93** | 10.38*** |
| Predicted correctly | 96% | 68% | 84% |

*Note:* The dependent variable for each model is binary = 1 if the state has the political reform, 0 if otherwise. Coefficients are unstandardized, values in parentheses are standard errors of the MLE. The coefficients and standard errors were derived using logistic regression in the SPSS program.

**$p < .01$, ***$p < .001$.

initiative is a statistically significant predictor of the adoption of TELs; states with high initiative use are more likely to adopt TELs. The model using initiative use only explains 68% of the variance in TELs adoption. Since twenty-one of the fifty states have state TELs (42% of the states), a model that predicts 58% of the states correctly would occur by chance. Thus, knowing whether a state has the initiative and how heavily the process is used improves our prediction by 10%. Model 2B in table 8.3 adds controls to this basic model and estimates the likelihood of a state's adopting TELs, controlling for total state and local tax burdens. Contrary to prevailing wisdom, state and local tax burdens appear to have little impact on the passage of TELs. Once again, only the coefficient for initiative use is statistically significant. Rather than a direct response to high taxes, the passage of state TELs is largely a function of a populist climate as expressed by initiative use.

Model 3A (table 8.2) estimates the impact of indicators of initiative use on the adoption of supermajority rules for tax increases. Like the previous policies, usage of the initiative process is positively associated with the adoption of supermajority rules and

**Table 8.3** The New Populism and Adoption of Legislative Term Limits (State Level Data) (Multivariate Models with Maximum Likelihood Estimates)

| | Term Limits Model 1B | TELS Model 2B | Supermajority Tax Rules Model 3B |
|---|---|---|---|
| Use of initiative historical | 5.30** (2.00) | .61** (.27) | 1.30*** (.41) |
| Legislative professionalism | −16.08* (7.95) | | |
| Legislative turn- over 1980s | −.12 (.09) | | |
| Total state taxes | | .23 (.22) | −.22 (.36) |
| Total local taxes | | .08 (.27) | −.75 (.45) |
| Constant | 6.34 (7.16) | −2.91 (2.30) | 1.51 (3.50) |
| N | 50 | 50 | 50 |
| Model $\chi^2$ (improvement) | 50.53*** | 6.62 | 16.14*** |
| Predicted correctly | 96% | 70% | 84% |

*$p < .05$; **$p < .01$, ***$p < .001$.

*Note:* The dependent variable for each model is binary = 1 if the state has the political reform; 0 if otherwise. The coefficients presented are unstandardized, values in parentheses are standard errors of the MLE. The coefficients and standard errors were derived using logistic regression in the SPSS program.

allows us to predict 86% of the cases correctly; states with higher usage of the initiative process are more likely to adopt supermajority tax rules. The controls for total state and local tax burdens in table 8.3 (model 3B) are not a significant predictor of the adoption of supermajority rules.

In sum, states with a higher number of initiatives on the ballot per year are more likely to adopt governance policies: legislative term limits, state TELs, and supermajority tax rules. Constitutional rules creating the initiative are not a sufficient condition for enacting governance policies. Nor are states experiencing high tax burdens, legislative professionalism, or lower turnover more likely to adopt governance policies. A state history of active citizen participation using the process is necessary to explain the adoption of governance policies. States that lack the initiative, and those with the initiative that make little use of it, are less likely to adopt political reforms.

## Conclusion

This analysis suggests that states vary in their reform climate. States with a populist climate and frequent initiative use are more likely to adopt three governance policies: legislative term limits, state TELs, and supermajority tax rules.

As with the direct election of U.S. senators and other early-twentieth-century reforms first adopted through the initiative, term limits, tax limitations, and supermajority rules for tax increases were first adopted in states that rely heavily on the initiative. In the past twenty years the initiative has been used to adopt a wide range of policies, from black bear–hunting regulations, euthanasia, legalization of gambling, open-space/environmental policy, to antigay laws. But its most important application is perhaps in the area of governance policy that changes the very operation of representative government. The resurgence in use of the initiative process for procedural reforms (often sponsored by conservative organizations) can have long-term impacts on state and local governments. Since these reforms have not been around very long, there is limited research as to their consequences. However, two studies on the effects of TELs suggest that states adopting these policies might incur greater long-term indebtedness as they attempt to maintain spending in the face of constrained tax revenue (Clingermayer and Wood 1995; Bowler and Donovan 1994d). Early studies of the effects of state term limits suggest that limits, while doing little to alter the social composition of legislatures, might lead to more frequent election of women. Term limits do appear to alter the behavior of state legislators by constraining members' district-oriented activities. Early research on the effects of limits also suggests a weakening of state legislatures' positions relative to executives and staff (Carey, Niemi, and Powell 1996).

Governance policies are an ever-growing component of political agendas. I discuss only three governance policies here, but there are a myriad of other salient procedural political reforms that might constrain the discretion of state legislators. These political reforms are sweeping state election ballots, dominating legislative sessions, and structuring candidate-centered campaigns. They include limitations on campaign spending, anti–affirmative action laws, ethics legislation, and restrictions on repeat criminal offenders. Such governance policies are often first adopted through the citizen's initiative, then later adopted through state legislatures as interest in the reforms diffuses through a process of cross-state policy contagion.

This research suggests that the reformist political climate of the 1980s–1990s can be compared to the late-nineteenth and early-twentieth century, which spawned a range of political reforms. Each era is distinguished by a rise in the use of direct democracy, the adoption of a significant number of institutional reforms, preference for procedural over substantive policies, and the pervasive distrust of representative government's institutions. Both eras may also be characterized by a backlash by upper-middle-class whites against the gains and political power of ethnic groups. Cain suggests this "New Populism" represents a voter backlash to reverse the gains of minority groups in the 1970s and to inhibit their access and influence in government (1992b).

Many Populist/Progressive Era political reforms (direct election of senators, direct primary, Australian ballot, home rule, nonpartisan local and state elections, women's suffrage) can also be characterized as governance policies, since they (1) are driven either directly or indirectly by citizen pressure; (2) change the internal rules that state and elected officials must follow; and (3) constitute procedural rather than substantive policy. Ironically, almost 100 years later, the success of 1980s-1990s reform politics is achieved by building on a procedural reform adopted during the Progressive Era (1900–1920): provisions for direct democracy.

The legacy of Progressive Era political reforms on U.S. politics sheds light on the long-term impact of current procedural reforms aimed at state and local governments. It also raises several questions. How will the procedural reforms we are enacting today fundamentally shape the structure of politics and policy in the next 100 years? What kind of 21st-century procedural reforms will produce

the fundamental changes in American politics that women's suffrage, the civil service, and direct democracy brought about in the
Progressive Era?

## NOTES

1. Similar reforms requiring voter approval of all tax increases have been
enacted through the initiative in Colorado (1992) and Washington (1993).

2. Survey conducted by Americans Talk Issues: *Improving Democracy
in America* (Washington, D.C: Americans Talk Issues Foundation, 1994).

3. Governance policies can be distinguished from Lowi's *constituent
policy*—essentially, administrative reorganization of national bureaucratic
agencies—in that governance policy is a *restructuring* of the institutions of
the state, rather than administrative *reorganization* (Lowi 1972). Governance policies are the building blocks for state-building (Skowronek 1982).

4. The impact of TELs on public policy is discussed briefly in chapter 12.

5. Both legislative term limits and TELs are commonly adopted by the
citizen initiative. These reforms are also adopted through legislative
statute. Since the late 1970s, the most common subject matter for initiatives has been taxes and government spending; three-fifths of all initiatives
have concerned government spending, public morality, or political reform
(Magleby 1994, 237). In the 1990s this trend is magnified, with nearly 30%
of all initiatives focusing on governmental and political reform (Magleby
1994, 238).

6. The governance policies examined here were adopted both by ballot
initiative and legislative statute. Governance policy is also not synonymous
with "constitutional" initiatives. Governance policies can be adopted either
by constitutional amendment or legislative statute.

7. As of July 1994 18 states had adopted legislative term limits. In the
1994 November general election, 4 more states adopted term limits.

8. From interviews with legislative party leaders in 4 states (Colorado,
Minnesota, New Jersey, and Washington) during the 1993–94 legislative
sessions.

9. Nevada and Rhode Island have nonbinding state expenditure limitations and are excluded from this analysis.

10. The measure of historical usage of the initiative (over roughly the
past 100 years) is highly correlated with measures of citizen usage of the

initiative process over the past 20 years. The same states with high initiative use over the past century are also high users of the initiative over the past 20 years. The variable with the broader time frame, historical use of the initiative, is used in this chapter to measure a populist climate, history, and "political culture" (Elazar 1984).

11. This measure is based on the total number of initiatives qualifying for state election ballots each year, not only those that were adopted (Neal 1993). The latter data are not readily available. Given that only half of all initiatives that qualify for the ballot are adopted, limiting this measure to only successful initiatives would unnecessarily reduce the sample size. Previous research in this area (cf. Magleby 1995) has included all initiatives qualifying for state election ballots.

12. The standardized number of initiatives on the ballot per year was calculated by dividing the total number of initiatives by the number of years the state has had the process. With regular elections every two years, this number can be multiplied by 2 for the average number of initiatives appearing on the ballot per election cycle. Eight states were coded high use of the initiative (above .9 initiatives per year), nine states were coded moderate (.43 [mean] to .90 per year), and six states were coded low (below .43 initiatives per year).

13. There are important variations in historical use of direct democracy. Some states use the process quite frequently, while other use the process rarely. What accounts for this variation? Variation in use of the initiative is a function of institutional rules for: (a) petition requirements, (b) geographical distribution requirements, and (c) the availability of other direct democracy options. Of the three, the signature threshold (petition requirements) for qualifying an initiative for the statewide ballot may be the most critical. Some states, such as Oregon and Colorado, require signatures from only 5% of the electorate voting for governor in the last election, compared with Wyoming, which requires signatures from 15% of the electorate. States such as Colorado and Oregon may provide a testing ground for new policy ideas because of low entrance costs for using the initiative process. Analysis (not shown) indicates that over 50% of the variation in historical usage of the initiative process is a function of the stringency of signature thresholds (petition requirements), geographic requirements for circulating petitions, and the number of available direct democracy options.

14. Both legislative professionalism and turnover in state legislatures are included as alternative explanations in the term limits models. The Pearson $(r)$ correlation between these two independent variables is -46, indicating they measure distinct features of state legislatures.

# 9

# Pressuring Legislatures through the Use of Initiatives: Two Forms of Indirect Influence

ELISABETH R. GERBER

One of the noteworthy facts of the modern initiative process is that most ballot initiatives fail. In the twenty-three American states that use initiatives, only 42% of the 271 statewide initiatives considered by voters between 1981 and 1990 passed.[1] In prior decades, the initiative passage rate in many states was considerably lower. In California, for example, the passage rate was less than 30% for the nearly seven decades between adoption of the initiative in 1911 through the late 1970s.[2] At the same time, the cost of qualifying and campaigning for initiatives is rapidly increasing. Proponents of five major California ballot initiatives spent an average of over $7 million per measure in 1994.[3]

Yet despite the low initiative passage rate and high cost, interest groups continue to use the process.[4] The number of initiatives appearing on statewide ballots increased from 67 initiatives in 1992, to 68 initiatives in 1994, to 92 initiatives in 1996.[5] One explanation for the use of initiatives in the face of high costs and low passage rates is that passing a new law is neither the only nor even perhaps the most important purpose for proposing an initiative.[6] Groups may propose initiatives without ever intending to pass the laws they propose. Instead, their motivation for proposing initiatives is often to exert pressure on other political actors. Groups that use initiatives to exert pressure hope that other actors will then pass or

191

block legislation in response to the interest group's proposal. To the extent that interest groups can pressure other actors through their initiative proposals, their activities may provide enough *indirect* influence to justify the costs of using the initiative process.

In this chapter, I focus on the use of initiatives to achieve indirect influence. I argue that groups pursue indirect influence for one of two different reasons. Some groups lack the resources to pass laws directly as initiatives (i.e., to achieve direct influence). For these groups, indirect influence is the only way that they can use initiatives to achieve their policy goals. Other groups have the resources to achieve direct influence. For these groups, indirect influence may represent a less costly way of achieving the same policy outcomes. In both cases, groups propose initiatives to pressure other actors, particularly the state legislature. To the extent that groups use initiatives to pursue indirect influence, the low passage rate, and the continued use of initiatives in the face of this low passage rate, are much less surprising.

Beyond addressing the immediate question of why groups use a process that seems to provide them with so little influence, my approach to studying indirect influence provides insight into the broader question of the overall extent of interest group influence in the initiative process. Acknowledging that groups may pursue either direct or indirect influence helps us to understand the motivations behind the choices interest groups make. Studies that focus solely on direct influence are likely to seriously underestimate the influence of groups that use initiatives to achieve indirect influence. My analysis also shows, however, that the ability of groups to achieve indirect influence is also severely limited. For most groups, achieving indirect influence is no more feasible than achieving direct influence. By identifying the conditions under which groups can and cannot achieve indirect influence, this analysis thus contributes to our understanding of interest group behavior and influence in the initiative process.

## Forms of Influence

Groups can promote their political interests by pursuing several forms of influence. Influence can be "status quo modifying" or "status quo preserving"; it can also be "direct" or "indirect." "Modifying" influence involves changing policy by passing a new law. "Preserving" influence involves protecting the status quo by preventing the passage of new laws. "Direct" influence involves immediately influencing policy, either modifying or preserving the status quo, through a given policy-making mechanism (i.e., the initiative process). "Indirect" influence involves using one policy-making mechanism (i.e., the initiative process) to bring about an effect on policy, again either modifying or preserving the status quo, in another policy-making arena (i.e., the legislative process). Thus, status quo–modifying influence can be either direct or indirect, as can status quo–preserving influence.

An example of direct modifying influence involves passing a law by initiative. Such influence is modifying in the sense that the policy consequence is to change the law from the status quo to the new initiative law. It is direct in the sense that the change comes about as a direct consequence of the initiative rather than as an indirect consequence (as when legislators respond to election outcomes). An example of direct preserving influence involves blocking the passage of an initiative. Such influence is status quo preserving in the sense that its consequence is to prevent passage of a new law; it is direct in the sense that the effect is made through the initiative process.

Indirect influence comes about when one actor pressures another actor to change or protect policy. An example of indirect modifying influence involves using initiatives to pressure state legislators to pass a new law. An example of indirect preserving influence involves using initiatives to pressure state legislators to block passage of new legislation. There are at least two ways an interest group can use initiatives to pressure the state legislature either to modify or preserve the status quo.[7] The first is to threaten to pass an initiative that legislators oppose. The second is to use initiatives to signal the group's support for (or opposition towards) an issue. Each of these approaches involves pursuing different activities, and each entails different relationships between interest groups, voters, and legislators. I describe each form of indirect influence below.

## Threatening to Pass an Adverse Initiative

An interest group may attempt to generate legislative action by threatening to pass an initiative that legislators oppose. The interest group may exert pressure either to modify current policy or to prevent the passage of new legislation. In response to such threats, legislators may or may not act. Whether legislators in fact respond to an interest group's threat, and hence whether the group can achieve indirect influence, depends upon the credibility of the group's threat. As I illustrate in the examples below, the credibility of a group's threat depends upon whether there exist majority-preferred initiatives that the group can propose and whether the group has sufficient resources to pay the costs of proposing, qualifying, campaigning for, and defending the initiative.[8] In other words, to pose a credible threat to the legislature, an interest group must have the electoral support and resources to pass their initiative directly; otherwise, legislators can ignore their threat. Interest groups pursue this form of indirect influence, then, when they have the choice of pursuing either direct or indirect influence and believe they can achieve their policy goals more cheaply by pressuring legislators to act on their behalf.

The following examples illustrate when groups will be able to use the initiative process to pressure the state legislature. The examples are based on a simple spatial model that is intended to capture the essential elements of the interaction between interest groups and legislatures.[9] Like all models, this spatial model represents a simplification of the actual policy process in many ways.[10] The purpose of the model is not to mirror all aspects of the policy process; rather, it is to isolate those fundamental features of the process that determine when groups can use initiatives to achieve this form of indirect influence.

In the model, there are three players: a Legislature, an Interest Group, and the median Voter.[11] I represent each player's policy preferences by an ideal point, which I refer to as $L$, $I$, and $V$, respectively, and a utility function relating each policy to the utility the player receives.[12] To facilitate illustration, I assume that players prefer policies that are "closer" to their ideal points to those that are further away.[13]

To understand the sequence of events, first consider the game tree represented in figure 9.1. The object of the game is to select a single policy. The Legislature moves first and decides whether or not to pass a new law $(L^*)$. If the Legislature decides to act, it passes

**Figure 9.1** Game Tree

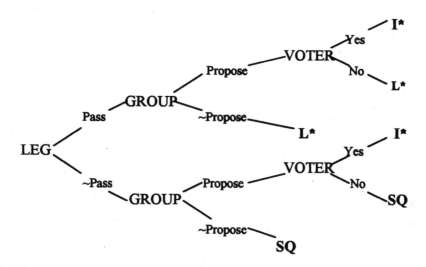

$L^*$ through normal legislative channels. If the Legislature does not act, the status quo *(SQ)* effectively becomes the "Legislature's law." The Legislature recognizes that some of its choices may provoke a challenging initiative. The Interest Group recognizes that it may be able to influence what the Legislature does and the content of the legislation it produces.

The Interest Group moves next and decides whether or not to propose an initiative *(I\*)*. If no initiative is proposed, the game ends and the Legislature's law remains. If an initiative is proposed, the Voter chooses between the initiative *(I\*)* and the Legislature's law *(L\* or SQ)* in a subsequent election. The policy (the law or the initiative) preferred by the median Voter prevails.

Whether the Interest Group can pressure the Legislature to pass a law other than its ideal policy *(L\* = L)*, and hence whether the group can achieve indirect influence by threatening to pass an initiative, depends upon the configuration of player preferences. Suppose the players' preferences are as depicted in figure 9.2.[14] In this example, the Interest Group's ideal point is moderate relative to the Legislature's and the Voter's, such that $L < I < V$.[15] If the Legislature and the Interest Group were to each propose their ideal policies, the initiative *(I\*)* would win because the Voter would prefer the Interest

**Figure 9.2** Player Preferences with Moderate Interest Group

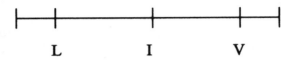

Group's moderate policy *(I\* = I)* to the Legislature's extreme policy *(L\* = L)*. Whether this translates into a credible threat by the Interest Group depends on the level of the Interest Group's costs.[16] In general, when the increase in utility the Interest Group expects to receive from proposing an initiative—compared with the utility received from the law—is greater than its costs, the Interest Group is tempted to make a proposal.[17] When the utility differential is less than the Interest Group's costs, the Interest Group cannot justify the costs and does not make a proposal.

In figure 9.2, when interest group costs *C = 0*, the Interest Group is willing and able to offer an initiative at its ideal point *(I)*.[18] This initiative will beat any law that the Legislature prefers to *I\**, that is, any point to the left of *I\**, since any such point is further from *V* than is *I\**. Anticipating this, the Legislature knows the best it can do is pass its law at the Interest Group's ideal point *(I)*. When *C > 0*, if the Legislature passes a law close enough to *I*, the Interest Group will not find it cost-effective to counter. In fact, the Legislature passes its law between *L* and *I*, just close enough to *I* to make the Interest Group indifferent between paying *C* and proposing an initiative, and keeping *C* and accepting *L\**.[19] Note that *L\** in this case is closer to the Legislature's ideal point than when *C=0*, as a function of the Interest Group's costs. However, it is further from the Voter's ideal point, implying that the Legislature need not be as responsive to the Interest Group and the Voters when the cost of using the initiative process is high. When *C* is sufficiently large (i.e., when *L* and *I* are less than *C* units apart), the Legislature can pass a law at *L\* = L* and the Interest Group will not act. A similar dynamic holds for the case where the Voter's preferences are relatively moderate.[20] In both cases, the important point is that both *I* and *V* are located on the same side of *L*.

By contrast, in figure 9.3, the Legislature's preferences are moderate relative to the Interest Group's and the Voter's such that

**Figure 9.3** Player Preferences with Moderate Legislature

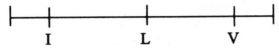

$I < L < V$.[21] When the players hold these preferences, there exists no initiative that the Interest Group and the Voter both prefer to the Legislature's ideal policy. For example, suppose the Legislature passes its law and the Interest Group proposes an initiative each at their ideal points. Clearly, the Voter prefers $L^*$, since it is closer to $V$. Indeed, if the Interest Group proposes any initiative that is to the left of $L^*$, the voter prefers $L^*$ and $I^*$ loses. Therefore, there exists no policy that the Interest Group prefers to the Legislature's policy that the Voter also prefers, and so no initiative is proposed. Knowing this, the Legislature passes its law at its ideal point *(L)* and ignores the Interest Group's potential threat.

To summarize, the legislature responds to an interest group's threat when there exists a majority-preferred initiative that the interest group can propose, and when the group can mobilize the necessary resources at sufficiently low cost to result in a positive net benefit. In other words, groups can successfully threaten to pass adversarial initiatives only when they know they can convince legislators both that their threat is credible and that they could, if they so chose, pass the initiative directly.

Whether or not a group can actually convince legislators that it has sufficient resources to obtain direct influence depends upon the amount of uncertainty regarding actors' preferences and resources. If all players have complete information about the other players' preferences and resources and the content of the policy alternatives, the interest group does not need to take any action at all. Under complete information, the legislature anticipates whether the group will propose an initiative, the content of its initiative proposal, and the median voter's preference. Furthermore, the legislature also knows that, as long as the other players have complete information as well, the voter will always vote for the policy that is closer to its ideal point, and the interest group will always propose the utility-maximizing initiative. Thus, the legislature can perfectly anticipate the interest group's activities and the median voter's response and moves to preempt them when the expected outcome is contrary to the legislature's preferences.

In the real world of politics, however, we know that political actors rarely have complete information. Uncertainty abounds. Legislatures can rarely predict the content of initiative proposals, let alone which groups might do the proposing. Interest groups have limited information about voter preferences, and voters themselves are often uncertain about the likely consequences of policy alternatives. All of these sources of uncertainty mean that interest groups may need to take steps to signal their intentions to the legislature. In particular, groups may need to reveal the content of their proposal by actually drafting and beginning to qualify their initiative. They may also need to signal public support for their initiative by organizing and mobilizing voters and by running and publishing polls. Finally, groups may need to signal their ability to mobilize other resources, especially financial resources, by holding fundraisers, hiring a consulting firm, paying signature gatherers to qualify the measure, and buying campaign advertisements. Note that once groups take these steps to signal their intentions, it may be relatively inexpensive to follow through with their initiative and pursue direct influence. Thus, when players have a great deal of uncertainty, groups may find indirect influence to be relatively costly and may choose direct influence instead.

While it is possible to identify conditions under which interest groups can theoretically achieve indirect influence, identifying examples where such indirect influence actually occurred is inherently problematic. Given the nature of the dynamic described above, it is often very difficult to infer intent from an interest group's actions. In fact, in equilibrium under complete information, the interest group never acts; simply being able to pose a credible threat is sufficient to induce the legislature to act favorably. Under incomplete information, the interest group takes actions such as drafting, qualifying, and campaigning for an initiative that could, in fact, be intended to achieve either direct or indirect influence. In other words, the interest group's strategy is often either unobservable or indistinguishable from strategies adopted for other purposes. This makes it very difficult to establish whether the legislature's policy is indeed the result of an interest group's threat or of some other cause.

Still, despite these problems, there are several examples that are strongly suggestive of the dynamic described above. One example in which interest groups clearly took steps to pressure a state legislature, and the legislature responded by passing favorable legislation, occurred in the area of environmental regulation. In 1993, the California state legislature passed a package of laws that reformed the California Environmental Quality Act [CEQA].[22] Before this package, numerous efforts to reform the environmental protection regulations contained in the CEQA had failed in the legislature. In response, a number of organizations formed a coalition called CART (Citizens Against Red Tape) to lobby in favor of reforming the CEQA. Several subsequent reforms were introduced in the legislature. Although the opponents of these reforms argued that they were too favorable to the California Chamber of Commerce and the petroleum industry, both well represented in CART, the measures ultimately passed. Whether or not their passage directly resulted from CART's effort is impossible to know; however, Barber notes that there was "fear that CART might try to change the law through the initiative route if it did not get its way in the Legislature. As evidence of this fear, environmentalists pointed to CART's hiring of Woodward-McDowell—a public relations company specializing in ballot measure campaigns. CART denied considering an initiative campaign" (Barber 1993, 37).

## Signaling the Group's Support or Opposition

Instead of threatening to pass an initiative that legislators oppose, groups may also seek indirect influence by signaling their support for a policy. Groups pursuing this second form of indirect influence recognize that there is no fundamental disagreement between their interests and legislators' preferences. Consequently, to influence legislative behavior, interest groups must simply be able to inform legislators about an issue and, most important, about their position on the issue. In the context of the model above, legislators must know an interest group's policy preferences to anticipate whether and how the group will act in response to the legislature's choices. More generally, legislators respond to interest group preferences in exchange for resources and services from the group such as campaign contributions, electoral support, information, and expertise.[23]

In recent years, the proliferation of interest groups, increased competition for campaign contributions, and other factors have made it more difficult for interest groups to signal their policy positions (Smith 1995). In fact, because interest groups face intense competition from other groups for a legislator's attention, and because legislators must cultivate relationships with many groups to fund increasingly expensive campaigns, it may now be extremely difficult for interest groups to make their positions known. Furthermore, this increased competition distorts interest group incentives; even if interest groups can attract a legislator's attention, policy makers may discount the group's statements, knowing that interest groups have incentives to mislead legislators, or at least overstate their positions, to attract the legislators' attention.

Initiatives provide a way of signaling a group's position on an issue. Groups can use initiatives to signal their support for, or opposition to, an initiative by expending two types of resources. Economic interest groups and other groups with abundant *monetary* resources can signal their policy position by contributing money to campaigns to support or oppose ballot measures.[24] This spending, of course, is voluntary in the sense that groups need only provide resources to support or oppose measures from which they expect to benefit and about which they feel intensely. By observing that a group chose to spend money to support or oppose a measure, legislators can rightly infer that the group expects to gain from the outcome of the election net of the costs of the campaign. Otherwise, the group would keep the money or spend it on some other purpose. Interest group spending on initiatives therefore serves as a costly signal of the interest group's preferences to the legislature.[25] In addition, spending on initiative campaigns is done outside of the direct market for interest group campaign contributions. Such spending may thus be viewed as less subject to the competitive pressures of campaign financing and therefore as more credible.

Citizen groups and other groups with abundant *personnel* resources (i.e., members, volunteers, and experts) can also use initiatives to signal their position on an issue. Since these groups tend to lack the monetary resources of economic groups, however, their strategy for achieving indirect influence must differ. Citizen groups signal their position to the legislature by mobilizing electoral support for an initiative. By placing initiatives on the ballot that draw a great deal of public support, organized interest groups serve as the links between legislators and voters by framing an issue on which legislators and voters agree. In providing this linkage, interest groups may be able to prompt legislators to behave as the group wishes by mobilizing electoral support that the legislators cannot ignore.

Under what conditions do we expect interest groups to be able to use initiatives to pressure the state legislature by signaling their policy positions? For the legislature to respond to an interest group's pressure, three conditions must be met. The first condition is that the group has sufficient resources to attract the legislature's attention. Some groups feel strongly about an issue but lack the monetary resources to organize and finance an initiative campaign. Other groups lack the personnel resources to mobilize electoral constituencies in support of or in opposition to an initiative. Groups that lack both monetary and personnel resources may be unable to engage in campaign activities that would attract the legislature's attention.

The second condition that must be met for the legislature to respond to an interest group's pressure is that the group must have something the legislature wants. In particular, groups must have either monetary resources that they can promise as future campaign contributions, or the backing of a large, important electoral constituency that they can pledge to mobilize in support of a candidate. If the group lacks both of these resources, it cannot promise future payment for the legislature's cooperation. Thus, even if the group successfully signals its position to the legislature, the legislature has no incentive to respond to the group's signal.

The third condition that must be met for legislators to respond to an interest group's pressure is that legislators must be electorally vulnerable. When legislators face tough competition and their jobs are at risk, they have a greater incentive to respond to the demands of important constituencies. Historically, numerous incumbency advantages meant that campaigns for legislative offices were rarely competitive and sitting legislators were rarely vulnerable. Nonetheless, legislators spent much of their time fund-raising and garnering the support of electoral and financial constituencies. Many observers argue that there are now few safe seats in state legislatures. In particular, in the era of term limits in many states, incumbency is likely to be much less important. I expect term limits and other recent changes in state political environments to result in more competitive elections and seats, and therefore more attention paid by state legislators to the issue preferences of their electoral constituencies.

Note that a ballot measure need not pass for it to provide an effective signal of an interest group's policy position. Indeed, to achieve indirect influence, it is the signal rather than the outcome that is key. When groups expend monetary resources to signal their position, the outcome of the election is irrelevant. What matters are the interest group's behavior and the cost it is willing to incur to support or oppose the measure. When groups expend personnel resources to signal their position, the outcome of the election is important insofar as it provides a gauge of support by important electoral constituencies for the measure.[26]

Note further the differences between this approach to indirect influence and the approach discussed earlier. In the first approach, legislators and interest groups have divergent policy preferences. The interest group's strategy is therefore to establish that it can and will propose an initiative in response to the legislature's action or inaction. If legislator, interest group, and voter preferences are configured such that the interest group can propose a majority-preferred initiative that makes it better off than the legislature's policy and makes the legislature worse off, the legislature responds to avert the initiative proposal. In this second approach, legislators and interest groups generally agree on policy. However, legislators are uncertain about the interest group's preferences on a particular issue. Therefore, the interest group's strategy is not to establish that it has the resources to punish the legislature with an adverse initiative. Instead, the interest group uses the initiative merely to signal its convergent position to the legislature. Note also that once the legislature obtains information about the group's preferences, it uses this information for very different purposes. In the first form of indirect influence, the legislature uses information about the group's preferences to avert initiative proposals. In the second form, the legislature learns about the group's preferences *from its initiative proposal and campaign activities* and uses this information as it formulates future legislative proposals.

Groups use initiatives to signal their policy positions to the legislature either because they lack the resources to pursue direct influence or because indirect influence represents a less costly way to achieve their policy goals. Groups that have monetary resources but little electoral support may find it extremely difficult to mobilize an electoral majority. By promising future campaign contributions, however, they may be able to pressure legislators who rely upon monetary resources to finance their ever more expensive campaigns. For these groups, direct influence is not an option, since they lack the resources and support to pass laws directly. Instead, they resort to indirect influence because they have no other options.[27]

Groups that have abundant personnel resources but limited monetary resources may have more direct legislation options available to them. If these groups have enough monetary resources to run a successful campaign, they may be able to pass laws directly by initiative.[28] These groups thus choose between direct and indirect influence. For some, indirect influence may represent a less costly way to achieve the same policy goals.

Recent California politics provide examples of groups expending both monetary and personnel resources in initiative campaigns to signal their positions to the legislature. An example of groups pressuring the legislature by expending monetary resources occurred in the area of health industry regulation. In 1996, labor organizations placed two initiatives, Propositions 214 and 216, on the California ballot. Nearly identical in content, these two propositions would have regulated many of the operations of Health Maintenance Organizations (HMOs) in the state. Proposition 214 was proposed, supported, and largely funded by the Service Employees International Union and AFL-CIO, while Proposition 216 was proposed, supported, and largely funded by the California Nurses Association. After a grueling campaign period and expensive opposing campaigns by the insurance industry, both initiatives failed. However, in the three months immediately following the 1996 general election, the legislature proposed at least 27 HMO regulation bills that included many of the provisions contained in the initiative measures.[29] While none of these bills have passed both houses of the state legislature, 23 are still under consideration. By contrast, only 1 HMO regulation bill was introduced during the entire 12-month period before the 1996 election. Thus, while the HMO regulation bills introduced in early 1997 may or may not have been introduced as a *direct* consequence of the failed initiatives, the increase in the number of bills in this area since their failure implies some connection.

An example of groups expending personnel resources to signal their position recently occurred in California as well. In 1993, an individual named Mike Reynolds drafted a measure to require a life prison sentence for persons convicted of three felonies. Known as the "Three Strikes and You're Out" law, or simply "Three Strikes," the measure received enthusiastic support from many individuals, citizens groups, and law enforcement organizations, and easily qualified for the ballot with primarily volunteer signatures. The measure was wildly popular, with an early Field Poll survey registering fully 84% approval (Field Research Institute, 1994).

Observing this overwhelming popularity, the legislature, not willing to miss the opportunity to act on such a popular issue, passed an identical law in 1993. Still, with little additional campaign effort, the measure remained on the ballot and passed with 72% of the vote in November 1994 (California Secretary of State, 1994). Thus, while the legislature's law was nullified by the passage of "Three Strikes" as an initiative, its action in passing the law was clearly in response to the signal of strong popular support for the initiative proposal.

## Implications

The discussion of indirect influence has several important implications for our understanding of the initiative process. First, the analysis provides a compelling explanation for both the low initiative passage rate and the continued use of initiatives in the face of low passage rates and high costs. When groups pursue indirect influence, they place propositions on the ballot that are never intended to pass. This is not to say that groups prefer for their initiatives to fail. Rather, groups recognize that even if their initiatives do fail, their efforts may still be worthwhile. If the legislature responds to a group's threats or signals, then the group may receive some policy benefit even from "unsuccessful" initiative proposals.

Second, the analysis of indirect influence shows that there are systematic patterns in how groups can indirectly influence policy through the use of initiatives. Groups can pressure the legislature by posing a credible threat to pass an initiative that the legislature opposes. Or they can propose initiatives as a means of signaling their support for a policy. Each of these approaches to pressuring the legislature involves undertaking particular activities, and each requires specific resources. Groups that are able to mobilize the necessary resources have the option of indirect influence open to them. Those same resources, however, may also be used to achieve other forms of influence, including status quo–modifying direct influence and status quo–preserving direct influence. Thus, while the two forms of indirect influence described above are available to groups that can mobilize the necessary resources, they may not represent the most valuable use of those resources.

Third, the analysis identifies some of the limits of indirect influence. Not all groups can achieve indirect influence, and a given group may be limited to influencing the legislature in certain issue areas only. Achieving indirect influence requires either prior access to the legislature or the resources and electoral support to pass initiatives directly. The groups that can mobilize those resources thus have other forms of political influence available to them, either through the initiative process or other political arenas. Thus, the ability to achieve indirect influence enhances the power of groups that are already successful politically. The two forms of indirect influence identified in this analysis do not provide a means for otherwise underrepresented groups to influence policy outcomes. Rather, they provide yet another way for politically important groups to promote their political interests.

NOTES

1. Public Affairs Research Institute 1992b.
2. California Commission on Campaign Financing 1992.

3. California Secretary of State 1994.

4. I use the term "interest groups" to refer to both preexisting organizations that engage in a range of political activities as well as newly formed organizations that form for the immediate purpose of proposing an initiative. See Gerber 1997.

5. Kennerk 1992; Mulligan, Lillienthal, and Gesmundo 1994; Mulligan 1996.

6. A second explanation is that interest group behavior is not, in fact, irrational in an economic sense. This explanation allows for the possibility that while the probability of a given initiative passing may be quite low, the potential benefit if it does pass may be extremely high. In fact, if the expected utility—that is, the expected benefit times the probability of passage—outweighs the cost, then the group is (economically) justified in pursuing even a low-probability initiative. Based on surveys with interest groups that use initiatives, both explanations appear to be important. See Gerber 1997.

7. In this chapter, I consider the use of initiatives to pressure legislators in an interest group's state. Interest groups may also use initiatives to pressure other policy actors, such as bureaucrats, legislators in other states, and members of Congress.

8. In fact, the group's initiative need not be majority preferred; rather, the legislature must believe that it is.

9. These examples are based on a model developed in Gerber 1996. There, I provide additional motivation for the model and consider the full set of equilibrium choices and behavior. For the current purposes of identifying the conditions under which interest groups can have certain kinds of indirect influence through their use of initiatives, the simple examples presented here suffice.

10. Since the game is an abstract, simplified representation of the policy process, I omit many of the details of legislator-interest group-voter interaction in order to isolate key aspects of the interaction. I relax some of these simplifications after presenting the basic model.

11. For the purposes of the examples, I assume the Legislature and the Interest Group each behave as unitary actors. A more detailed description of the policy process would also model the complex interactions between actors within the state legislature and the proposing interest group. See Gerber 1996 for a discussion of these interactions. I also simplify my treatment of voter behavior and focus strictly on the decisions of the median Voter. Since voters in the model ultimately choose between two policy alternatives, the preferences of the median Voter are decisive.

12. This formulation implies that all players, including the Legislature,

receive utility from policy *outcomes.* An alternative assumption treats legislators strictly as position-takers, i.e., they only care about how they vote, rather than about the ultimate policy consequences of their actions (Mayhew 1974). My formulation allows legislators to be reelection oriented, so long as their constituents hold them accountable for policy outcomes.

13. This assumption implies that player utility functions are linear, symmetric, and single-peaked at their ideal point.

14. Assuming a unidimensional policy space greatly simplifies the game and exposition of the results.

15. Comparable results hold for the reverse case, where $V < I < L$.

16. These costs represent the costs of qualifying and campaigning for an initiative.

17. What is important with respect to costs is not the absolute level of resources required to draft, qualify, campaign for, and defend the initiative, but rather the ease with which the group amasses and mobilizes those resources.

18. Since the proposer (either alone or in coalition with other groups) must pay the costs of proposing, qualifying, and campaigning for the initiative, I assume the Interest Group must absorb these costs. By contrast, I assume the Legislature has already committed to considering policies in a given policy area, and so its costs are effectively zero. If we assume the Legislature must also absorb the costs (both direct costs and opportunity costs) of passing its law, the results extend straightforwardly.

19. Specifically, the Legislature passes its law $C$ units from $I$.

20. When $L < V < I$ and $C = 0$, the Legislature and the Interest Group each tries to obtain the policy outcome closest to their own ideal point, and both converge to the median Voter's ideal point. When $C > 0$, the Legislature only needs to move $L^*$ to the point that its law is a distance equal to half the Interest Group's costs. At that point, the Interest Group is willing to keep $C$ and accept a policy $C$ units from its best response on the other side of $V$.

21. Comparable results hold for the reverse case, where $V < L < I$.

22. Much of this discussion draws from Barber 1993.

23. See Smith 1995 for a review of the recent literature on legislator–interest group exchanges.

24. See Gerber 1997 for a discussion of the relationship between a group's internal characteristics, resources, and strategies.

25. See Banks 1991 for a review of the literature on costly action in signaling games in political science.

26. The legislature may respond to support by a constituency that makes up far less than an electoral majority. See Fenno 1978.

27. Groups that have the monetary resources to signal their position to

the legislature and promise future campaign contributions may have other options *outside the initiative process.* Specifically, they may be able to effectively lobby the legislature through traditional means.

28. Running a successful modern initiative campaign requires at least some monetary resources to purchase campaign ads. To some extent, personnel resources substitute for monetary resources. Groups that lack monetary resources may also rely on free media to publicize their initiative.

29. Lexis-Nexis State-track, search by keywords HMO and California.

# 10

## Race/Ethnicity and Direct Democracy: The Contextual Basis of Support for Anti-Immigrant and Official English Measures

CAROLINE J. TOLBERT AND RODNEY E. HERO

While race/ethnicity is often seen as important in U.S. politics, it has not always been systematically incorporated into political science research (Hero and Tolbert 1996; Radcliff and Saiz 1994). This chapter examines voting patterns on two initiatives adopted by ballot initiative in California: "Official English," commonly referred to as Proposition 63 (1986), and the "illegal immigration" initiative, referred to as Proposition 187 (1994). Consistent with a "racial/ethnic diversity" interpretation of politics and policy in the states, we find that racial/ethnic context and diversity play an important role in explaining county-level support for both anti-immigrant and Official English propositions (Hero and Tolbert 1996; Hero, Tolbert, and Lopez 1996; cf. Wolfinger and Greenstein 1968).

California voters adopted an English Language Amendment (Proposition 63) to the state's constitution in 1986, which aimed to enforce the status and primacy of English as the state's official language and to "preserve, protect and strengthen the English language, the common language of the people of the United States." That measure was the model for initiatives adopted two years later in Colorado, Florida, and other states. In all three states Official English measures were adopted by wide margins; the popular vote in favor was 64% in Colorado, 73% in California, and 84% in Florida. In each state, the initiative amended the state's constitution and prevented the state legislature from making any law that diminishes or ignores the role of English as the state official language. The sentiments expressed in the Official English measures continue to resonate. The U.S. Congress proposed an English Language Amendment to the U.S. Constitution in 1996.

In 1994, California voters supported Proposition 187 by a 59% to 41% overall margin. The ballot initiative denies social services, nonemergency health care, and education to illegal immigrants and requires public agencies to report suspected illegal immigrants to state and federal authorities. Although federal courts placed an injunction on implementation of parts of the measure days after the election, this policy has important implications for both national and subnational politics.

Proposition 187 and the Official English initiative are not unique in the history of California, or in other states, but are part of a series of policies that are more likely to be adopted in states with high racial/ethnic populations (Hero and Tolbert 1996). Other policies relevant to minority groups considered or adopted by ballot initiative in California include the repeal of fair housing legislation in 1965 and the California Civil Rights Initiative (Proposition 209) on the 1996 statewide ballot, which would prevent the consideration of race, ethnicity, or gender in awarding governmental contracts, college admissions, and a range of other government-funded programs (Wolfinger and Greenstein 1968; Citrin et al. 1990a; Cain 1992b; Citrin et al. 1990b).

## A Racial/Ethnic Interpretation of Anti-Immigrant and Official English Measures

Interpretations of state (and substate) politics tend to focus primarily on how political-governmental factors on one hand, or economic conditions on the other, drive policy adoptions (Gray 1990; Dye 1966; Plotnick and Winters 1985; Lewis-Beck 1977; Carmines 1974). In contrast, we contend that a state's racial/ethnic diversity—the mixtures or cleavages of various minority and or racial/ethnic groups—is central to explaining public policies, especially policies adopted by ballot initiative that affect minority groups (Key 1949; Giles and Evans 1986; Blalock 1970; Hero and Tolbert 1996). We suggest in this chapter that the passage of California's Official English and illegal-immigration initiatives can be understood in terms of the state's racial/ethnic composition.

State racial and ethnic diversity includes a state's black (African American), Latino/Hispanic, and Asian populations, i.e., those groups that are defined as "minority groups" or "protected classes" in (implicit) recognition of unique historical experiences in the United States. The diversity interpretation brings careful attention to these emerging minority groups in the states. A state's politics are a product of the cooperation, competition, and/or conflict between and among (pre)dominant and subordinate groups within a state. The extent of cooperation or conflict is, in turn, significantly affected by racial/ethnic similarity or dissimilarity (Hero and Tolbert 1996).

This interpretation, and related measures of racial/ethnic diversity, also distinguish between northern and western European populations versus nonnorthern and nonwestern Europeans who immigrated in large numbers to the U.S. in the late nineteenth century. Based on the size of the minority population and "white ethnic" populations, the states are ranked (or indexed) on two scales. State racial/ethnic diversity is a product of both minority and white ethnic diversity.

The states can be delineated into three broad categories, according to the degree of racial/ethnic diversity: "homogeneous," "heterogeneous," and "bifurcated." States with large minority populations (primarily black or Latino) and large white (nonethnic) populations are classified as having a *bifurcated* social structure. States with large white ethnic populations (nonnorthern and nonwestern European white) and moderately sized minority populations have a *heterogeneous* social structure. Finally, states low in both racial and ethnic diversity, i.e., with small minority and white ethnic populations, are relatively *homogeneous.*

A racial/ethnic diversity interpretation predicts that policies targeting minority groups are more likely to be adopted in bifurcated political jurisdictions (Hero and Tolbert 1996; Key 1949; Giles and

Evans 1986; Blalock 1970). Large minority populations are perceived to pose the greatest "threat" to the dominant white population. Thus, the adoption of policies such as Official English and Proposition 187 can be understand as a product of high minority diversity within states. Homogeneous political jurisdictions with low racial/ethnic diversity may also be concerned about minority populations. A racial/ethnic interpretation of California politics contrasts with others that have viewed California as a "progressive" or a "moralistic" state (Elazar 1966, 1984).

## California's Racial/Ethnic Composition

Based on its large minority population and relatively small white ethnic population, California can be classified as having a bifurcated social structure (Hero and Tolbert 1996). Although the state has a diverse population, it is dominated by a white (nonethnic) majority and a large minority (primarily Latino) population. Internally, the state's racial/ethnic composition varies by region. The southern and south-central part of the state has a bifurcated racial/ethnic composition, the central/coastal regions of the state are more heterogeneous, and the extreme northern part of the state is relatively homogeneous. California's 1990 population includes 57% whites, 26% Latinos, 9.5% Asian-Americans, and 7.5% African-Americans. While whites make up 57% of California's population, they constituted 81% of voters in the 1994 election. Latinos make up 26% of the state's population, but only 8% of the voters (Hayes-Bautista and Rodriguez 1994).

Ten of California's 58 counties have a sizable Latino population of between 30% and 66% of the population. These counties are concentrated primarily in the southern and south-central part of the state. Latinos make up between 20% and 29% of the population in 12 counties, and an additional 10 counties have between 11% and 20% Latino population. Thus 55% ($N = 32$) of the counties in California have a Latino population over 10%. The average Latino population per county is 17.5%, ranging from a low of 3.3% to a high of 65.8%. Counties with the largest Latino populations include Los Angeles (33%) and Imperial County (66%).

Cain (1992a) suggests that a "new populism" has arisen in California politics, a product of white/Anglo concerns over the increased size and political influence of blacks and Latinos in the state. This new populism represents a voter backlash against the gains of minority groups in the 1970s to inhibit their access and influence in government. A clear manifestation of this new populism is the use of ballot initiatives to circumvent representative institutions, especially the state legislature, where blacks and Latinos have gained influence. Previous research found that bifurcated states with large minority populations are more likely to adopt Official English laws and other policies aimed at minority groups (Citrin et al. 1990a).

## Voter Self-Interest and the California Initiative Process

A growing body of research has examined the role of the initiative process in shaping state policy and the role of voter self-interest in direct democracy elections (Donovan and Snipp 1994; Citrin et al. 1990a; Bowler and Donovan 1994a, 1994b; Lupia 1994a, 1994b). States with the initiative process provide a mechanism for policies to be adopted directly by the voters. With whites representing 80% of the electorate in California's 1994 elections, the initiative process provides a mechanism for the dominant white majority to adopt policies they prefer, over the opposition of minority groups. The presence of an electoral institution such as the initiative process— in combination with high racial/ethnic (minority) diversity—may help explain past and present state policy adoptions.

## Background on Official English

California was the first state in the nation to adopt an Official English amendment via ballot initiative in 1986. A U.S. senator from California, S. I. Hayakawa (R), first proposed an amendment to the U.S. Constitution in 1981 to declare English the nation's official language. This English Language Amendment was reintroduced in 1983 and 1985, but did not win legislative approval. In 1983,

Hayakawa founded the advocacy group "U.S. English," which sponsored ballot initiatives to declare English the official language across the states. Proponents of Official English argue that their goal is to speed assimilation and end bilingual education that keeps children in their native tongue. Recently, some proponents of Official English support it because they claim it will discourage immigration itself (Woodward 1995). They contend that historical experience teaches that linguistic diversity threatens political cohesion and stability. Proponents contend that previous generations of immigrants understood that English proficiency was necessary for economic mobility and social integration, creating the great "melting pot" that defined American society. Opponents argue that Official English targets linguistic minorities (primarily Latinos and Asians). Such measures are seen as mechanisms of exclusion rather than assimilation that threaten the cultural traditions of minority populations. Official English laws also imply future discrimination against language minorities and threaten the continuation services that are necessary for participation in the political process. Critics contend that the campaign for Official English is "at best unnecessary and at worst a thinly veiled form of racism and xenophobia" (Citrin et al. 1990a, 539).

Public opinion polls conducted after the 1986 election in California indicate that the Official English initiative polarized the electorate along ethnic lines, with strong support among white voters and lower levels of support among other ethnic groups. In California, whites voted almost 2 to 1 in support of Official English (72% approval rate). Blacks also widely supported the measure. Latinos, in contrast, opposed the measure 61% to 39% (Citrin et al. 1990a, 1994 [see table 10.1]; also see Hero 1992).

Currently 20 states have laws designating English as the official language. Racial/ethnic diversity explains much of the pattern of states' adoptions (Hero and Tolbert 1996; cf. Citrin et al. 1990a). Of the states with Official English measures, a number (California, Colorado, Arizona, and Florida) were passed by ballot initiative that amended the state constitution. Although the majority of these measures were adopted in the late 1980s, this issue has resurfaced in popular discussion. Three "homogeneous" states (Montana, New Hampshire, and South Dakota) adopted measures in 1995.

## Background on Proposition 187

Proposition 187 was commonly referred to as the "Save our State" (SOS) initiative. Supporters (including GOP Governor Pete Wilson) argued that California could not afford the cost of serving a large and growing illegal immigrant population. The ballot measure was devised as a means to save billions of dollars in state tax dollars and to "send a message to Washington" about the economic and social problems posed by the estimated 1.6 million illegal immigrants in the state.

Opponents argued that the proposition bordered on being racist and its passage would create a two-tiered society if implemented. They argued that the proposal did nothing to strengthen border enforcement or prevent employers from hiring illegal immigrants. Opponents also argued that the measure would foster a police-state mentality in which legal residents would be questioned simply because of their accent and/or skin color.

A *Los Angeles Times* exit poll found that the illegal immigration initiative polarized the electorate along racial lines, getting broad support among white voters while losing among other ethnic groups (see appendix). Whites voted almost 2 to 1 in support of Proposition 187. Latinos, in contrast, opposed the measure 77% to 23%. The poll also shows that 53% of black and Asian voters opposed the measure, suggesting the measure may have been broadly conceived of as antiminority or anti-Latino.

## County-Level Race/Ethnicity and the Official English and Anti-Immigration Vote

This analysis examines the hypothesis that racial/ethnic diversity is a central explanation for county-level variations in the vote for two policies targeting minority groups: Official English and Proposition 187. We suggest that racial/ethnic diversity and context are critical *beyond* individual-level factors; social context shapes individual perspectives on politics and policy. To measure this context, we use 1986 and 1990 census data from California's 58 counties on the percent of Latino, black, Asian, and white populations. California counties are powerful governmental entities and the direct providers of major social services, the same services Proposition 187 would deny to illegal aliens or Official English would deny to non-English speakers. There was a wide range in the county-level vote for each measure. The vote for Official English initiative ranged from a low of 53% in San Francisco County to a high of almost 90% in a number of counties. The vote for Proposition 187 ranged from a low of 29% in San Francisco County to a high of 77% in Colusa County (Colusa is over 33% Latino).

## The Vote for Official English (1986)

We first examine the relationship between racial/ethnic context and the county-level vote for Official English. A series of Ordinary Least Squared (OLS) regression equations are used to estimate the impact of racial/ethnic context on county-level support for Official English. In each model, racial/ethnic populations are the independent variables and the county-level vote for Official English is the dependent variable. Bivariate regression analysis (not shown) indicates that larger Latino, black, and Asian populations are inversely related to support for Official English in California; as the size of the Latino, black, and Asian populations rose in a county, the vote for the language proposal decreased. As expected, the size of the white population is positively correlated with the vote for this policy in each state (cf. Citrin et al. 1990a).

Table 10.1 (models 1, 2, and 3) displays the estimates of the impact of race on the county vote for Official English controlling for the percent Latino. This control is used because the Official English measure was widely perceived to target Latinos, who represent the largest linguistic minority in California and in the United States. Controlling for the percent Latino does not change the strength of the inverse relationship between higher black and Asian populations and lower approval levels.

Across counties, the size of the white population was positively associated with higher approval levels for the ballot initiative: as the size of the white population increased, so did the vote for Official English. White voters in California counties with quite small minority (and Latino) populations strongly approved of the English

**Table 10.1** Race/Ethnicity and the Vote for Official English in California Controlling for % Latino Population, Party, and Economic Conditions (County-Level Data)

|  | Model 1 | Model 2 | Model 3 | Model 4 |
|---|---|---|---|---|
| % Latino | -.10 | -.09 | .32*** | -.23*** |
|  | (.05) | (.05) | (.10) | (.05) |
| % Black | -.69*** |  |  | .35* |
|  | (.20) |  |  | (.17) |
| % Asian |  | -.63*** |  | -.23* |
|  |  | (.12) |  | (.12) |
| % White |  |  | .40*** |  |
|  |  |  | (.08) |  |
| Unemployment rate (%) |  |  |  | .79*** |
|  |  |  |  | (.17) |
| Republican Party (% Registered) |  |  |  | 71.12*** |
|  |  |  |  | (9.78) |
| Constant | 81.12*** | 81.62*** | 41.45*** | 46.29*** |
|  | (1.32) | (1.20) | (7.58) | (4.81) |
| Adjusted $R^2$ | .22 | .36 | .35 | .68 |
| Standard error | 5.42 | 4.93 | 4.96 | 3.50 |
| N | 58 | 58 | 58 | 58 |
| F | 9.07*** | 16.72*** | 16.36*** | 24.71*** |

*Sources:* Bureau of the Census, *City and County Data Book* 1986; and the Secretary of State's office in California, Colorado, and Florida.

*Note:* Entries are unstandardized regression coefficients; standard errors in parentheses. "Minority": % Latino, black, and Asian population.

*$p < .05$, ***$p < .001$ (two-tailed).

Language Amendment. In California, when we control for the white population, the coefficient for Latino is positively related to the vote for Official English. Individual-level data also indicate Latinos strongly opposed the initiative. This suggests that white voters in bifurcated counties with large Latino populations *and* white voters in homogeneous counties with quite small minority (and Latino) populations strongly supported Official English.

Historically, economic conditions have been an important factor in white responses to immigration and ethnic groups, often resulting from concern over competition for jobs (Hayes 1957; Hofstadter 1955). Therefore, model 4 (table 10.1) extends the analysis to account

for county unemployment rates and for political party affiliation
(cf. Citrin et al. 1990a; *City and County Data Book,* 1986 California).
In California, poor economic conditions are positively associated
with the vote for Official English. As the county unemployment rate
increased, so did the vote for the language initiative.

Model 4 also examines the impact of political party, measured by
the percentage of registered Republicans per county in California
(1986). Republican Party leaders tended to be more supportive of Official English, although many Republican leaders called the measure unnecessary and said that it could arouse resentment among
minority groups. State Democratic Party leaders generally opposed
the measure. Counties with higher Republican Party affiliation
were much more likely to vote for the language proposal. Model 4
accounts for nearly 70% of the variation in the county-level vote for
Official English. Previous research found strikingly similar county-
level voting patterns on Official English initiatives in Colorado and
Florida (cf. Hero, Tolbert, and Lopez 1996). We suggest that racial/
ethnic diversity accounts for similar voting patterns not only across
states but also across policy areas.

## The Vote for Proposition 187 (1994)

We next examine the relationship between racial/ethnic context
and the county-level vote for Proposition 187, adopted by California
voters eight years after Offical English. Since Latinos account for
the majority of illegal immigrants in California, first analyzed is the
relationship between percent Latino and the county-level vote for
Proposition 187. Figure 10.1 suggests that the relationship between
the size of the Latino population and support for this policy is more
complex than a simple linear relationship (see figure 10.1). As the
size of the Latino population increased, voters were significantly
more likely to support the initiative (upper-right quadrant of graph).
But individual-level data indicates that Latinos voted against the
measure by almost a 4 to 1 margin (see appendix). White voters in
bifurcated counties with large Latino populations (over 20%)
strongly supported the measure.

The vote for Proposition 187 was also high in homogeneous
counties with very small minority populations. Homogeneous

**Figure 10.1** California's Latino Population and the Vote for Proposition 187

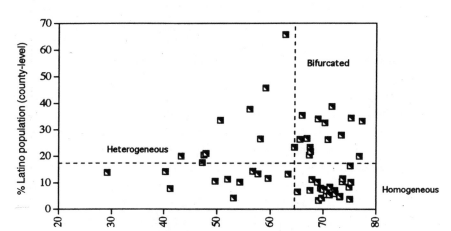

counties with a predominant white (nonminority) population and small Latino population (less than 10%) are concentrated in the lower-right quadrant of the graph. The vote ranged between 70% and 80% in these counties, well over the county-level mean of 64%. This may suggest that illegal immigration was viewed as a statewide problem, irrespective of the size of the Latino (and/or illegal alien) population. Indeed, the measure was referred to as "Save Our State," i.e., framing the issue as one of statewide importance. It also suggests that the immediate presence of Latinos (or illegal immigrants) is not necessary for whites to be concerned with growing minority populations (cf. Key 1949; Giles and Evans 1986). On the other hand, the *lowest* levels of voter support occurred in heterogeneous counties, those with moderately large black and Asian populations.[1]

Again, a series of OLS regression equations are also used to estimate the impact of race/ethnicity on county-level support for Proposition 187. In each model, racial/ethnic populations are the independent variables and county-level vote for Proposition 187 is the dependent variable. Bivariate regression analysis (not shown) indicates that larger black and Asian populations are inversely related to support for Proposition 187; as the size of the black and Asian population rose in a county, the vote for the immigration proposal decreased. The size of the Asian population alone accounts for 40% of the variation in support for the initiative at the county level. As expected, the size of the white population is positively correlated with the vote for this policy.

Table 10.2 estimates the impact of race on the vote for Proposition 187 controlling for the percent Latino. This control is used because the initiative was widely perceived to target Latinos, who represent the majority of illegal aliens in the state. In Model 3 the size of *both* the Latino and white populations is positively correlated with the vote of the proposition at the county level. As the size of the Latino population increases and/or as the size of the white population increases, so did the vote for the initiative. But individual-level data make clear that Latinos strongly opposed the measure. Thus, white voters in counties with large Latino populations *and* in counties with quite small minority (and Latino) populations strongly approved of immigration control. A similar voting pattern

**Table 10.2** Race/Ethnicity and the Vote for Proposition 187 Controlling for % Latino Population (County-Level Data)

|                       | Model 1    | Model 2    | Model 3    |
| --------------------- | ---------- | ---------- | ---------- |
| % Latino              | .03        | .06        | .87***     |
|                       | (.10)      | (.09)      | (.17)      |
| % Black               | -1.33***   |            |            |
|                       | (.35)      |            |            |
| % Asian               |            | -1.28      |            |
|                       |            | (.20)      |            |
| % White               |            |            | .81***     |
|                       |            |            | (.14)      |
| Constant              | 68.44***   | 69.66***   | -11.02     |
|                       | (2.41)     | (2.00)     | (12.87)    |
| Adjusted $R^2$        | .19        | .40        | .37        |
| Standard error        | 9.60       | 8.27       | 8.41       |
| $N$                   | 58         | 58         | 58         |
| F                     | 7.48***    | 19.64***   | 18.02***   |

*Sources:* California Secretary of State's Office.

*Note:* Entries are unstandardized regression coefficients; standard errors in parenthesis.

***$p < .001$ (two-tailed).

was found for the Official English initiative. Controlling for the percent Latino does not change the inverse relationship between higher black and Asian populations and lower approval levels.

These findings are not unlike those of Key concerning the 1940s South (1949). Key found that "black belt" counties with large black populations were more strongly segregationist than neighboring counties and regions where blacks represented a smaller segment of the population. Blacks did not, of course, support segregationist policies; rather, blacks in these counties were largely prevented from participating in elections by various legal constraints. Key also found especially high white-voter turnout in "black belt" counties. Similarly, turnout in California's 1994 election was unusually high—60%—in counties with large white populations for a midterm election. These findings suggest California's white/Latino bifurcated racial/ethnic composition may parallel the white/black bifurcation of the Deep South in an earlier era.

Economic conditions also appear to have an impact on support for Proposition 187. Table 10.3 introduces controls for county unemployment rates, historically an important factor in responses to high immigration (Hayes 1957; Hofstadter 1955). County-level data on the percentage unemployed of the civilian workforce is from the *City and County Data Book* (1990). In each model, as the unemployment rate increased, so did the county-level vote for the statewide initiative; the coefficients for racial/ethnic composition remain strong and statistically significant. These findings suggest that economic conditions and racial/ethnic context had a combined impact on support for the illegal immigration initiative, especially among white voters.

Table 10.4 includes controls for the impact of economic conditions and party registration levels. Party is measured by the percentage of registered Republicans per county in 1994 (California Secretary of State 1994). California's Republican Party members, including incumbent Republican Governor Pete Wilson, were vocal advocates of Proposition 187, while the state's Democratic Party leaders, including Assembly Speaker Willie Brown, generally opposed the measure. It is not surprising, then, that Republican-dominated counties were much more likely to vote for the immigration proposal. The models in table 10.4 account for between 86% and 89%

**Table 10.3** Race/Ethnicity and the Vote for Proposition 187 Controlling for Economic Conditions (County-Level Data)

|                        | Model 1     | Model 2     | Model 3     |
|------------------------|-------------|-------------|-------------|
| % Latino               | -.15        | -.08        | .57**       |
|                        | (.11)       | (.10)       | (.17)       |
| % Black                | -.91**      |             |             |
|                        | (.36)       |             |             |
| % Asian                |             | -1.04***    |             |
|                        |             | (.21)       |             |
| % White                |             |             | .65***      |
|                        |             |             | (.14)       |
| Unemployment           | 1.24***     | .93**       | .91**       |
| rate (%)               | (.38)       | (.34)       | (.35)       |
| Constant               | 58.70***    | 62.33***    | -2.14       |
|                        | (3.68)      | (3.30)      | (12.72)     |
| Adjusted $R^2$         | .31         | .46         | .43         |
| Standard error         | 8.85        | 7.83        | 8.01        |
| N                      | 58          | 58          | 58          |
| F                      | 9.43***     | 17.05***    | 15.47***    |

*Sources: City and County Data Book 1986;* and the Secretary of State's Office.

*Note:* Entries are unstandardized regression coefficients; standard errors in parenthesis.

Correlation diagnostics indicate no problems of multicolinearity between unemployment rate and racial/ethnic composition. Largest Pearson (r) correlation is .43 between county unemployment rate and % Latino.

**$p < .01$, ***$p < .001$ (two-tailed).

of the variation in the county-level vote for the initiative, using only three or five parameter estimates.

Controlling for political party and economic conditions further clarifies the relationship between race/ethnicity and county-level voting patterns. Model 1 (table 10.4) indicates that when we control for these factors, percent Latino is inversely related to the vote for the ballot measure. Controlling for party and unemployment rates statistically eliminates the effect of the high vote for Proposition 187 in counties with large Latino populations, because these counties have the highest unemployment and registered Republicans. The remaining (homogeneous) counties show a slight negative relationship. Similarly, controlling for percent white statistically elimi-

**Table 10.4** Racial/Ethnic Diversity and the Vote for Proposition 187 (County-Level Data)

|  | Model 1 | Model 2 | Model 3 | Model 4 | Model 5 |
|---|---|---|---|---|---|
| % Latino | -.16*** |  |  |  | -.15*** |
|  | (.05) |  |  |  | (.05) |
| % Black |  | .06 |  |  | .54** |
|  |  | (.18) |  |  | (.17) |
| % Asian |  |  | -.36*** |  | -.42*** |
|  |  |  | (.12) |  | (.12) |
| % Minority |  |  |  | -.12*** |  |
|  |  |  |  | (.03) |  |
| Unemployment | 1.32*** | 1.09*** | .95*** | 1.18*** | 1.26*** |
| rate (%) | (.16) | (.16) | (.15) | (.14) | (.19) |
| Republican Party | 1.19*** | 1.23*** | 1.08*** | 1.12*** | 1.16*** |
| (% Registered) | (.07) | (.09) | (.09) | (.08) | (.08) |
| Constant | 8.36** | 5.45 | 14.76*** | 12.28*** | 9.93** |
|  | (3.18) | (4.39) | (4.21) | (3.58) | (3.93) |
| Adjusted $R^2$ | .86 | .83 | .86 | .86 | .89 |
| Standard error | 3.93 | 4.33 | 4.02 | 3.95 | 3.55 |
| $N$ | 58 | 58 | 58 | 58 | 58 |
| F | 120.68*** | 96.14*** | 114.93*** | 119.78*** | 92.12*** |

*Sources:* Bureau of the Census, *City and County Data Book 1986;* and California Secretary of State's Office.

*Note:* Entries are unstandardized regression coefficients; standard errors in parenthesis. "Minority": % Latino, black, and Asian population. Correlation diagnostics indicate no problems of multicolinearity.

**p < .01, ***p < .001 (two-tailed).

nates the effect of high support for the measure in counties with very low Latino populations, because it is in these counties that we find the largest white populations. The remaining (bifurcated) counties indicate a positive relationship (see table 10.2, model 3). Both models are correct; counties with both high and very low Latino populations strongly supported the measure (see figure 10.1). Thus, while unemployment and party may be important, these factors alone are not sufficient to explain the complex voting patterns on Proposition 187. Race/ethnicity remains critical.

Counties with moderately large Asian populations strongly opposed the measure, even controlling for party and economic conditions. When we control for party and high unemployment, however, larger black populations are associated with *higher* levels of support for the initiative. This suggests that an interminority competition may exist between Latinos and blacks for employment and even governmental social services. Previous studies support this finding. McClain (1993) found evidence for competition among blacks and Latinos for municipal unemployment (399-414).

## Proposition 187 and the Wilson Gubernatorial Campaign

Proposition 187 was also related to several candidate-based races in California, especially for governor. In 1993, public opinion of the incumbent governor, Pete Wilson (Republican), reached record lows in the face of recession, tax increases, and defense cutbacks that weakened the California economy. In the early stages of the campaign, Democratic candidate Kathleen Brown was leading Wilson in the opinion polls by as much as 23%. Wilson made illegal immigration the central issue of his reelection campaign. In contrast, the Democratic candidate linked her campaign closely to the opposition to Proposition 187.

Since Wilson allied his reelection campaign closely with his support for Proposition 187, it is not surprising that race/ethnicity also played a central role in the 1994 vote for governor. The county-level vote for Wilson and Proposition 187 are strongly related (Pearson [$r$] correlation = .85; $R^2$ =.72; $p$ = .0001) in California's 58 counties. The *Los Angeles Times* exit poll indicates 61% of whites voted for the Republican incumbent candidate, Wilson, and 35% for the Democratic candidate. Seventy-two percent of Latinos voted for Brown and 23% for Wilson. Blacks strongly supported the Democratic candidate (77% to 20%), while Asian Americans split their vote evenly between the Republican and Democratic gubernatorial candidates. This suggests issue elections (ballot initiatives) may play a role in structuring candidate-based elections.

## Conclusion

Official English and Proposition 187 appear to be two policies in a series of policies adopted through the initiative process in "bifurcated" racial/ethnic contexts. Our findings suggest that states with bifurcated racial/ethnic populations may be more likely to adopt policies, especially through the initiative process, that target minority groups. These findings directly parallel and reinforce those of a state-level analysis of racial/ethnic diversity. Although voter approval was expected to increase with the size of the Latino population, the relationship was more complex. Support for Official English and Proposition 187 were high in bifurcated counties, with above-average Latino populations and a dominant white population. Surprisingly, support for both policies was also very strong in homogeneous counties with very small minority populations. Previous research on race and public policy in the states does not anticipate or explain the dynamics of race/ethnicity in homogeneous contexts. The lowest support occurred in racially heterogeneous counties with sizable black and Asian populations. These patterns are consistent with state-level findings examining the impact of racial/ethnic diversity on various policy outcomes (cf. Hero and Tolbert 1996).

Economic conditions (unemployment) and party (registered Republicans) also played a role in county-level voting patterns. The analysis shows that racial/ethnic diversity (context) was important in shaping voting patterns, even when these factors are accounted for.

The importance of the theory and empirical findings presented here extend beyond California to national and subnational politics. It is likely that measures similar to Proposition 187 (and Official English) will diffuse to other states with bifurcated racial/ethnic contexts, especially large Latino (and illegal immigrant) populations, such as Arizona, Colorado, Florida, and Texas. Previous research leads us to expect that the diffusion will occur first in "populist" states with high usage of the initiative process (Tolbert 1996; see chapter 8, this volume). However legitimate concerns over immigration and the primacy of the English language may be, this response to immigration and ethnic groups follows patterns familiar in California, state politics, and indeed, in U.S. history.

## APPENDIX

| Voter<br>Demographics | | Voted for<br>Prop 187 (%) | Voted against<br>Prop 187 (%) |
|---|---|---|---|
| RACE/ETHNICITY | | | |
| White | 81% | 63 | 37 |
| Black | 5% | 47 | 53 |
| Latino | 8% | 23 | 77 |
| Asian | 4% | 47 | 53 |
| EDUCATION | | | |
| High school or less | 20% | 66 | 34 |
| Some college | 30% | 62 | 38 |
| College graduate | 50% | 53 | 47 |
| AGE | | | |
| 18–29 years old | 14% | 47 | 53 |
| 30–49 years old | 45% | 55 | 45 |
| 50–64 years old | 25% | 63 | 37 |
| More than 65 years old | 16% | 68 | 32 |
| PARTY AFFILIATION | | | |
| Democrat | 40% | 36 | 64 |
| Independent | 16% | 62 | 38 |
| Republican | 41% | 78 | 22 |
| POLITICAL IDEOLOGY | | | |
| Liberal | 17% | 26 | 74 |
| Moderate | 46% | 55 | 45 |
| Conservative | 37% | 78 | 22 |

*Source: Los Angeles Times* exit poll of 5,336 voters as they exited 85 polling places across the state. Precincts were chosen based on the pattern of turnout in the past general elections. The survey was by confidential questionnaire. The margin of sampling error for percentages based on the entire sample is plus or minus 3 percentage points. Davis Market Research Services Inc. of Calabasas assisted the *Times* in this poll. (Contact: Rob Cioe, *Los Angeles Times*, email: cioer@news.latimes.com or cioer@aol.com)

## NOTES

1. These data might be interpreted as showing that, at moderate levels of minority population, a process of social contagion goes on in these hetero-

geneous counties that generates more tolerance (or less fear) of minorities. Contrary to Key (1949), Huckfeldt and Sprauge (1987) and others (Carsey 1995) contend that interaction among races encourages acceptance of the minority groups. Higher levels of support for Official English and Proposition 187 in counties with the largest minority populations might suggest that, beyond some threshold of minority populations' share, white acceptance of minorities decreases.

# 11

## Direct Democracy and Minorities: Changing Attitudes about Minorities Targeted by Initiatives

JAMES WENZEL, TODD DONOVAN,
AND SHAUN BOWLER

The advocates of some forms of direct democracy claim that use of these institutions can stimulate political interest and facilitate learning about politics (Barber 1984; Butler and Ranney 1994; Dolbare and Hubble 1996). Democratic theorists (Macpherson 1977; Pateman 1980) have suggested that direct participation in policy making can play a pedagogic role, and some empirical studies of highly salient national referenda illustrate that voters absorb considerable information on the issues from referenda campaigns (Elklit and Peterson 1973; Hansen et al. 1975; Siune 1993).

Critics, on the other hand, note the potential for majoritarian tyranny, particularly when unpopular minority groups are made the subject of an initiative (Gamble 1997; for a review, see Cronin 1989, chapter 5; Butler and Ranney 1994, 19–21; Magleby 1984, 30). Those even more critical of direct democracy suggest that these institutions provide an opportunity for highly visible political discourse that can have a stigmatizing effect on minority groups made the subject of the initiative (Bell 1978; Fountaine 1988; Goetz 1987; Gunn 1981; Linde 1989, 1993). This chapter builds upon these insights and questions by examining how direct democracy affects mass attitudes and opinions about minority groups targeted by citizen's initiatives.

## Initiatives and the Tolerance of Unpopular Groups

Issues that clearly subject minority groups to critical public scrutiny are by no means the most frequent topics to reach the ballot.[1] On occasion, however, initiatives qualify that appear designed to restrict the services provided or rights accorded to a relatively unpopular group. Examples of initiatives from the 1990s include those targeting the rights of homosexuals, services provided to welfare recipients, and the status of immigrants.[2] If we assume that voters' attitudes about the specific policies proposed by these various initiatives are somewhat uncertain and malleable, and that opinions about these groups are also uncertain, what effects might the institution of direct democracy have on attitudes and opinions?

One major problem for the maintenance of democratic institutions is that tolerance of (or empathy for) political outgroups is not necessarily a "normal" response, particularly if the group in question is perceived as potentially threatening. On the contrary, as Stouffer (1955) suggested, initial responses to outgroups, or to attempts to suppress them, are almost universally intolerant. Tolerant outcomes occur only when individuals are able to devote significant cognitive resources to the consideration of the broader implications of the proposed repression. Although Stouffer confined his analysis principally to the question of the level of tolerance of communists, his findings are supported by similar studies using alternate reference groups (Gibson and Bingham 1985; Nunn, Crockett, and Williams 1978). Our interest is in the process by which the "sober second thought" on which Stouffer depended to generate tolerant outcomes is influenced by the initiative process.

A useful way to conceptualize the impact of initiatives on citizen willingness to support the rights and benefits accorded unpopular minorities is to model the process as one involving attempts at persuasion. Let us assume that mass opinion on the subject of the rights and status of political minorities is quite diffuse initially. Some members of the public may have positive views about the group while many harbor distinctly negative feelings toward the group. As a rule, however, few give the group or its members much direct thought. When an initiative is proposed that would restrict or rescind rights and benefits granted (generally by statute) to the group, the campaigns in favor of and opposed to the initiative expose members of the public to stimuli designed to sway their opinions.

In general, political tolerance at the individual level has been found to be a function of individuals' general commitment to the norms of democracy and the perceived threat posed by the target group. The stronger one's commitment to democratic norms, the more likely one is to respond in a tolerant fashion to the urge to repress. Conversely, the greater the degree of threat perceived, the more likely it becomes that the initial intolerant reaction will hold sway. The problem for tolerance, and hence for democratic government, is that while the urge to repress potential threats has a strong, potentially genetically transmitted (see Willhoite 1977), affective component, a tolerant response requires the commitment of substantial cognitive resources. This ingrained propensity to respond in an intolerant fashion must be overcome by resort to reasoned argument. Citizens must be convinced that reason requires that they ignore their initial impulses toward what they perceive as self-preservation and extend rights to those whom they view as threatening and potentially destructive. Ballot choices involving unpopular minority groups create a context where citizens must make choices about these groups on the basis of their affect toward the groups, in combination with the information received during the petition drive and campaign.

## The Dynamics of Opinion in Direct Democracy

Given the absence of panel data, and the absence of survey instruments designed for the purpose of studying direct democracy, there are virtually no existing studies that examine change in individual opinions within the course of a direct democracy election or across years (with at least one exception being Mendelsohn's 1994 study of the Canadian Referendum of 1992). This being the case, there is little empirical knowledge about how the institutions of direct democracy affect citizen attitudes, preferences, or opinions about subjects of the initiatives and referenda. There are a number of theoretical points of departure for viewing the potentially dynamic nature of voter preferences and opinions on initiative topics.

One perspective on opinion formation suggests that mass opinions on many if not most policies are shaped by elites. Rather than assuming that individual preferences are preexisting and stable (Ordeshook 1992), opinions are assumed to be malleable during campaigns (Converse 1964; Key 1966). Depending upon campaign intensity and responsiveness to information, citizens can be exposed to information that alters their opinions about subjects of the campaign (Converse 1962; Zaller 1989, 1992).

Zaller (1991) notes that when looking at mass opinions in general, if there are ideological or partisan cues in the messages that elites send (that is, if elite messages display clear partisan/ideological differences), then subgroups in the mass public can respond in a manner consistent with messages supplied from elites of their respective groups. If partisan or ideological elites are divided, voters can respond to the positions taken by partisan and/or ideological elites they identify with. Considering this, we might expect that attentive partisans respond to the positions and messages advanced by elites in their respective parties regarding the subjects of ballot initiatives.

Gerber and Jackson (1993, 640), drawing from Cohen and Axelrod (1984), describe a similar "adaptive utility model" that assumes voters in candidate contests have uncertain preferences about programs being debated publicly. As parties propose and discuss their programs in public, individuals acquire information about possible outcomes. Gerber and Jackson identify shifts in party positions as providing the spark that causes voters to "update" their preferences. Following March and Olsen, their findings illustrate the important role that political institutions play in "helping individuals learn preferences and roles" (1994, 654).

But what of the institutions of direct democracy? If the adaptive utility model is appropriate in the direct democracy setting, then what, if anything, might individuals learn when they are exposed to information about policies that have clearly identifiable minority groups as subjects? If preferences (attitudes and opinions) are flexible or malleable, what happens to mass attitudes when the institutions of direct democracy are used in attempts to restrict the political status of minorities? The fear of majority tyranny over minorities, after all, is one of the fundamental criticisms of direct democracy.

If the successful inculcation of the mass public to norms of democracy such as tolerance is to have an impact on public policy, citizens must be able to identify situations in which tolerance is an appropriate response. One palliative for this problem may be the role that social and political elites play in providing guidance for the public. Many theorists, Stouffer (1955) included, have suggested that elites, by virtue of their having better inculcated the norms of democracy, and being able to better identify situations in which tolerance is a democratically appropriate response, are more likely to respond in a tolerant fashion (see also Nunn, Crockett, and Williams 1978; McCloskey and Brill 1983).

Initiatives and referenda present the potential for substantial difficulties for the maintenance of broad democratic values. What happens when, as in the situation of a citizen's initiative, the role of elites in promoting tolerance is negligible, or at least reduced? By assuming the mantle of policy promoters, the organizers of the initiative movement may tend to usurp the traditional role that elites play in mitigating intolerant mass opinion. This apparent inversion of the elite role from one that promotes tolerance and democratic values to one calling for a recision of those values may well have substantial consequences for the maintenance of tolerance and democracy.[3]

Models estimated in this chapter are designed to test hypotheses derived from the assumption of adaptive (flexible) mass opinions and preferences. We anticipate that the process of contesting the ballot issue can affect the attitudes and preferences that citizens hold about things made the subject of an initiative. Prior to a topic's appearing as an initiative (T1), voters can have some relatively uncertain preexisting opinions about the group that the initiative deals with and the general policy issues associated with the topic. These opinions and preferences might be, in part, associated with the voter's stock of political information, past political socialization, education, partisanship, and demographic traits. Later (T2), the voter is placed in a position of evaluating a specific proposal in the form of an actual policy proposal. At this time, the voter can be exposed to new information about the (new) policy proposal, about the group, and about how the group is affected by the policy. Information regarding the initiative proposal can come from a variety of sources—political parties, political elites, the news media—and may provoke changes in mass opinion distributions from that seen early in the campaign (Darcy and Laver 1990; Magleby 1989; Karp, chapter 7 in this volume).

To the extent that opinions are relatively malleable, the influence of messages about groups targeted by initiative efforts ought to be observable in opinion data. It would seem that they are. Sniderman et al. (1991), for example, found attitudes toward racial policy to be quite susceptible to persuasion. Moreover, the degree of susceptibility to persuasion was asymmetric with respect to the respondents' initial policy positions. On the subject of government assistance to nonwhites, those who initially professed support for assistance were substantially more vulnerable to conservative arguments than those initially expressing opposition to assistance were to liberal arguments. In fact, after both counterarguments were applied, a 5–4 majority in favor of government assistance to blacks had been converted to a 5–4 majority in opposition to such assistance.[4]

If information received during the initiative campaign affects preference and opinions, voters residing in places experiencing an initiative on topic Y should be more likely to display changes in opinions and preferences related to Y from T1 to T2, above and beyond that displayed by voters residing in states having no such initiative. A simple dummy variable indicating that a respondent resides in states with certain initiative movements is not likely to capture completely the relationship between an individual's opinion change and that person's experiences associated with direct democracy. If the initiative context actually creates the opinion change, we expect that change from T1 to T2 should be affected by an interaction between living in the direct democracy state and some indicator of attentiveness to politics, or be affected by an interaction between the direct democracy context and identification with the political party supporting the initiative. This follows from our assumption that attentive and partisan voters will be more likely to be exposed to and receptive to messages about the initiative (Converse 1962; Zaller 1989).

Consider initiatives dealing with the civil rights of gays and lesbians. Prior to the 1990s, very few of the state initiatives that were circulated dealt explicitly with gay rights.[5] Voters had (possibly uncertain) opinions about gay rights policies and about gays and lesbians as a group. In 1994, however, anti-gay rights initiatives were filed in eight states and broached in another (Donovan and Bowler n.d.).[6] We assume that this issue was not as highly salient in these states in the early 1990s as it was by the mid-1990s. Many voters might been unaware of the positions that state, party, and ideological elites took on gay rights prior to 1992.[7] However, by the time a state's antigay initiative is drafted and circulated, parties and elites are often forced to take visible public positions (Witt and Mc-Corkle 1997). As the petition campaigns progressed in each state, editorials, news coverage, "decline to sign" efforts, and even occasional commercials focused not only on the policy proposals, but on the group targeted, the group's lifestyle, and the policy and the positions that elites were taking on the policy. This was particularly true in those states where initiatives qualified for the ballot. By late 1994, some voters, particularly those attentive to political information or those responsive to party cues, might have shifted their opinions about gay rights and gay and lesbian lifestyles. In terms of this example, we are interested in determining if there were significantly larger shifts in opinions about gays from 1992 to 1994 among citizens living in states having antigay petition efforts in 1994. We expect the effect to be most pronounced among partisan and attentive voters in these states.

This begs the question, however, of the expected direction of opinion change. From one perspective, the intervention of choices and discourse presented by direct democracy might have an impact on moving attitudes toward greater tolerance if elites assume a consensus in favor of the tolerant position and these messages are transmitted through the campaign. March (1970) and March and Olsen (1984, 739) see such a situation as a classic model of political leadership in democracy. If, however, we consider the critique of direct democracy offered by Hans Linde, Derrick Bell, and others (as well as that implicit in Madisonian theory) who suggest that the mere existence of initiatives targeting minorities can stigmatize the group—particularly if visible elites of at least one party or ideological group promote the intolerant position—evidence of "learning" or attitude change might be reflected in opinions shifting toward less acceptance of the target group. What if opinion change associated with direct democracy choices breeds greater disdain of minorities? If there is any evidence of this, we might have to conclude that there is some merit to the idea that heated public debates generated by placing such questions on the ballot can have adverse consequences for targeted groups, regardless of the policy implications of the proposals.

## Cases, Data, and Methods

This study makes use of 1990–1992 and 1992–1994 NES panel studies to model changes in opinions about groups made the subject of ballot initiatives. Emphasis is given to attitudes about gays and lesbians, welfare recipients, and illegal immigrants. Hypotheses about the effects that exposure to initiative campaigns, political attentiveness, and partisanship have on feeling thermometer ratings are tested. We also test hypotheses about changes in attitudes about public policies related to these initiatives. Lagged endogenous models of individual-level opinion change are estimated to test our hypotheses (Marcus 1979, 47).

The NES provides some opportunities for examining how direct democracy might affect attitudes about minorities targeted by initiatives. Since we are interested, in part, in testing if these initiatives stigmatize groups, we examine change in perceptions of relevant groups as reflected in panel studies. Perceptions are measured with standard feeling thermometer scores. Multiple wave of NES panels repeated questions asking respondents to rate their feelings about gays, illegal immigrants, and welfare recipients on a scale from 0 to 100, with 100 being warm, 0 cold, and 50 neutral.[8] We are also interested in assessing the impact the initiative has on citizens' attitudes toward the treatment of these groups. Since the NES is not designed to assess opinions about specific initiatives, tests of these policy-related hypotheses are based on NES questions that deal with questions related to, but not specifically drawn from, the policies proposed in the various initiatives.

Our measures of change in attitudes about treatment of these groups are different across the three targeted groups we examine.

For example, concurrent with the filing of antigay initiatives in 1994, NES panel respondents were asked in 1992 and 1994 how strongly they agreed/disagreed that "different moral standards should be tolerated." Likewise, a California initiative appeared on that state's November 1994 ballot (Proposition 187) ostensibly designed to reduce illegal immigration by denying state and local services to illegal immigrants and their children. Corresponding with this, 1992–1994 panel respondents were asked their opinions about how much illegal immigration should be increased or decreased nationally. California also had a "welfare reform" initiative on the November 1992 ballot (Proposition 165) that would have reduced AFDC payments in the state by 25%. Corresponding with this, 1992 NES respondents were asked if "spending on welfare" should be increased, left the same, or decreased.[9]

We expect that attitudes change as people are exposed to new information about policies concerning which they have only loosely formed preferences. Since we are interested in testing if opinion change is associated with something emanating from the process of direct democracy, we need to isolate the effect of information exposure that is unique to citizens residing in states having relevant initiatives. NES has no direct measure of exposure to information about initiatives during these campaigns. We can, however, use measures of state residence to isolate individuals who reside in states having relevant initiatives. Thus, we create a dummy variable representing potential exposure to antiminority initiatives and their associated campaign messages. For the models of opinion change associated with antigay initiatives, individuals residing in states where the antigay initiatives were filed in 1994 are coded as 1, others as 0. For the models of opinion change associated with the 1992 welfare and 1994 immigration initiatives, individuals residing in California in 1992 and 1994 (respectively) are coded as 1, others as 0. These variables isolate the contextual effect of exposure to campaign discourse associated with direct democracy.[10]

In testing for the interaction between partisanship and potential responsiveness to messages emanating from these initiative contests targeting these minority groups, we focus on Republican identifiers. In each of the cases we examine, elites within the Republican Party were more likely to be associated with advocacy of the initiative petitions. This is most clear in the case of the two California initiatives. Proposition 187, the anti-immigration measure, was supported by GOP Governor Pete Wilson[11] and was sponsored by a GOP state assemblyman (*California Journal,* September 1994, 10). Proposition 165, the antiwelfare measure, was sponsored and supported by Governor Wilson (*California Journal,* September 1992, 6).

Identifying distinct partisan advocacy of the antigay initiatives is a bit less certain. Nevertheless, the antigay measures in some states were sponsored by conservative activists who had displaced traditional Republican state party officials and were assuming control of state party organizations (i.e., Oregon, Idaho). In other states (i.e., Washington, Michigan) initiatives were sponsored by conservative groups associated with, but not in control of, their state's GOP organizations (Liechtling et al. 1993). Advocates of the antigay initiatives were clearly conservative and often involved with their state's Republican party; however, unlike the California situation, these proponents typically came from outside the circle of elected officials (Witt and McCorkle 1997). To test for responsiveness to the initiative context associated with Republican partisanship, we include an interaction term in our models that represents Republicans residing in states having a relevant antiminority initiative.

## A Bivariate Example

Before estimating models of opinion change, we illustrate, in simple form, the dynamic nature of opinions associated with one group targeted by a ballot initiative. Consider, for example, the impact of the campaigns surrounding the proposed citizen's initiatives to rescind the provision of public services to illegal immigrants and their children. In a world where opinion is perfectly consistent (time and the campaign have no impact) a scatterplot plotting opinion toward illegal immigrants before the initiative (T1) against opinion toward this group after the initiative (T2) should reveal all respondents lining up on the diagonal. In regression terms, the intercept would equal zero and the slope and R-square would equal 1.0.[12] A uniform aggregate shift in opinion (in the positive or negative direction) would result in an intercept of greater than or less than zero. Our expectations as to the slope and R-square, however, do not change. If, however, the structure of opinion changes in response to the campaign, we would expect this to be reflected in a change in the slope. Higher slopes (greater than one) indicate that opinion at the extremes of the distribution became more intense. Lower slopes (less than one) indicate a general attenuation of opinion. R-square in this model becomes a measure of consistency. Low values indicate a greater degree of scattering of responses around the regression line.

Although in the real world mass opinion is not perfectly consistent, a comparison of the relationship between opinions toward illegal immigrants before Proposition 187 was filed and opinions toward illegal immigrants after the initiative was filed should offer some insights into the impact of the initiative process on mass opinions. By comparing the impact of pre-initiative opinion on post-initiative opinion in California with the rest of the United States, we should be able to observe any obvious differential shifts in the structure of opinion associated with residence in a direct democracy state.

As we suspected initially, the presence of an anti-immigrant initiative campaign does appear to exert some influence, although limited, on individual affect toward the group. Using panel data from the 1992–1994 National Election Survey, we conducted two regressions, reported in table 11.1. In each, the dependent variable is the respondent's 1994 feeling thermometer evaluation of illegal immigrants, and the independent variable is the 1992 response to the same question. The first estimation includes only that portion of the respondents living in states in which no immigrant-related initiatives were filed during the 1992–1994 time period ($N = 624$). This produces an intercept of 15.22, and a $b$ of .52, with an R-square of .23. Given the positive intercept, it would seem that for these respondents, illegal immigrants are better liked in 1994 than in 1992 (or disliked less), that opinion has moderated somewhat over the time period (indicated by a slope of less than 1), and finally, that opinion is somewhat inconsistent.

The second regression is identical to the first, with the exception that only those respondents residing in California ($N = 62$) are included. The lower intercept (8.05) and significantly steeper slope (.77) suggest that, compared to the population as a whole, affect toward illegal immigrants among respondents in these states was sub-

**Table 11.1** Changes in Attitudes about Illegal Immigrants, 1992–1994 (Dependent variable = feelings toward illegal immigrants in 1994, *after* initiative campaign)

|  | Estimate | Std. Error | Cases | $R^2$ |
|---|---|---|---|---|
|  |  | Rest of U.S. |  |  |
| Feelings, 1992 | .52 | .03 |  |  |
| Intercept | 15.22 | 1.62 | 624 | .23 |
|  |  | Californians |  |  |
| Feelings, 1994 | .77 | .11 |  |  |
| Intercept | 8.05 | 4.86 | 62 | .45 |

*Source:* American National Election Study, NES 1992–1994 Panels, variables 317 (1994) and 5331 (1992).

*Note:* The slopes are significantly different—test comparing the slopes produces a value of 2.20 ($p < .025$). A comparison of intercepts produces a $t$ of 1.40 ($p < .10$).

stantially less influenced by the thaw that pervaded the rest of the electorate, while retaining a bit more of the intensity of the earlier period.[13] Interestingly, the value of R-square (.45) suggests that the presence of an initiative campaign served to increase substantially the relative degree of consistency of opinion.

## Models of Opinion Change

Potential exposure, however, is likely to be too crude a measure of any relationship between direct democracy and attitude formation/change. Beyond contextual measures of potential exposure, we require measures that tap the likelihood that someone in this context will receive and respond to information associated with groups made the subject of these initiatives.

For Zaller, the greater a person's level of general political knowledge or awareness, "the more likely he or she is to be exposed to and comprehend . . . political messages" (Zaller 1992, 42–43). He assumes that people who are knowledgeable about politics are habitually attentive to communications on most issues. We follow

Zaller's lead and create an additive index from correct responses to six factual questions about politics.[14] Our models of opinion change include this to represent the independent effect of knowledge on opinion change. We also include measures of the respondent's education to account for potential exposure to political information.

In addition to indicators of stored factual knowledge, our models of opinion change in direct democracy also include two measures of likelihood of receiving and responding to messages and discourse emanating from the initiative campaign context. We expect that voters in these initiative states who are most attentive to media coverage of politics should be more likely to receive information and thus be more likely to change their attitudes about groups and policies made the subject of the initiative. To assess this, we create an additive index of political attention that summarizes the respondent's self-reported interest in politics, frequency of political discussions, and attentiveness to television news coverage.[15] If the relationship between attentiveness and opinion change is accentuated or amplified by the context of direct democracy, we should see a significant interaction between our attentiveness measure and the variable representing the direct democracy context. In other words, attentive voters residing in states having antiminority initiatives are expected to be more likely to change their opinions about groups and policies associated with these initiatives.

Likewise, we also expect that Republican voters residing in initiative states should be more likely to change their opinions about groups and policies associated with these initiatives. Existing research indicates that political parties (and party strategies and positions) affect and shape individual attitudes over time (Gerber and Jackson 1993; Carmines and Stimson 1989; Zaller 1991). As noted above, the initiatives included here were either proposed by or supported by elites within the Republican party (some more than others), while opposition was most visible from mainstream Democratic elites.

Thus, we expect that GOP identification will be associated with opinion change, and that the relationship between partisanship and opinion change was amplified in states with initiatives. GOP voters nationally might be exposed to and respond to elites' messages about groups targeted by ballot initiatives, but not in the context of clearly defined policy choices. However, GOP voters residing in states having initiatives on these subjects are more likely to receive additional cues and/or become aware of state-level partisan elites taking positions on actual ballot initiatives. For these reasons, we include a measure of GOP identification in our models, as well as a variable that represents the interaction between GOP identification and residence in states having initiatives. Our models also include controls for age, for respondents' opinions at $T_1$, and in the case of opinions on welfare, for an indicator of respondent's race.

## Findings

Results from these lagged endogenous models are decidedly mixed. They neither wholly relieve direct democracy from the critique that antiminority initiatives stigmatize targeted groups, nor do they totally acquit direct democracy of these charges. Furthermore, the evidence of accentuated attitude change among attentive and partisan voters exposed to direct democracy contests is also mixed.

Table 11.2 presents the results of our analysis of the impact of the initiative process on individual affect toward the targeted groups. In general, Republican voters nationally were less sympathetic to each group in latter stages of the panels. This effect can be seen as being consistent with cues given by GOP elites during the 1990–1994 period. The effect, however, is most pronounced among GOP identifiers from California asked to evaluate illegal immigrants in 1994. After exposure to California's heated Proposition 187 campaign, a GOP identifier in California rated their feelings for illegal immigrants nearly 20 points lower in 1994 than they did in 1992. This compares to a change of 4 points associated with the independent effect of GOP identification. There appears to be no significant partisan effect interacting with direct democracy from the models estimating feelings about welfare recipients and gays and lesbians.

Looking at the interaction between attentiveness and feelings about these groups, there is also mixed evidence that the direct democracy context might be associated with opinion shifts that reflect stigmatization of targeted groups. After Pete Wilson's 1992 initiative campaign to reduce AFDC (Aid to Families with Dependent Children) payments, politically attentive voters living in

**Table 11.2** Individual-Level Changes in Attitudes toward Groups Targeted by Initiatives

|  | Illegal Immigrants | Welfare Recipients | Gays and Lesbians |
|---|---|---|---|
| Knowledge | -.47 | -.37 | .10 |
|  | (.54) | (.43) | (.51) |
| Feelings (t - 1) | .52** | .38** | .73** |
|  | (.03) | (.02) | (.03) |
| Age | -.02 | .05+ | -.04 |
|  | (.05) | (.03) | (.04) |
| Attention | .19 | .37* | -.37* |
|  | (.19) | (.15) | (.19) |
| Attention* Direct Democracy | .78** | -.26+ | -.01 |
|  | (.29) | (.19) | (.19) |
| GOP | -3.99** | -4.55** | -5.54** |
|  | (1.87) | (1.26) | (1.91) |
| GOP* Direct Democracy | -19.91** | 3.01 | 2.79 |
|  | (5.91) | (3.73) | (3.80) |
| Education | 1.76** | .22 | 1.05* |
|  | (.57) | (.37) | (.51) |
| Black |  | 4.49** |  |
|  |  | (1.72) |  |
| Constant | 9.85** | 26.68** | 11.90** |
|  | (3.67) | (2.50) | (3.37) |
| Adj $R^2$ | .26 | .27 | .53 |
| N | 703 | 1032 | 686 |

$^+p < .10$ (one-tailed), $^*p < .05$, $^{**}p < .01$.

California had slightly lower feelings for welfare recipients than they had in 1990. Conversely, our models indicate that attentive voters in California actually had warmer feelings for illegal immigrants after the 1994 immigration initiative than they did in 1992.

Turning to table 11.3, we present the results of models estimating opinion change on policies related to the treatment of targeted groups. These results indicate that these same attentive respondents from California, although significantly more sympathetic to immigrants, were more likely by 1994 to have shifted their opinions to a position calling for less immigration.[16] Similarly, political attentiveness was associated with shifts to opinions less tolerant of alternative lifestyles among voters living in states where antigay

**Table 11.3** Individual-Level Changes in Attitudes toward Group-Oriented Policy

|  | *Illegal Immigrants* | *Welfare Recipients* | *Gays and Lesbians* |
|---|---|---|---|
| Knowledge | -.07 | -.00 | .05* |
|  | (.02) | (.01) | (.02) |
| Opinion (t - 1) | .42** | na | .42** |
|  | (.03) |  | (.03) |
| Age | .00 | .00 | .00 |
|  | (.00) | (.00) | (.00) |
| Attention | -.10 | .008* | -.003 |
|  | (.008) | (.004) | (.01) |
| Attention* | .023* | -.00 | .012+ |
| Direct Democracy | (.012) | (.00) | (.010) |
| GOP | .03 | .26** | .28** |
|  | (.09) | (.03) | (.10) |
| GOP* | -.34 | .11 | .38* |
| Direct Democracy | (.35) | (.11) | (.20) |
| Education | -.04* | .01 | -.03 |
|  | (.02) | (.01) | (.02) |
| Black | na | .25** | na |
|  |  | (.05) |  |
| Constant | 2.82** | 2.11** | 1.46** |
|  | (.19) | (.07) | (.18) |
| Adj R$^2$ | .23 | .05 | .23 |
| N | 695 | 1,936 | 727 |

*Note:* Low scores on the dependent variable are associated with greater aceptance of a liberal policy (more immigration, more welfare spending, greater tolerance).

+$p < .10$ (one-tailed), *$p < .05$, **$p < .01$.

initiatives were filed in 1994, although this effect fails to attain conventional levels of statistical significance ($p < .10$, one-tailed). There is also additional evidence here of direct democracy turning opinion against targeted minority groups. By 1994, GOP respondents living in states where antigay initiatives circulated were significantly less likely to respond favorably about tolerating different lifestyles and moral standards. While GOP identifiers nationally shifted to opinions less tolerant of these lifestyles, the effect was even more pronounced among GOP voters in states where antigay initiatives were filed.

## Discussion and Conclusions

Recent scholarship has challenged one of the primary assumptions of many formal/positive theories about attitude formation and electoral processes. As Gerber and Jackson note (1993, 654), "most theoretical models of electoral processes treat preferences as being fixed in order to study properties of different electoral systems." Spatial election models and the Median Voter Theorem, for example, assume voters have fixed, single-peaked preferences on issues in order to predict candidate convergence toward the median voter's preference (Black 1958; Downs 1957; Enelow and Hinich 1984).

Empirical studies, however, often provide insights that run counter to this central premise. Empirical results illustrate that attitudes and policy preferences are not necessarily stable across elections (Zaller 1991; Granberg and Holberg 1990; Converse 1964) or within elections (Tedin and Murray 1981; Zaller 1989). Among other things, these studies note the role that campaign events, information, and party leadership cues can play in changing mass attitudes over time. Findings also illustrate that opinions move predictably in response to the strategies and messages sent by parties and candidates (e.g., Gerber and Jackson 1993; Zaller 1991, 1992; Carmines and Stimson 1989).

Such findings have implications for democratic theory and for evaluations of the role that institutions play as vehicles for making social choices. Many existing formal theories consider institutions simply as vehicles for aggregating the preexisting preferences of individuals into outcomes (e.g., Riker 1982). Citizen preferences and attitudes are supposed to be produced and changed by some process that is exogenous to the process of choice, and not by the rules and institutions that structure choices. Institutions are important to many formal theorists, but their main concern with rules and institutions deals with how political systems produce outcomes that may or may not be reflective of majority preferences assumed to be preexisting in the electorate.

As March and Olsen note, conventional theories of politics assume that a voter's exposure to the process of choosing does not change the voter's beliefs about the subject of the choice (1984, 739). Conversely, political institutions themselves (such as various electoral rules, systems, and forms of party competition) are seen by March and Olsen and others as having an important role in the formation of individual policy preferences, attitudes, and opinions.

We have illustrated instances where some changes in individuals' opinions over time appear associated with the process and institution of direct democracy. Most notably, partisan voters in direct democracy states shifted their opinions about groups made the subject of one initiative in a manner that corresponds to party positions on the initiative. These voters also appear to shift opinions about policy-related attitudes in the direction of the position associated with their party. Furthermore, we find some evidence that opinions about targeted groups shift as a result of the interaction between political attentiveness and residence in a state having an initiative targeting the group. There is also some evidence that politically attentive voters living in direct democracy states change their opinions about policies associated with some initiatives. Our evidence also indicates that these shifts associated with direct democracy— particularly with Republicans' feelings about immigrants and tolerance of different "moral standards"—are clearly toward less tolerant opinions. These results are particularly interesting (and disturbing) given that some opponents of antigay initiatives claim that hate crimes against gays increased when some antigay initiatives appeared on state ballots.

These results also suggest that, as a system for directly transforming citizen preferences into policy, direct democracy might operate to the detriment of the toleration of political outgroups. The same, however, might well be said of any sort of campaign. If, as was the case with Proposition 187 in California, state and local political elites use the presence of an initiative as a platform for furthering their own political ambitions, which is responsible for the appeals to mass intolerance—the initiative process itself or elite demagoguery? At this point, with the data at our disposal, we are unable to completely differentiate between the two. Answers to these questions, among others, however, are required if we are to understand the impact direct democracy has on the deliberative processes that animate the "sober second thought" on which Stouffer placed so much reliance.

NOTES

The authors contributed equally to this chapter. The order of names is reverse-alphabetical simply to spite Bowler, who usually goes first in these situations.

1. Magleby notes that the subject matter of initiatives "is fairly evenly distributed across such issue categories as health, welfare, housing, business regulation, revenue and taxes and public morality" (1984, 74).

2. The relative unpopularity of these groups can be illustrated by responses to standard NES feeling-thermometer questions that ask voters to rate how they feel about various social groups. In 1992, the question was asked about 25 groups. These three groups targeted by initiatives in the 1990s received mean ratings of 51.1 (people on welfare), 37.8 (gays and lesbians), and 36.1 (illegal immigrants). Only lawyers (49.9) and liberals (50.1) were also ranked as low as these groups.

3. Gibson (1990) has suggested that this may well be the case more often than we would suspect. He contends that contrary to the expectations of an elite theory of democracy, much political repression in the modern United States, in particular the Red Scare of the 1950s, is or has been elite driven (see also Jackman 1972).

4. These findings are consistent with Gibson and Wenzel (1988). Conceptualizing tolerance as a two-stage process, they conducted a quasi-experiment in which respondents to the 1987 General Social Survey were first asked to respond to a set of questions regarding their willingness to allow members of a group the respondent disliked or found threatening to engage in a variety of acts of political participation. Those respondents giving an initially tolerant response were presented with a set of arguments designed to persuade them to adopt an intolerant position. Conversely, those giving an initially intolerant response were exposed to an argument presenting the virtues and benefits of tolerance. They found it significantly easier to persuade those giving initially tolerant responses to adopt an intolerant position than to convince the initially intolerant of the efficacy of tolerance.

5. Prior to the 1990s, most antigay initiative battles were local. Colorado and Oregon had explicitly anti–gay rights initiatives on their ballots since 1992. These were the first since California's 1978 Briggs Initiative.

6. These states included Arizona, Florida, Idaho, Maine, Michigan, Missouri, Oregon, and Washington. The Florida petition was eventually invalidated by the courts and blocked from the ballot. An effort to qualify a petition in Ohio began but was not filed with the state. The Oregon and Idaho initiatives qualified for a ballot listing in 1994 (National Gay and Lesbian Task Force 1994). The Maine initiative appeared on the 1995 ballot. In sev-

eral states where these initiatives were filed but failed to qualify, there were well-organized and visible "decline to sign" campaigns opposing the petition efforts (see Witt and McCorkle 1997).

7. At the national level, gay rights issues likely became more salient in 1993 after President Clinton's executive order on gays in the military. The effect of this on mass opinions should be relatively uniform across states. We test for state-specific effects associated with direct democracy by isolating respondents residing in states with antigay rights initiative movements.

8. 1994 feeling thermometer scores for gays and lesbians and illegal immigrants are from NES questions 318 and 317, respectively. 1992 scores for these groups and welfare recipients are from NES vars 5335, 5331, and 5318, respectively.

9. 1994 policy attitudes on moral standards and attitudes on immigration rates are measured with NES questions 1032 and 1016, respectively. Corresponding questions from the 1992 wave of the panel are 6116 and 6235. 1992 attitudes about welfare spending are measured with NES question 3726. No corresponding welfare question was asked on the 1990 wave of the panel.

10. The NES sample for 1994 resulted in 22.5% of respondents residing in states where antigay initiatives were filed. This reflects some fortuitous oversampling by NES in states where these petitions were circulated. Californians comprise 9.5% of the sample.

11. Wilson was clearly associated with each of these issues. In 1992, he linked the welfare issues in Proposition 165 to the protracted budget deadlock with the Democratic-held legislature. Proposition 165 would also have given the governor substantially more control of the state budget (*California Journal*, September 1992, 6–7).

In 1994 illegal immigration became a major theme in the governor's reelection campaigns as he linked the state's difficulties to illegal immigration. The first commercial he aired during the November campaign "featured lurid scenes of illegals rushing across the southern border, then fanning out to disappear in the maw of California" (Martis and Block 1994, 21).

12. Random inconsistency should be reflected in the measure of R-square. Inconsistent responses should depress R-square, leaving the slope and intercept static.

13. The retention of intensity is indicated by the regression coefficient. A slope of 1.0 would indicate that intensity remained more or less stable. In other words, those who expressed positive evaluations in 1992 expressed similarly valenced evaluations in 1994. A slope of less than 1 would suggest that opinion became less intense during the period as those expressing strongly negative or strongly positive initial evaluations tended to respond

with less extreme evaluations. Conversely, a slope of greater than 1 would suggest that opinion became more intense.

14. For 1992, knowledge is a summary of correct responses to NES questions 5916, 5917, 5918, 5919, 5920, and 5921. For 1994: 1006, 1007, 1008, 1009, 1010, and 1011.

15. For 1992, attentiveness is a summary of NES variables 5102, 5107, and 5104. For 1994, variables 124, 126, and 130.

16. In table 11.3, higher scores on the dependent variable measuring attitudes about treatment of the groups represent responses least sympathetic to the targeted group. For immigrants, low scores represent a preference for more ease of immigration, higher values reflect a preference for decreased immigration. For welfare recipients, low values reflect a preference for more spending on welfare; higher values represent a preference for decreased. For gays and lesbians, low values reflect strong agreement with the statement that different moral standards and lifestyles should be tolerated, while higher values reflect strong disagreement with this statement.

# 12

## Responsive or Responsible Government?

### TODD DONOVAN AND SHAUN BOWLER

As academic interest in direct democracy waxes and wanes, variants of the process seem periodically to attract fans advocating its use and expansion (see for example Dolbare and Hubbell 1996; Schultz 1996; Barber 1984; Fishkin 1991). Critics of direct democracy, as noted in the preceding chapters, are numerous and every bit as ardent in challenging its use as supporters are in defending it. This clear dichotomy between advocates and critics, and the unfavorable reviews direct democracy typically receives, stand in contrast to research on representative democracy. Beyond issues of limiting terms, regulating campaign finances, and applying some limits to legislative discretion, one is hard pressed to find much heated contemporary debate over the existence of the legislative process itself.[1]

Scholarship associated with direct democracy frequently concludes with some evaluation about the fundamental merits or legitimacy of the process, often with reference to how well it compares to representative democracy (e.g., Magleby 1984, 180–200). The standard normative critiques of direct democracy, furthermore, often emerge from these comparisons. Under direct democracy, voters are seen as being less competent, outcomes less likely to make sense, policies more abusive of minorities, and special interests somehow more advantaged. We hope that the chapters in this volume have illustrated that some of this criticism is unfounded. In this chapter, we assess in general terms how direct democracy might measure up to the Progressives' goal of producing responsive and responsible policy.

Evaluating direct democracy on these or any grounds is no simple task. First of all, direct and representative democracy are not mutually exclusive. Briffault (1985) notes that they coexist and interact in the United States. If we are to evaluate the responsiveness or responsibility of the process, we need to recognize that the question is not just how much better (or worse) direct democracy performs when compared to representative democracy, but "whether the initiative corrects some of the defects of the legislative process" (Briffault 1985, 1350). In our introduction, we also pointed out that responsiveness could be evaluated, in part, in terms of *whom* the process is responsive to (i.e., what gets on ballots, who has access to professional campaigns, who can pass what, etc.). At various points in the book, we have suggested that well-financed interests might have defensive advantages, but that the process still results in policy making that might be seen as being responsive to the interests of broad, diffuse constituencies.

Additional lines of reasoning can provide us some basis for making concluding assessments about representative versus direct democracy, and about state-level direct democracy's potential ability to remedy problems associated with legislative government.

The field of institutional analysis illustrates that we cannot idealize representative processes when making comparisons. This literature illustrates how legislatures create incentives for representatives to behave in ways that often cause them to fail to respond to public preferences. In evaluating direct democracy we should first consider how it affects institutional rules, or how it facilitates the "regulation of politics." Briffault (1985, 1368) argues that the best case for direct legislation is that it can play a key role in making legislative institutions—and policy outcomes—more responsive to the public's will. Representative institutions create one paramount incentive for individual legislators: the need to get reelected (Mayhew 1974). In pursuing this self-interest, legislators might be motivated to maintain policies such as weak campaign-finance regulations, unlimited discretion in fiscal policy, designing safe partisan districts, unlimited tenure, and ballot access restrictions that increase their chances for reelection.

These legislators might also give particular advantages to politically active interest groups that contribute to their campaigns and mobilize voters. Such groups can have strong incentives to influence the fiscal decisions of a legislature, and might cause resulting spending policy to deviate from the preferences of the mass public (Buchanan and Tullock 1962; Niskanen 1971). By forming "coalitions of high demanders" inside a legislature unchecked by direct democracy, they may drive total spending above that preferred by most voters (Briffault 1985, 1368; Denzau, Mackay, and Weaver 1981). As illustrated in chapter 8, "governance policies" affecting the regulation of legislative taxing and spending powers are often adopted by the initiative.

The field of electoral studies provides another basis for analysis. This literature examines, among other things, the effects of variation in election rules on representation and policy outcomes. Proponents of various electoral reforms point out that institutional rules produce different outcomes—different winners and losers. In this chapter, we provide some final evidence about how variation in institutional rules, between direct versus representative democracy states, affects what governments do and who potential winners and losers might be. By exploring this issue we can evaluate, at least in part, the Progressives' goal that direct democracy would produce public policies more responsive to the general public (Eaton 1912).

Thus, in addition to considering how direct democracy might alter institutional rules, we need to examine the effects of rules on winners and losers. We do this in two ways. First, we review existing literature to examine what effect direct democracy has on state tax and spending policies. We seek to identify how tax and spending policies might be more (or less) responsive to mass preferences under direct democracy. We then look at responsiveness a second way, focusing on how direct democracy might determine who bears the burden of paying for state services.

We also try to assess if the process produces "responsible" public policies. In an attempt to avoid a normative morass of contestable definitions of responsible or (irresponsible) policy, we examine if direct democracy produces policies that might be viewed as irresponsible given two fairly narrow criteria: fiscal prudence and treatment of minorities. We accept that there are numerous other criteria that can be used to assess what responsible policy might be, but these two issues are frequently raised by critics of direct democracy. We examine if state-level direct democracy results in policies that create long-term fiscal problems. We also examine what is perhaps the overarching critique of direct democracy, that it is overly responsive to majority preferences in the area of civil liberties, and that being *too* responsive, it is more likely than legislatures to produce policies that are abusive of minorities.

## Direct Democracy: Changing the Rules of the Game

As we have seen, ballot propositions can generate heated opinions about the substantive policies put before voters. Some of the reasons for this are quite straightforward: distribution issues (who wins, who loses) are often obvious, particularly when elites try to mobilize various sections of the population to take sides. Symbolic and moral issues, and questions about minority rights, can also enflame passionate opinions and debate. But often, the *policy* consequences of these conflicts are very short-lived. Although they may affect a large number of people, possibly in a very harmful way, subsequent court challenges and legislative acts do much to blunt their impact. Time and changing political fashions do even more to temper the heat of the moment. The criticism linking the desirability of the initiative process to specific policies that result from the process (gay rights, services for immigrants, coastal protection, bottle bills, etc.) is, then, often based on short-term and quite possibly faddish normative evaluations of the observer.

A concern about the desirability of specific policies that might emerge from the process also says little about the longer-term consequences of the initiative process itself. And over the long haul, many of the specific policies that generate so much initial heat and anger may do much less to shape a state than initiatives that put longer-term political and institutional reforms in place. That is, an emphasis on the immediate policy proposal at hand often distracts attention from the broader institutional reforms resulting from citizen's initiatives, which are likely to be of longer-lasting consequence. It is in these changes to institutional rules regarding the conduct of politics that the major consequences of the initiative process might be found.

If anything, direct democracy opens a door that allows people other than legislators to regulate how politics are conducted. If we assume these "outsiders" do not share the same incentives as legislators (i.e., reelection, maintaining party control, etc.), over time, rules about the conduct of politics can be different in direct democracy states—or new innovations in the regulation of politics will be first adopted in these states. Historically, groups from outside the mainstream of politics have used the initiative process to change state institutions in order to further their own goals. A classic example here is that of the women's movement, which used the initiative process to gain women's rights at the state level before gaining them at the federal level (Banaszak 1996). Term limits are just one recent example of a whole series of institutional-reform initiatives that relate to the political process. Campaign finance reform, open primaries, and reporting of contributions and expenditures are all examples of ways in which the initiative process has been used to change the political system itself. The initiative process may, therefore, bring about a different way of doing politics, in large part because the groups and policy entrepreneurs using the process are not part of the standard cast of characters found in state capitols.

The initiative process can also have profound long-run effects on the "getting and spending" of state revenues, not so much by targeting specific policies but by altering the rules under which fiscal politics are conducted. Tolbert (chapter 8) identifies several of these kinds of policies, most notably term limits, supermajority requirements, and tax and expenditure limits (TELs). The importance of policies such as these lies in the long-term effects they have over the conduct of state politics after adoption by initiative.

While specific policies may come and go, cycling up into being very contentious and then down again into being ignored or overturned, institutional provisions that govern how policies may be dealt with have a much longer lasting impact. In Riker's apt phrase, institutions represent "congealed preferences." In general, we may distinguish between two sorts of ballot initiatives: those that attempt to change a specify policy outcome, and those that attempt to change the procedures by which outcomes are produced—i.e., the rules of the game. The formal literature shows that, while shifts in specific policies involve a change from one point to another along a given dimension, shifts in rules can involve a shift in the permissible range or set of choices, possibly over more than one dimension. Changing policy may involve shifting points within a given policy space, and altered rules can change the shape of the very policy space, removing some options from the agenda while creating new opportunities for others (Shepsle and Weingast, 1993).

Changing the rules of the game, then, can produce far more profound change over policy outcomes, over a long period of time, than can changes in a given policy outcome, no matter how thoroughgoing. The importance of TELs is especially striking in light of recent California history and reveals something both of the importance of changing institutions and of a dynamic to the initiative process. Perhaps no other proposition has the level of name recognition over such an extended period of time as California's Proposition 13. This policy put limits on the extent to which property taxes could be raised and also included a subsequent requirement that property tax rates could only be changed by a supermajority in a referendum. Proposition 13 has had profound effects on revenue sources in California, and the "spirit" of Proposition 13 (including policy entrepreneurs who worked on the measures in California) has diffused beyond the state to affect revenue policies elsewhere. By one estimate it has reduced California's tax revenues by $200 billion since 1978 (Price and Bell 1996, 246). Even for an economy the size of California's this is quite a loss—a loss which has led to a series of bitter fights and disputes between the counties and the state over jurisdiction and revenue sources.

## What Difference Does Direct Democracy Make? Taxes and Spending

If it is the case that direct democracy provides a means to change rules about how politics are conducted, questions about the effect of initiatives on the responsiveness and responsibility of government should be examined in terms of the long-term consequences of these rule changes. To date, there is limited but informative research that can illuminate these questions.

Direct democracy can affect how government responds to groups or the mass public in a variety of ways. Tolbert (chapter 8) demonstrates that the initiative can allow citizens to *directly* draft and adopt laws affecting a state's governance structure—laws that legislatures would not usually impose on themselves (i.e., term limits, rules for tax increases, TELs). Gerber (chapter 9) demonstrates that the threat of a potential initiative also affects policies on parental consent and notification for abortion *indirectly*, causing state policies to match popular preferences more closely.

We might expect, then, that if initiative states adopt term limits, TELs, and abortion policies that more closely mirror public preferences than the policies adopted in representative states, then other policies in initiative states, particularly tax and spending policies, could also more closely reflect mass preferences. Yet existing research suggests that responsiveness associated with initiatives might not be constant across all policy areas.

In one study of the relationship between mass opinion and policy in initiative versus noninitiative states, Lascher et al. (1996) found no evidence that spending policy was more responsive to mass preferences in initiative states. Indeed, their data show that state activity in initiative states on AFDC (Aid to Families with Dependent Children), education, and Medicaid was significantly less than mass opinion would otherwise predict. Matsusaka (1995) also demonstrates that government spending from 1960 to 1990 is significantly lower in initiative states when other factors are accounted for. He attributes this very generally to the theory that initiatives can force legislatures closer to the median voter's preferences, which, it is implied, means less spending. However, Lascher et al. (1996) test this directly and find that initiative states are not just spending less, but less than mass opinion would predict.

One possible explanation for conflicting interpretations of findings, such as those in chapter 9 and those reported by Matsusaka (1995) and Lascher et al. (1996), is that by facilitating responsiveness to public demands to lower specific taxes (or general increases in spending), the long-run operation of direct democracy constrains the revenue available to state legislatures. This process, while potentially effective in translating demands for lower taxes into policy, might be less effective in resolving conflicts about finding alternative, publicly acceptable tax sources that would fund programs—such as education—that voters might simultaneously support.

We suggest that by being very responsive to citizen demands for adopting rules that constrain overall taxation, direct democracy can have the effect of institutionalizing rules (perhaps unintentionally) that might subsequently cause state spending policies to deviate from public preferences. As chapter 8 illustrates, several states have passed initiatives requiring that new taxes be approved only after a popular referendum (i.e., Colorado, Nevada, Washington). Some have changed rules such that all tax increases must be approved by legislative supermajorities (i.e., Arizona, Washington, Colorado). As Tolbert illustrates, direct democracy states are more likely to adopt TELs and supermajority requirements (table 8.2).

Voter approval of these rules can reflect popular demand for constraint on taxation and expenditure growth, self-interest on the part of citizens who pay the most in taxes (Donovan and Bowler n.d.), or both. Yet it is another thing to expect that support for antitax policies reflects systematic popular judgments about the mixtures of tax sources and spending that legislatures must subsequently make after their powers are constrained via initiatives (or threat of initiative). Once legislative taxing and spending powers are constrained, legislators could have a difficult time funding programs at levels the public might prefer, so we could see lower spending in these states as well as a gap between popular preferences for spending and actual spending. Implicit in this logic is the assumption that some voters might prefer to cut taxes while still expecting that government should be able to continue funding programs. If anything, voters are more likely to cut taxes than raise taxes (see table 12.1). All of this can create a paradoxical situation where the long-term consequences of the fiscal rules adopted in direct democracy states might cause some spending policies to be less responsive to popular preferences. Responsiveness on one level (changing tax rules) hinders responsiveness at another level.

Some of our previous research illustrated that voters are highly sensitive to property tax levels, and that this is the most unpopular tax used by any level of government in the U.S. (Bower and Dono-

**Table 12.1** Direct Democracy and the Public's Preferences for Budget Policy: Proposition Voting, California, 1979–1994

|  | *Mean Yes Vote (%)* | *N* | *N Pass* | *% Pass* |
|---|---|---|---|---|
| Tax Limits[a] | 62 | 26 | 21 | 81 |
| Tax Hikes[b] | 39 | 14 | 2 | 14 |
| Bonds[c] | 56 | 68 | 52 | 76 |
| Other Propositions[d] | 54 | 216 | 132 | 61 |

*Source:* Voting records, California Secretary of State's Office, various years.

[a]Includes tax exemptions referred by legislature, in addition to tax limitation and rollbacks initiated by citizens.

[b]Includes tax increases and votes to make future increases easier.

[c]Referred to voters by the state legislature.

[d]This includes all noneconomic propositions. These include issues of public morality, business regulation, governmental organization, etc.

van 1995). Many of the tax limitation rules adopted via direct democracy that continue to shape fiscal policies in states like Colorado, Oregon, and California are directed at property taxes. Voters are thus highly responsive to property tax levels, and direct democracy can be very efficient at translating dissatisfaction with property taxes into rules limiting taxation. As table 12.1 illustrates, tax limitations and exemptions (typically associated with property taxes) are more popular with California voters than tax increases. This does not mean that voters are necessarily against funding programs; they are likely to approve borrowing to fund projects when given the chance. In the long run, if antitax propositions cause less tax revenue to be available for state governments (and borrowing cannot be a perfect substitute for revenue), spending in direct democracy states can end up lower than in other states, and lower than what mass opinion might demand.

All of this should not be interpreted as suggesting that the voting public is, by nature, fiscally irresponsible. We should stress that these tax limitation initiatives are rarely, if ever, linked to cuts in specific programs or the adoption of alternative revenue sources. Indeed, single-subject restrictions might make it difficult to link such issues in one ballot measure. This being the case, voters are typically allowed to express only one side of their potential fiscal preferences (e.g., a desire for property-tax relief), and these become institutionalized. Direct democracy, however, provides no comparable, readily used mechanism for aggregating preferences about numerous decisions and tradeoffs that must be made about spending over hundreds of programs and agencies. It is not just that most voters might "want something for nothing" (Sears and Citrin 1982), but that they are typically faced with one-half of the fiscal equation when deciding on ballot initiatives. Thus, voters seeking property-tax relief might institutionalize rules limiting the tax, but the same voters who might also favor continued funding of programs like parks or libraries are rarely asked simultaneously to find alternative funding sources. Legislatures are then forced to improvise within a constitutionally constrained revenue situation, and might be unable to deliver services that match mass preferences for spending.

## What Difference Does Direct Democracy Make? The Distribution of Tax Burdens

One of the persistent critiques of contemporary direct democracy is that wealthy elites hold sway at the expense of the general public interest. This might seem somewhat counterintuitive, given classic arguments that the expansion of direct popular participation in government would produce leveling and redistribute tendencies. The modern critique, however, is in part based on the idea that elites and "special interests" are advantaged by having an additional point of access to the policy-making process that, due to high campaign costs, broad-based groups might not have (see chapters 3 and 4). Wealthy interests are expected to pursue their own narrow ends, while quashing broad-based attempts at redistributive policies. Ultimately, then, if narrow groups are advantaged by the process, rather than producing redistributive outcomes, direct democracy might shift the burden of paying for government services to those who can least afford to pay (Dwyer et al. 1994).

As we have seen, however, the influence of narrow interests using the initiative industry is more muted than critics suggest. Broad-based groups still pass policies via direct democracy. Voted ballots also show evidence of ideological structure to voter choices, and campaign spending data show that there is far more value in spending money to defeat propositions than to pass them. In short, few special interests will be able to find an ignorant, unanchored electorate and use vast sums of money to sell them a policy that is inconsistent with the voting public's ideas or interests. The difficulty of this is increased since many people also decide on the basis of elite cues, or on a tendency to just vote "no." When we consider this, it appears that one of the primary (if not exclusive) advantages that well-funded interests have in direct democracy is a sort of veto over many things that reach the ballot. In fact, the initiative device can be seen as a fairly conservative process in which the odds are stacked against proponents of any scheme.

Yet there are reasons to expect distributional effects of direct democracy independent of elite advantages in the campaign process. In addition to initiative states' spending less on some policies than state opinion might predict, there is also evidence suggesting that state legislatures respond to initiatives by making those who use public services pay a greater share of costs. Matsusaka has demonstrated that initiative states rely more on user fees and charges than representative states, and Lascher et al. (1996) also found that initiative states have less-progressive taxation systems than other states. So there is some evidence that the poor bear a greater share of the burden of funding public services in direct democracy states.[2]

However, these findings might not reflect upon direct democracy per se but can reflect the corresponding weakness of political parties in states that experienced Progressive Era reforms (Hofstadter 1955). Consider the theory of representation proposed by Dwyer et al. (1994). Echoing V. O. Key (1949), they focused on the role of access to the policy-making process: states having well-organized parties that incorporate the "have nots" into electoral politics are expected to produce more-progressive taxation. On the other hand, the "fragmented" access created by "disorganized" Progressive Era institutions, such as weak parties and direct democracy, should disadvantage "have nots." According to Dwyer et al. (1994), narrow interests have access to state legislatures regardless of the party system, and initiatives can offer them additional access (even if only as a veto). The poor and unorganized groups, however, who are typically incorporated into legislative politics via strong parties are excluded by Progressive Era laws that weaken parties. Dwyer et al. (1994) concluded that direct democracy and weak parties are two of the primary reasons that New York State has more-progressive taxation than a direct democracy state such as California. In the former, the poor are, to some extent, "at the table" in the legislature. In the latter, they have less say in the legislature, and the initiative can be used to roll back progressive fiscal policies that might get through a legislature.

In table 12.2, we extend this analysis to the 50 states by examining levels of tax progressivity in initiative and noninitiative states, while accounting for characteristics of the state's party system. Our simple model includes a dummy variable representing if a state allows the initiative, a measure of the strength of traditional local party organizations, and a measure of party competition. These data do suggest that noninitiative states have slightly more progressive income and property taxation, with the effect of the initiative being largest on property taxes. The effect, however, is substantively small, even in this simple model, which fails to control for other economic factors that are likely to affect the distribution of tax burdens.[3] The initiative dummy (as well as an alternative measure of frequency-of-initiative use) explains very little variance in each

**Table 12.2** Direct Democracy and the Distribution of State Tax Burdens

| Variable | Property Tax | Sales Tax | Income Tax |
|---|---|---|---|
| Intercept | 1.67** | 1.82** | -0.10 |
| Initiative (dummy) | 0.21+ | 0.10 | 0.15* |
| Traditional party Organization score | 0.07* | 0.03 | 0.84** |
| Very competitive Party state | -0.24* | -0.11 | -0.52 |
| N | 50 | 50 | 43 |
| $R^2$ | .11 | .05 | .24 |

*Sources:* Tax data from McIntyre et al. (1991); TPO scores from Mayhew (1986); party competitiveness data from Bibby et al. (1990).

*Note:* Dependent variables = index of tax progressiveness; low scores reflect more-progressive taxation.

Cell entries = OLS regression coefficients.

**significant at $p < .05$ (two-tailed), *significant at $p < .10$ (two-tailed), +significant at $p = .11$ (two-tailed).

model. The two party variables, for example, explain 17% of the variance in income tax progressivity, while the initiative alone explains only 1.4%.

## Responsible Policies? State Debt and Direct Democracy

When the long-term fiscal effects of direct democracy are considered, we see reasons that initiative-enhanced tax policy responsiveness might cause fiscal policies to depart from mass preferences. Over the long run, direct democracy might have other effects on state fiscal policies, effects associated with the tax-limitation rule changes discussed above. Table 12.1 illustrated that while citizens might typically approve tax cuts, they also might prefer debt financing to new taxes. We expect that legislators could also view debt financing as an attractive way to fund things that the public might continue to expect after tax-limitation rules have been put in place (Buchanan and Wagner 1977). But state operating budgets are required by law to balance, and borrowing is often limited to capital projects. In the long run, however, rules that are often institutionalized via direct democracy (TELs, supermajority requirements for tax increases, and public referenda on increases) might create incentives for a government not only to spend less, but to find "creative" uses of debt that maintain some programs within the bounds of balanced budget requirements.

It has been shown that direct democracy plays a role in affecting state and local budgeting (Sharp and Elkins 1987). State and local government indebtedness, furthermore, increased in the 1980s after the first wave of the "tax revolt" (Regens and Lauth 1992). Although the roots of this increase are complex, there is evidence that legislatures might circumvent citizen-initiated TELs by issuing nonguaranteed debt or by offering voters' proposals to issue more full faith and credit debt (Clingermayer and Wood 1995). Thus, TELs and the initiative process can possibly contribute to greater levels of state indebtedness. This might occur, since full faith debt and "off-budget" debt are used by some legislatures to avoid the constraints of TELs (Bahl and Duncombe 1993; conversely, see Kiewiet and Szakaly 1992).

As table 12.3 illustrates, from 1977 to 1990 initiative states using TELs do have higher long-term debt than other states. In a pooled cross-sectional analysis, we use several variables to predict the amount of annual full faith debt each state carries as a proportion of its revenue. First, the model accounts for the presence of population and economic pressures on states.[4] We control for the growth in real per capita income over the 1980s in each state, and also the rate of growth in population. Second, we account for the presence of divided government, since Fiorina (1992, 92–95) notes that divided government might promote deficits and debt. Third, we include variables that account for constitutional rules affecting debt issue. We include indicators that reflect (a) whether or not a supermajority in the legislature is required to issue bonds; (b) whether a public referendum is required to approve bonds; (c) whether there are explicit dollar limits on debt; and (d) whether "casual" debts are allowed (see Hackbart and Leigland 1990).

**Table 12.3** State Full Faith and Credit Debt as a Proportion of State Revenue, 1977–1990 (GLS-ARMA Estimates)

| Variable | B | SE | t-value |
|---|---|---|---|
| Constant | 0.147 | 0.014 | 10.488** |
| Economic growth | 0.033 | 0.004 | 8.280** |
| Population growth | -0.001 | 0.000 | -3.206** |
| Divided D | -0.006 | 0.005 | -1.225 |
| Divided R | -0.002 | 0.002 | -1.005 |
| Supermajority | 0.038 | 0.017 | 2.180* |
| Referendum | -0.075 | 0.011 | -6.411** |
| Dollar limit | -0.044 | 0.012 | -3.547** |
| Casual | -0.024 | 0.013 | -1.830* |
| Intervention | 0.010 | 0.004 | 2.142* |
| Combination | 0.038 | 0.013 | 2.876** |
| GLS $R^2$ | 0.058 | | |
| Equivalent OLS $R^2$ | 0.179 | | |
| N | 700 | | |

Sources: *Significant Features of Fiscal Federalism*, various years; *Book of the States*, various years; Bureau of the Census, "Government Finances" (Washington, D.C.: Government Printing Office, various years).

**p < .01 (one-tailed), **p < .05 (one-tailed).

We also include a dummy variable ("Combination") indicating whether a state has the initiative process and bond referenda simultaneously. This variable represents those states having the institutional arrangements that allow voters the sort of choices illustrated in table 12.1: the ability to say "no" to taxes while simultaneously saying "yes" to debt.[5] Finally, we include an intervention term that notes when TELs were adopted. This intervention variable takes a value of 1 for each state in each cross-section only after such a limit was introduced, and 0 otherwise.

Table 12.3 illustrates that most of the institutional limitations have an impact of limiting the debt burden in states. Referenda for debt issue, casual debt limits, and dollar limits are associated with lower debt burdens. Legislative supermajority requirements appear to be associated with higher debt burdens, however. This latter finding is not surprising when we consider that a certain amount of logrolling might be required to pass capital budgets (funded by debt), and when we consider that capital projects yield particularistic benefits that can be concentrated in individual legislative districts. Supermajority rules thus might require that larger, "universal" legislative coalitions are formed to pass these budgets, thus causing greater debt appropriation (Weingast 1979).

The potential long-term effects of direct democracy are illustrated by the coefficients for "Combination" (indicating states that allow initiatives and require referenda for debt) and "Intervention" (demarking the adoption of a TEL, in time). States having the combination of bond referenda and citizen's initiatives tend to have significantly higher levels of debt relative to revenue when other factors are controlled for. These are states where many direct choices over the taxing and borrowing are made by voters, with legislatures left to do budgeting later on. There also appears to be a longitudinal intervention associated with adoption of TELs that increases borrowing in the long run. After these policy interventions are in place, states appear eventually to increase their debt burden as a proportion of revenue.

This suggests that direct democracy, by possibly being "responsive" on one level to popular expressions of antitax sentiment, can lead to uses of debt that do not necessarily meet standard definitions of fiscal responsibility. Indeed, we have shown elsewhere (Bowler and Donovan 1994d) that credit markets are sensitive to the debt levels estimated in table 12.3. States with more debt relative to revenue receive lower bond ratings, and those having the combination of bond referenda and citizen's initiative receive even lower ratings.[6]

Thus far, we have attempted to evaluate the responsiveness of direct democracy by asking several questions: Does it affect how state politics is conducted? Does it affect what states spend money on? Does it affect who pays what for public services? In evaluating responsibility, we asked, does it affect the long-term fiscal health of the state?

On some levels, our findings are somewhat paradoxical. Direct democracy does allow citizens the ability to change rules about how legislatures do business, and it might be highly responsive to voter hostility to the property tax. But contrary to what classical democratic theorists might have feared about direct legislation, it does not cause a state to have more redistributive policies (i.e., progressive taxation). Contrary to what Progressive advocates might have expected, it does not necessarily cause more "responsible" budgeting in the long run. The problem is not simply with direct democracy as a process, but with how it interacts (or fails to interact) with the legislative process. By frequently presenting voters with only part of the fiscal equation (cutting taxes, maybe borrowing, but rarely spending choices or raising new revenue), direct democracy places state legislatures in a position where it might be extremely difficult for them to write a budget.

## Responsible Policies? Direct Democracy and Minorities

Perhaps the most resounding criticism leveled against direct democracy is that it will produce policies that are more hostile to minority interests than those passed by a legislature (Butler and Ranney 1994, 19–21; Bell 1978; Magleby 1984, 30; Linde 1993; Gunn 1981; Fountaine 1988). It is said that the problem is magnified by the fact that state courts are directly elected in these states, making them unlikely to protect unpopular minorities (Eule 1990,

1994). Gamble argues (1997) that policies adopted via direct democracy, lacking the filter of a deliberative legislative process, are more likely to facilitate majority tyranny. Echoing many critics of direct democracy in finding it abusive of minorities, Gamble concludes that "direct legislation only weakens us" as a nation (1997, 262).

We do not dispute the possible validity of the antiminority critique as it might apply to the local level, but we suggest the criticism is overstated and not supported by data when examined at the state level. The central question Gamble and others raise is, When citizens have the power to legislate issues directly, will the majority tyrannize the minority? (1997, 245). Gamble notes that Madison advocated a constitution that must control for the "mischief of (majority) factions," since if factions were "united by a common interest, the rights of the minority will be insecure." She suggests that his cure for this "was not direct legislation," and that this was institutionalized with "the absence of the initiative process" (1997, 247).

We suggest that Publius's full treatment of the majority faction problem should be considered, since it offers additional insights into managing the threat of democracy in general (which was their primary concern), rather than the particular threat of direct democracy. Publius's theory for controlling an abusive majority included much more than indirect democracy, which was fairly "progressive" at the time (Roche 1961). In *Federalist* no. 9 Hamilton argued that the tyrannical capacity of majority factions in any democracy would be constrained by the "enlargement of the orbit" (Hamilton [1788] 1961, 73) of a political system over a large territory, a warning he addressed to anti-Federalist advocates of small homogeneous societies (Storing 1981).

Madison further elaborated this theory of the extended republic. Speaking of democracy in general, in *Federalist* no. 10 he warned that in smaller, homogeneous jurisdictions "more frequently will a majority be found of the same party [and the] more easily will they concert and execute their plans of oppression. Extend the sphere and you take in a greater variety of parties and interests; you make it less probable that a majority of the whole will have a common motive to invade the rights of other citizens" ([1788] 1961, 83).

In *Federalist* no. 51 he argues explicitly that minority rights and civil rights are protected by extending the scale of the physical area governed by democratic practice so that "society itself will be broken into so many parts, interests and classes of citizens, that the rights of individuals, or of the minority, will be in little danger from interested combinations of the majority" (1961, 324).

This emphasis on the calming effects of the size and scale is a central element of the federal argument about protecting minorities and is distinct, but complementary, to the role that representative democracy plays for Publius. Independent of the form of democracy, the scale over which it is practiced should also determine the prospects for majority tyranny of a minority. Larger units offer the social heterogeneity of interests that make it difficult for a politically cohesive majority to form and tyrannize a minority.

This theory suggests distinct types of evidence that could be used in assessing democracy's capacity to oppress minorities. It suggests we should expect differences between examples drawn from smaller or larger jurisdictions regardless of the form of democracy. We suggest that Publius's theory of democracy also indicates that *local* direct democracy can be far more injurious to minorities than direct democracy at the *state* level, since states are typically larger and more socially diverse than localities.[7] Evidence used by Gamble and others to support claims about direct democracy's abuse of minority civil rights should take this distinction into consideration.

Most scholars who evaluate the antiminority critique of direct democracy offer only anecdotal examples to support their claims (e.g., Cronin 1989; Magleby 1984; Zimmerman 1986; Linde 1993). Gamble (1997) is perhaps the only scholar who has attempted to examine a sample of initiatives and referenda in order to assess how frequently voters limit the civil rights of minorities. She claims to have found "strong evidence that the majority has indeed used its direct legislative powers to deprive political minorities of their civil rights" (1997, 246). We use her study as a point of departure for evaluating how direct democracy might abuse minorities.

Gamble's evidence includes results from state and local referenda on civil rights issues spanning three decades. She examines five areas where ballot measures limited minority rights: AIDS testing, gay rights, language, school desegregation, and housing/public accommodations desegregation. The relatively high approval rates for referenda in these five areas are compared to lower approval rates for all ballot measures. Evidence of a high approval rate is used to conclude that representative democracy protects minorities better than direct democracy.

Yet rather than constructing a random sample or universe of cases, most of the cases Gamble examines are local measures that happened to attract the attention of journalists and academics. The use of this evidence is problematic. As noted above, there are theoretical reasons to expect that small, local democracies—through representative or direct means—might be relatively more abusive of minorities. For example, Wald, Button, and Rienzo use an "urbanism/diversity theory," similar to our reading of Publius, to establish that population size is the single largest factor differentiating between communities that adopt gay rights ordinances and those that do not. Councils in smaller places are less likely to adopt policies protecting the rights of gays and lesbians.

Since Gamble's sample is so heavily weighted by a nonrandom draw of local cases, it is difficult to use it to evaluate how often places adopt antiminority policies via direct democracy, and it is impossible to compare this to what legislatures or councils do. However, since the population of state measures in these five areas is much smaller and known for some categories, we can examine claims about direct democracy's abuse of minorities with state-level data. For example, we (1997) have identified all state-level measures appearing from 1977 to 1995 dealing with civil rights of gays and lesbians, including measures dealing with AIDS.[8]

Table 12.4 illustrates approval rates for these state-level gay rights and AIDS measures. Three passed (27%), but only two (18%) can be said to have produced decidedly antiminority policy outcomes.[9] This compares to a 38% approval rate for all state initiatives from 1898 to 1992 (Magleby 1994, 231), and the 82% approval rate of local antiminority outcomes that Gamble identified. Although the number of cases here is small, we can be sure that our state-level sample is not biased. Contrary to Gamble's claim that voters are prone to abuse minorities via the initiative, we find strong evidence that *state* electorates do not deprive minorities of civil rights in these areas. Consistent with Publius's theory of the extended republic, antiminority policies tend to pass in smaller, homogeneous jurisdictions, not in larger, diverse jurisdictions (states).

**Table 12.4** Approval of Statewide Antigay and Anti-AIDS Initiatives, 1978–1995

| State | Year/ Proposition | Pass or Fail | Vote in Favor (%) | Anti- minority Result? | Court Overturned? |
|---|---|---|---|---|---|
| California | 1978, Prop. 6 | Fail | 41 | No | n/a |
| California | 1986, Prop. 64 | Fail | 29 | No | n/a |
| California | 1988, Prop. 69 | Fail | 32 | No | n/a |
| California | 1988, Prop. 96 | Pass | 62 | No[a] | No |
| California | 1988, Prop. 102 | Fail | 34 | No | n/a |
| Oregon | 1988, Meas. 8 | Pass | 57 | Yes | Yes[b] |
| Colorado | 1992, Amnd. 2 | Pass | 53 | Yes | Yes[c] |
| Oregon | 1992, Meas. 9 | Fail | 43 | No | n/a |
| Idaho | 1994, Prop. 1 | Fail | 49 | No | n/a |
| Oregon | 1994, Meas. 13 | Fail | 44 | No | n/a |
| Maine | 1995, Meas. 1 | Fail | 47 | No | n/a |

Average yes vote                                     44.6
% approved = 27.2
% approved with antiminority result = 18.2

*Source:* Donovan and Bowler (1997).

[a]Applied to violent criminals, not to AIDS population.

[b]Initiative overturned by U.S. Supreme Court in *Romer v. Evans,* 116 S. Ct. 1620, 134 L. Ed. 2d. 1996.

[c]Initiative overturned by Oregon Court of Appeals, in *Merrick* decision, 1992.

Even when we extend the analysis to include also all the state-level cases from each policy area included in Gamble's sample, evidence from the state level points to lower approval rates for anti-civil rights issues than Gamble identified with her sample. In table 12.5, we illustrate that when all state-level initiatives in these policy areas are considered, 50% had policy outcomes that may have constrained the civil rights of a minority.[10]

Still, finding that state voters pass 18% or 50% of the few initiatives that limit minority rights says nothing about how much better minorities are treated by a legislature. State voters and state legislatures alike approve policies that are abusive of minority rights (see Cronin 1989 on legislatures). Despite serious questions about the constitutionality of their efforts, in 1996 state legislatures across the U.S. rushed to ban recognition of same-sex marriages—all while

**Table 12.5** Approval of Statewide Civil Rights Initiatives, 1960–1995

| Subject | State/ Year | Pass or Fail | Anti- minority outcome | Court Overturned? |
|---|---|---|---|---|
| Accommodations | California, 1964 | Pass | Yes | Yes[a] |
| Accommodations | Maryland, 1964 | Fail | No | n/a |
| Accommodations | Maryland, 1964 | Fail | No | n/a |
| Accommodations | Maryland, 1968 | Pass | Yes | No[b] |
| Accommodations | Wash., 1968 | Fail | No | n/a |
| Schools | Arkansas, 1960 | Fail | No | n/a |
| Schools | California, 1970 | Pass | Yes | Yes[a] |
| Schools | Colorado, 1974 | pass | Yes | No[c] |
| Schools | Mass., 1978 | Pass | Yes | No[c] |
| Schools | Wash., 1978 | Pass | Yes | Yes[c] |
| Gay Rights | California, 1978 | Fail | No | n/a |
| Gay Rights | Oregon, 1988 | Pass | Yes | Yes[a] |
| Gay Rights | Oregon, 1992 | Fail | No | n/a |
| Gay Rights | Oregon, 1994 | Fail | No | n/a |
| Gay Rights | Idaho, 1994 | Fail | No | n/a |
| Gay Rights | Maine, 1995 | Fail | No | n/a |
| English | California, 1986 | Pass | No[d] | n/a |
| English | California, 1988 | Pass | Yes | No[c] |
| English | Arizona, 1988 | Pass | Yes | Yes |
| English | Colorado, 1988 | Pass | Yes | No[c] |
| English | Florida, 1988 | Pass | Yes | No[c] |
| AIDS | California, 1986 | Fail | No | n/a |
| AIDS | California, 1988 | Fail | No | n/a |
| AIDS | California, 1988 | Fail | No | n/a |
| AIDS | California, 1988 | Pass | No[e] | n/a |

pass = 52%
yes = 44%

*Source:* Gamble (1997); Donovan and Bowler (1997).
[a]State court ruled unconstitutional.
[b]State law nullified by federal legislation.
[c]Federal court ruled unconstitutional; affected future initiatives in this area.
[d]A nonbinding initiative that did not affect policy.
[e]Applied to violent criminals only.

none of these states recognized such marriages. Legislatures were motivated by the fear that one state (Hawaii) might grant such a right. No state adopted the marriage ban via direct democracy. The problem with direct democracy is said to be that courts are willing to act as a check against legislatures, but are unwilling to take on the voting public for fear of electoral reprisal. Gamble and others (Eule 1994) claim that the judicial system grants "deference" to direct democratic processes. Yet the data do not support this claim. The two antigay initiatives with clear antiminority policy outcomes listed in table 12.4 were both overturned by courts. In this policy area then, only two antiminority initiatives passed at the state level, and none have withstood court scrutiny. Indeed, in each policy area Gamble identifies, state or federal courts rejected in principle the antiminority elements of the major state initiatives that did pass. For each policy included in table 12.5, the observations are largely time-bound: court rulings chilled future initiative efforts in each area.

These data suggest that it is not direct democracy per se that is abusive of minorities. Given Publius's theory, we could expect that the very same democratic process, indeed the very same initiative measure, could abuse a minority locally but not at the state (or perhaps national) level. Consider what happened in Oregon during and after the battle over Measure 9. This anti–gay rights measure failed statewide, but opponents of gay rights subsequently petitioned to place very similar measures on local ballots in smaller, typically homogeneous, rural Oregon communities where support for Measure 9 was high. Indeed, 18 of the 39 local antigay measures that Gamble identified were these "sons of Measure 9." Nearly all of them passed. In this example, is it direct democracy that is abusive, or democracy as practiced in a social homogenous community? *Publius* predicts that minorities will find little protection *from democracy in any form* in such a context.

## Conclusion

Along with findings reported in other chapters, all of this suggests, quite strongly we believe, that direct democracy "matters" greatly in our understanding of state politics and policy. It matters in terms of the sorts of public preferences government is more or less responsive to, but it matters in ways that might be different than expressed in the fears and concerns of observers writing at the time these institutions were adopted. Although initiatives might make policy and policy-making more responsive in terms of some issues (abortion policy, tax limitation rules, term limit proposals, etc.), it cannot easily "budget" or negotiate the long-term consequences of all issues. Policy, and rules about making policy, might better reflect mass opinion on some accounts, but this sort of responsiveness might cause things in other areas to be less representative of preferences over spending. If responsiveness to the actual spending priorities of voters is something that is desired, direct democracy in the American states might need to be reformed in some way that links decisions over tax cuts and tax rule changes to decisions about spending. As it stands, direct democracy thus interacts with representative democracy in ways that might partially remedy one defect of legislatures (regulating politics) but exacerbate other things legislatures already have a difficult time doing (budgeting).

There is evidence suggesting that the process of state-level direct democracy ends up being somewhat conservative—not only in terms of the tendency for most initiatives to fail, but in the some of the fiscal patterns that emerge. When legislatures face fiscal constraints created by direct democracy, they might respond by shifting the burden of paying for government to those who are least likely to participate in elections and least likely to have access to legislatures. In the end, then, "moneyed interests" are not advantaged in direct democracy by their ability to "buy" favorable policies via the initiative industry, but by the structural disadvantages that the poor might have in fiscal decisions in weak party legislatures over the long haul. Direct democracy, by altering rules by which budgeting is done and possibly constraining revenue, might force legislatures to make choices about spending trade-offs that cause the least harm to those interests who have constant access to the legislature.

In our evaluation of how responsible outcomes might be under direct democracy, we find that on one level it might do better (or less badly) than many suggest. State-level direct democracy seems less likely to translate opinions about unpopular minorities into anti–civil rights policies than critics would suggest, or state voters might have less hostility to minority civil rights than some would have us expect. Although we do find that initiatives affect how people think about some minority groups, we find that in some areas, state voters are less likely to pass policies that abuse minority rights than they are to pass initiatives in general. When these policies do pass, courts consistently act to protect minority interests. Thus, one of the most enduring critiques of state direct democracy—that it is somehow more abusive of minorities than representative processes—rings a bit hollow. However, at another level—one that might receive less attention historically—the initiative and tax rules adopted via the initiative appear to lead to less responsible fiscal policies in the long run by causing states to use debt in a manner that has negative effects on their credit ratings.

We conclude by stressing, again, that some of the observed faults of the initiative process are perhaps a product of rules affecting how it is used today, not of any inherent flaw in the mass public. Initiatives are a means by which citizens can remake the constitutional contract and amend the original terms of constitutions in a peaceful manner. As such they represent a fundamentally important mechanism that deserves more consideration by scholars than is presently given. These issues have long been central to some of the research on law and policy. At least since Buchanan, political science has also had an interest in the idea of constitutional contracts. A whole series of rational-choice scholars—Nozick perhaps most prominently—have reconsidered the contractarian basis of society. Constitutions as contracts bind future generations to a contract specified at one point in time. Rigid constitutional rules, then, are not simply "congealed preferences" but frozen ones. If the initiative process is good for facilitating responsiveness to simple questions about unpopular taxes, but bad for sorting out complex choices across multiple policies and multiple revenue sources (i.e., budgeting), the preferences it freezes as institutionalized rules might only reflect part of what citizens expect or desire from government.

## NOTES

1. We acknowledge that contemporary critiques of representative government do exist (e.g., Buchanan and Tullock 1962; Buchanan and Wagner 1977; Brennan and Buchanan 1985); however, they share different concerns

than those visible in many analyses of direct democracy. We suggest only that there are more observers who are quick to challenge the use of direct democracy than there are observers challenging the use of representative government (e.g., Riker 1982). Critics of representative government who advocate greater use of direct democracy might see it as a means of improving upon or constraining legislative processes (e.g., Brennan and Buchanan 1985; Buchanan 1979), rather than as a virtue in and of itself.

2. Bias in who participates could affect these observations. Lascher et al. (1996) assess opinions of the general public, not of participants in elections.

3. These models are probably underspecified, but are included here for the purpose of illustration. For more complete models, see Lowery (1987) and Berch (1995).

4. With use of the control variables, this dependent variable serves as a rough indicator of a state's debt extension relative to its ability to service its debt.

5. We expect that this combination of direct democracy rules is particularly problematic for the long-term fiscal health of a state given the voting patterns reflected in table 12.1.

6. Results are reported in Bowler and Donovan 1994d. A model estimating Moody's Bond ratings similar to that in table 12.3, and including state full faith and nonguaranteed debt per capita, results in a fit ($R^2$) of .23.

7. By extension, this theory would suggest that within localities minority rights would receive better protection in larger localities. We also suggest that most American states in the late twentieth century have more social diversity than the American republic did when *Publius* wrote. Homogeneous localities in contemporary American society might be seen as analogous in diversity to the states that Publius wrote of.

8. Gamble includes most but not all of these measures in her sample. Gay rights and AIDS issues comprise 65% of cases in Gamble's sample; however, 83% of her cases are local issues drawn from an unknown population.

9. One AIDS-testing initiative applied only to a category of criminals.

10. Thirteen of 26 measures identified can be said to have policy outcomes that limit or restrict minority rights. Two of the measures that Gamble coded as limiting rights were not included in our count as having antiminority results: a nonbinding advisory measure on language in California, and an initiative repealing busing in Colorado. She also coded two public accommodations referenda that Maryland voters rejected as a single case. We count it as two. We also do not include a 1960 initiative Gamble identified from Mississippi, since Mississippi did not adopt the initiative until 1991.

# References

Abramson, Paul R. 1983. *Political Attitudes in America: Formation and Change*. San Francisco: W. H. Freeman.

Abramson, Paul R., John H. Aldrich, Phil Paolino, and David W. Rohde. 1992. "Sophisticated Voting in the 1988 Presidential Primaries." *American Political Science Review* 86: 55–69.

Achen, Christopher. 1975. "Mass Political Attitudes and the Survey Response." *American Political Science Review* 69: 1218–31.

Advisory Commission for Intergovernmental Relations (ACIR). 1994. "Significant Features of Fiscal Federalism," vol. 1. Washington D.C.: Advisors Commission for Intergovernmental Relations Publication.

———. Various years. "Significant Features of Fiscal Federalism." Washington, D.C.: Advisory Commission, GPO.

Ainsworth, Bill. 1990–91. "Initiative Wars: If You Can't Beat 'Em, Swamp 'Em." In *California Government and Politics Annual*, edited by Thomas Hoeber and Charles Price, vol. 21, pp. 96–97. Sacramento: California Journal Publications.

Allsop, Dee, and Herbert F. Weisberg. 1988. "Measuring Change in Party Identification in an Election Campaign." *American Journal of Political Science* 32: 996–1017.

American National Election Study. 1994. American National Election Study Enhanced File #6507. Inter-university Consortium for Political and Social Research, Ann Arbor, Mich.

Anderson, Dennis M. 1985. "Referenda Exit Interviews: What Do Referendum Voters Know?" Paper presented at the annual meeting of the American Political Science Association, August 29–September 1, New Orleans, La.

Ansolabehere, Stephen, Roy Behr, and Shanto Iyengar. 1993. *The Media Game: American Politics in the Television Age*. New York: Macmillan.

Ansolabehere, Stephen, and Shanto Iyengar. 1994. "Of Horseshoes and Horse Races: Experimental Studies of the Impact of Poll Results on Electoral Behavior." *Political Communication* 11: 413–30.

275

Asher, Herbert B. 1980. *Presidential Elections and American Politics.* 2d ed. Homewood, Ill.: Dorsey.

Atkeson, Lonna R., James A. McCann, Ronald B. Rapoport, and Walter J. Stone. 1996. "Citizens for Perot: Assessing Patterns of Alienation and Activism." *In Broken Contract? Changing Relationships between Citizens and Government in the United States,* edited by Stephen Craig. Boulder, Colo.: Westview.

Attiyeh, Richard, and Robert F. Engle. 1979. "Testing Some Propositions about Proposition 13." *National Tax Journal* 32: 131–57.

Bahl, R., and W. Duncombe. 1993. "State and Local Debt Burdens in the 1980s: A Study in Contrasts." *Public Administration Review* 53: 31–40.

Baine, H. M., Jr., and D. S. Hecock. 1957. *Ballot Position and Voter's Choice.* Westport, Conn.: Greenwood Press.

Baker, Lynn. 1991. "Direct Democracy and Discrimination: A Public Choice Perspective." *Chicago-Kent Law Review* 67: 707.

Balmer, Donald G. 1972. S*tate Election Services in Oregon.* Princeton: Citizens' Research Foundation.

Banaszak, Lee Ann. 1996. *Why Movements Succeed or Fail: Opportunity, Culture and the Struggle for Women's Suffrage.* Princeton: Princeton University Press.

Banducci, Susan. 1992. "Voter Confusion and Voter Rationality: The Use of Counter Proposal in the Direct Democracy Process." Paper presented at the annual meeting of the American Political Science Association, September 3–6, Chicago, Illinois.

Banducci, Susan A., and Jeffrey A. Karp. 1994. "Campaigns, Elite Endorsements and Public Support for Term Limits." Paper presented at the annual meeting of the Western Political Science Association, March 10–12, Albuquerque, N.Mex.

Banks, Jeffrey S. 1991. *Signaling Games in Political Science.* Chur, Switzerland; New York: Harwood Academic.

Barber, Benjamin R. 1984. *Strong Democracy: Participatory Politics for a New Age.* Berkeley: University of California Press.

Barber, Mary Beth. 1993. "Compromising on CEQA." *California Journal* 24 (October): 35–37.

Barnett, J. 1915. *The Operation of the Initiative and Referendum in Oregon.* New York: Macmillan.

Bartels, Larry. 1988. *Presidential Primaries and the Dynamics of Public Choice.* Princeton: Princeton University Press.

———. 1996. "Uninformed Voters: Information Effects in Presidential Elections." *American Journal of Political Science* 40: 194–230.

Beard, Charles, and Birl E. Schultz. 1912. *Documents on the State-wide Initiative, Referendum and Recall.* New York: Macmillan.

Beneson, Robert. "Initiatives and Referendums." *Editorial Research Reports* 2: 775–92.

Bell, Charles G., and Charles M. Price. 1984. *California Government Today*. Homewood, Ill.: Dorsey Press.

Bell, Derrick A., Jr. 1978. "The Referendum: Democracy's Barrier to Racial Equality." *Washington Law Review* 54: 1–29.

Benedict, Robert C. 1975. "Some Aspects of the Direct Legislation Process in Washington State, 1914–1973." Ph.D. diss., University of Washington.

Benjamin, Gerald, and Michael J. Malbin, eds. 1992. *Limiting Legislative Terms*. Washington, D.C.: Congressional Quarterly Press.

Bennet, Stephen Earl. 1988. "'Know-Nothings' Revisited: The Meaning of Political Ignorance Today." *Social Science Quarterly* 69: 476–90.

Berch, Neil. 1995. "Explaining the Changes in Tax Incidence in the States." *Political Research Quarterly* 48: 629–42.

Berelson, Bernard, Paul Lazarsfeld, and William McPhee. 1954. *Voting*. Chicago: University of Chicago Press.

Berg, L., and C. Holman. 1989. "The Initiative Process and its Declining Agenda Setting Value." *Law and Policy* 11: 451–69.

Berk, Richard A. 1979. "Estimation Procedures for Pooled Cross-Sectional and Time Series Data." *Evaluation Quarterly* 3: 385–410.

Berkman, Michael B. 1993. *The State Roots of National Politics: Congress and the Tax Agenda, 1978–1986*. Pittsburgh: University of Pittsburgh Press.

Bibby, John, Cornelius Cotter, James Gibson, and Robert Huckshorn. 1990. "Parties in State Politics." In *Politics in the American States*, edited by V. Gray, H. Jacob, and R. Albriton. Glenview, Ill.: Scott, Foresman.

Bishop, George F., A. J. Tuchfarber, and R. W. Oldendick. 1978. "Change in the Structure of American Political Attitudes: The Nagging Question of Question Wording." *American Journal of Political Science* 22: 250–69.

Black, Duncan. 1958. *The Theory of Committees and Elections*. Cambridge: Cambridge University Press.

Black, Jerome H. 1978. "The Multicandidate Calculus of Voting: Application to Canadian Federal Elections." *American Journal of Political Science* 22: 609–38.

Blair, G.S. 1967. *American Legislatures: Structure and Process*. New York: Harper and Row.

Blalock, Hubert M. 1970. *Toward a Theory of Minority-group Relations*. New York: Capricorn Books.

Bogardus, E. 1959. *Social Distance*. Yellow Springs, Ohio: Antioch Press.

Bogart, L. 1957. "Opinion Research and Marketing." *Public Opinion Quarterly* 21 (1): 129–40.

Bone, Hugh. 1975. *The Initiative and the Referendum.* New York: National Municipal League, State Constitutional Studies Project.

Bone, Hugh A., and Robert C. Benedict. 1978. "Perspectives on Direct Legislation: Washington State Experience 1914–1973." *Western Political Quarterly* 28: 330–51.

*The Book of the States.* Various years. Lexington, Ky.: Council of State Governments.

*The Book of the States, 1994–95.* Lexington, Ky.: Council of State Governments.

Borland, John. 1996. "*California Journal* Ballot Book: Tort Reforms." *California Journal* 27 (September): 4–6.

Boskoff, Alvin, and Harmon Zeigler. 1964. *Voting Patterns in a Local Election.* New York: J. B. Lippincott.

Bowler, Shaun, and Todd Donovan. n.d. *Demanding Choices: Opinion, Voting and Direct Democracy.* Ann Arbor: University of Michigan Press. Forthcoming.

———. 1992. "Economic Conditions and Voting on Ballot Propositions." Paper presented at the annual meeting of the American Political Science Association, September 3–6, Chicago, Ill.

———. 1993. "Information and Opinion Change on Ballot Propositions." Paper given at the annual meeting of the Western Political Science Association, March 17–22, Pasadena, Calif.

———. 1994a. "Self-Interest and Voting in Direct Democracy." Paper presented at the annual meeting of the American Political Science Association, September 1–4, New York, N.Y.

———. 1994b. "Economic Conditions and Voting on Ballot Propositions." *American Politics Quarterly* 22: 27–40.

———. 1994c. "Information and Opinion Change on Ballot Propositions." *Political Behavior* 16: 411–35.

———. 1994d. "Is Direct Democracy Good for Public Budgets? The 'Constitution' of State Indebtedness." Paper presented at the Annual Meeting of the Western Political Science Association, March 10–12, Albuquerque, N.Mex.

———. 1995. "Popular Responsiveness to Taxation." *Political Research Quarterly* 48: 79–100.

Bowler, Shaun, Todd Donovan, and Ken Fernandez. 1996. "The Growth of the Political Marketing Industry and the California Initiative Process." *European Journal of Marketing* 30 (10): 173–75.

Bowler, Shaun, Todd Donovan, and Trudi Happ. 1992. "Ballot Propositions and Information Costs: Direct Democracy and the Fatigued Voter." *Western Political Quarterly* 45: 559–68.

Bowler, Shaun, and David Farrell, eds. 1992. *Electoral Strategies and Political Marketing*. London: Macmillan.

Bradley, Martin B. 1992. *Churches and Church Membership in the United States, 1990*. Atlanta: Glenmary Research Center.

Brady, David W. 1993. "The Causes and Consequences of Divided Government: Toward a New Theory of American Politics?" *American Political Science Review* 87: 189–94.

Brady, Henry E. 1990. "Dimensional Analysis of Ranking Data." *American Journal of Political Science* 34: 1017–48.

Brady, Henry E., and Stephen Ansolabehere. 1989. "The Nature of Utility Functions in Mass Publics." *American Political Science Review* 83: 143–63.

Brady, Henry E., and Paul M. Sniderman. 1985. "Attitude Attribution: A Group Basis for Political Reasoning." *American Political Science Review* 79: 1061–78.

Brennan, G., and J. Buchanan. 1985. *The Reason of Rules*. Cambridge: Cambridge University Press.

Briffault, Richard. 1985. "Distrust of Democracy." *Texas Law Review* 63: 1347–75.

Broder, David S. 1994. "Democracy by Poll." *Washington Post*, 25 April 1994, A17.

Buchanan, James. 1979. "The Potential for Taxpayer Revolt in American Democracy." *Social Science Quarterly* 59: 691–96.

———. 1987. "The Constitution of Economic Policy." *American Economic Review* 77: 243–50.

Buchanan, James, and Gordon Tullock. 1962. *The Calculus of Consent*. Ann Arbor: University of Michigan Press.

Buchanan, James, and Richard Wagner. 1977. *Democracy in Deficit: The Political Legacy of Lord Keynes*. New York: Academic Press.

Bureau of the Census. 1986. *City and County Data Book*. Washington, D.C.: GPO.

———. Various years. "Government Finances." Washington, D.C.: GPO.

Butler, David, and Austin Ranney. 1978. *Referendums: A Comparative Study of Practice and Theory*. Washington, D.C.: American Enterprise Institute for Public Policy Research.

———. 1994. *Referendums around the World: The Growing Use of Direct Democracy*. Washington, D.C.: American Enterprise Institute Press.

Cain, Bruce E. 1984. *The Reapportionment Puzzle*. Berkeley: University of California Press.

———. 1992a. "The Varying Impact of Legislative Term Limits." Paper presented at the annual meeting of the American Political Science Association, September 4, Chicago, Ill.

————. 1992b. "Voting Rights and Democratic Theory: Toward a Color-Blind Society?" In *Controversies in Minority Voting,* edited by Bernard Grofman and Chandler Davidson. Washington, D.C.: Brookings Institution.

Cain, Bruce E., John Ferejohn, and Morris Fiorina. 1987. *The Personal Vote.* Cambridge, Mass.: Harvard University Press.

California Commission on Campaign Financing. 1992. *Democracy by Initiative: Shaping California's Fourth Branch of Government.* Los Angeles: Center for Responsive Government.

California Fair Political Practices Committee. 1988. "Historical Overview of Receipts and Expenditures by Ballot Measure Committees." Sacramento, CA.

*California Green Book.* 1990. Sacramento: Dutra Communications.

*California Journal.* 1990. "Term Limits." 21 (December): 578–88.

————. 1992. "A California Journal Analysis: November 1992 Ballot Propositions" (insert). 23 (September).

————. 1994. "A California Journal Analysis: November 1994 Ballot Propositions" (insert). 25 (September).

————. 1996. "Propositions." 27 (December): 9–11.

California Roundtable. 1979. *California Tax Study.* Burlingame: California Roundtable Task Force Publication.

California Secretary of State. 1988. "Summary of Receipts and Expenditures by Committees Formed to Qualify, Support, or Oppose a State Measure." Sacramento, Calif.: Office of the Secretary of State.

————. 1990. "Summary of Receipts and Expenditures by Committees Primarily Formed to Qualify, Support, or Oppose a State Measure." Sacramento, Calif.: Office of the Secretary of State.

————. 1994. "Statement of the Vote, General Election." Sacramento, Calif.: Office of the Secretary of State.

————. 1996. "Campaign Receipts and Expenditures." Sacramento, Calif.: Office of the Secretary of State.

*California Senate Journal.* 1923. May 14: 1780–89.

California State Assembly. 1972. Elections and Reapportionment Committee. *Public Hearings on the Initiative Process.* Sacramento, Calif.

Campbell, Angus, Philip E. Converse, Warren E. Miller, and Donald E. Stokes. 1960. *The American Voter.* New York: Wiley & Sons.

Campbell, Anne. 1997. "The Citizen's Initiative and Entrepreneurial Politics: Direct Democracy in Colorado, 1966–1994." Paper presented at the annual meeting of the Western Political Science Association, March 13–16, Tuscon, Ariz.

Campbell, James E. 1986. "Forecasting the 1986 Midterm Elections to the House of Representatives." *PS: Political Science and Politics* 19: 83–87.

Capell, Elizabeth A. 1993. "The Impact of Term Limits on the California Legislature: An Interest Group Perspective." Paper presented at the annual meeting of the Western Political Science Association, March 18–20, Pasadena, Calif.

Carey, John, Richard Niemi, and Lynda Powell. 1996. "The Effects of Term Limits on State Legislatures." Paper presented at the annual meeting of the American Political Science Association Meeting, August 29–September 1, San Francisco, Calif.

Carmines, Edward G. 1974. "The Mediating Influence of State Legislatures on the Linkage between Interparty Competition and Welfare Policies." *American Political Science Review* 68: 1118–24.

Carmines, Edward G., and James A. Stimson. 1980. "The Two Faces of Issue Voting." *American Political Science Review* 74: 78–91.

———. 1989. *Issue Evolution: Race and the Transformation of American Politics.* Princeton: Princeton University Press.

Carsey, Thomas. 1995. "The Contextual Effects of Race on White Voter Behavior: The 1989 New York City Mayoral Election." *Journal of Politics* 57: 221–28.

Cassel, Carol A. 1984. "Issues of Measurement: The 'Levels of Conceptualization' Index of Ideological Sophistication." *American Journal of Political Science* 28: 418–29.

Cataldo, E., and J. Holm. 1983. "Voting on School Finances: A Test of Competing Theories." *Western Political Quarterly* 36: 619–31.

Charlow, Robin. 1994. "Judicial Review, Equal Protection and the Problem with Plebiscites." *Cornell Law Review* 79: 527.

"Citizen Initiatives: Direct Democracy Advocate Grover Norquist Joins Campaign Experts Dick Woodward and Rick Arnold in a Roundtable Discussion of a Hot National Trend." 1994. *Campaigns & Elections* 5 (May): 33–37..

Citizens Conference on State Legislatures. 1972. *State Legislatures: An Evaluation of Their Effectiveness.* New York: Praeger.

Citizens for Tax Justice. 1991. *A Far Cry from Fair: CTJ's Guide to State Tax Reform.* Washington, D.C.: Citizens for Tax Justice.

———. 1992. *How Taxes Affect Elections: The Politics of Paying for Government.* Washington, D.C.: Citizens for Tax Justice.

Citrin, Jack. 1979. "Do People Want Something for Nothing: Public Opinion on Taxes and Spending." *National Tax Journal* 32: 113–29.

———. 1996. "Who's the Boss? Direct Democracy and Popular Control of Government." In *Broken Contract? Changing Relationship between Americans and Their Government,* edited by Stephen C. Craig. Boulder, Co.: Westview Press.

Citrin, Jack, Beth Reingold, and Evelyn Walters. 1990. "The 'Official English' Movement and the Symbolic Politics of Language in the United States." *Western Political Quarterly* 43: 553–60.

Citrin, Jack, Beth Reingold, and Donald P. Green. 1990. "American Identity and the Politics of Ethnic Change." *Journal of Politics* 52: 1124–54.

Clingermayer, James, and B. Dan Wood. 1995. "Disentangling Patterns of State Indebtedness." *American Political Science Review* 89: 108–20.

Clucas, Richard A. 1993. "Amateur Legislators in a Professional House: California after Term Limits." Paper presented at the annual meeting of the American Political Science Association, September 4, Washington, D.C.

Cohen, Michael, and Robert Axelrod. 1984. "Coping with Complexity: The Adaptive Value of Changing Utility." *American Economic Review* 74: 30–42.

Coleman, James S. 1957. *Community Conflict.* New York: Free Press.

Conover, Pamela Johnston, and Stanley Feldman. 1984. "Group Identification, Values, and the Nature of Political Beliefs." American Politics Quarterly 12: 151–75.

———. 1984. "How People Organize the Political World: A Schematic Model." *American Journal of Political Science* 25: 617–45.

Converse, Philip. 1962. "Information Flow and the Stability of Partisan Attitudes." *Public Opinion Quarterly* 26: 578–99.

———. 1964. "The Nature of Belief Systems in Mass Publics." In *Ideology and Discontent*, edited by David Apter. New York: Free Press.

Converse, Philip E., and Gregory B. Markus. 1979. "Plus ça change . . . : The New CPS Election Study Panel." *American Political Science Review* 73: 32–49.

Copeland, Gary W. 1992. "Term Limitation and Political Careers in Oklahoma: In, Out, Up, or Down." In *Limiting Legislative Terms*, edited by Gerald Benjamin and Michael J. Malbin, Washington, D.C.: CQ Press.

———. 1993. "Legislative Career Planning under Term Limitations." Paper presented at the annual meeting of the American Political Science Association, September 4, Washington, D.C.

Copeland, Gary W., and John David Rausch. 1991. "The End of Professionalism? The Dynamics of Legislative Term Limitations." Paper presented at the annual meeting of the Southern Political Science Association, November 1, San Antonio, Tx.

Corrado, Anthony. 1996. "The Changing Environment of Presidential Campaign Finance." In *In Pursuit of the White House*, edited by William Mayer. Chatham, N.J.: Chatham House.

Cottrell, E. 1939. "Twenty-Five Years of Direct Legislation in California." *Public Opinion Quarterly* 3 (1): 30–45.

Craig, Barbara Hinkson, and David M. O'Brien. 1993. *Abortion and American Politics*. Chatham, N.J.: Chatham House Publishers.

Craig, Stephen C. 1996. "The Angry Voter: Politics and Popular Discontent in the 1990s." *In Broken Contract? Changing Relationship between Americans and Their Government*, edited by Stephen C. Craig. Boulder, Colo.: Westview Press.

Croly, Herbert. 1912. "State Political Reorganization." *Proceedings of the 8th Annual American Political Science Association.* February.

———. 1914. *Progressive Democracy*. New York: Macmillan.

Cronin, Thomas. 1988. "Public Opinion and Direct Democracy." *PS: Political Science and Politics* 21: 612–19.

———. 1989. *Direct Democracy: The Politics of Initiative, Referendum, and Recall*. Cambridge, Mass.: Harvard University Press.

———. 1990. "Term Limits—A Symptom, Not a Cure." *New York Times*, 23 December, sec. A, p. 11.

Darcy, Robert, and Michael Laver. 1990. "Referendum Dynamics and the Irish Divorce Amendment." *Public Opinion Quarterly* 54 (1): 1–20.

Davidson, Roger H., and Walter J. Oleszek. 1994. *Congress and Its Members*. Washington, D.C.: Congressional Quarterly.

Delli Carpini, Michael X., and Scott Keeter. 1993. "Measuring Political Knowledge: Putting First Things First." *American Journal of Political Science* 37: 1179–1206.

Denzau, A., R. Mackay, and C. Weaver. 1981. "On the Initiative-Referendum Option and the Control of Monopoly Government." In *Tax and Expenditure Limitations*, edited by H. Ladd and T. Tideman. Cambridge, Mass.: Department of Regional Planning, Harvard University.

DiCamillo, Mark, and Mervin Field. 1994. "The Field Poll." Release date, January 26, 1994. San Francisco: The Field Institute.

Dionne, E. J., Jr. 1991. *Why Americans Hate Politics*. New York: Simon and Schuster.

———. 1996. *They Only Look Dead: Why Progressives Will Dominate the New Political Era*. New York: Simon and Schuster.

Dodd, Lawrence C. 1995. "The New American Politics: Reflections on the Early 1990s." In *The New American Politics*, edited Byron D. Jones. Boulder, Co.: Westview Press.

Dolbare, Kenneth, and Janette Hubbell. 1996. *USA 2012: After the Middle-Class Revolution*. Chatham, N.J.: Chatham House Press.

Donovan, Todd. 1993. "The Social and Political Basis of Support for Legislative Term Limitation Initiatives." Paper presented at the annual meeting of the Western Political Science Association, March 18–20, Pasadena, Calif.

———. 1994. "Anti-Gay and Lesbian Ballot Initiatives and Public Opinion." Paper presented at the annual meeting of the Pacific Northwest
Political Science Association, October 13–15, Portland, Ore.

Donovan, Todd, and Shaun Bowler. 1997. "Direct Democracy and Minori-
ties: Opinions on Anti-Gay Rights." *In Anti-Gay Rights: Assessing
Voter Initiatives*, edited by Stephanie Witt and Suzanne McCorkle.
Westport, Conn.: Praeger.

Donovan, Todd, and Joseph R. Snipp. 1994. "Support for Legislative Term
Limitations in California: Group Representation, Partisanship, and
Campaign Information." *Journal of Politics* 56: 492–501.

Douglas, Michael. 1980. "Judicial Review of Initiative Constitutional
Amendments." *UC Davis Law Review* 461: 468–74.

Downs, Anthony. 1957. *An Economic Theory of Democracy*. New York:
Harper and Row.

Dubin, Jeffrey A., D. Roderick Kiewiet, and Charles Noussair. 1992. "Voting on Growth Control Measures: Preferences and Strategies." *Economics and Politics* 4: 191–213.

Durand, Roger. 1972. "Ethnicity, 'Public Regardingness,' and Referenda
Voting." *Midwest Journal of Political Science* 16: 259–68.

Duscha, Carla Lazzareschi. 1975. "The Koupals' Petition Factory." *California Journal* 8: 83.

Duverger, Maurice. 1954. *Political Parties*. New York: Wiley & Sons.

Dwyer, Diane, M. O'Gorman, J. Stonecash, and R. Young. 1994. "Disorganized Politics and the Have Nots: Politics and Taxes in New York and
California." *Polity* 27: 25–47.

Dye, Thomas R. 1966. *Politics, Economics, and the Public: Policy Outcomes in the American States*. Chicago: Rand McNally.

Eaton, Allen. 1912. *The Oregon System: The Story of Direct Legislation in
Oregon*. Chicago: McClurg and Co.

Egan, Timothy. 1991. "Campaign on Term Limits Taps a Gusher of
Money." *New York Times*, 31 October, sec. A, p. 10.

Elazar, Daniel J. 1966. *American Federalism: A View from the States*. New
York: Crowell.

———. 1972. *American Federalism: A View from the States*. 2d ed. New
York: Crowell.

———. 1984. *American Federalism: A View from the States*. 3d ed. New
York: Harper and Row.

Elklit, Jorgen, and Nikolaj Peterson. 1973. "Denmark Enters the European
Communities." *Scandinavian Political Studies Yearbook*, 198–213.

Enlow, James, and Melvin Hinich. 1984. *The Spatial Theory of Voting*.
Cambridge: Cambridge University Press.

Erikson, Robert S., Gerald C. Wright, and John P. McIver. 1993. *Statehouse Democracy*. New York: Cambridge University Press.

Erickson, Robert. 1989. "Economic Conditions and the Presidential Vote." *American Political Science Review* 83: 567–73.

Eule, Julian. 1990. "Judicial Review of Direct Democracy." *Yale Law Journal* 99: 1504.

———. 1994. "Crocodiles in the Bathtub: State Courts, Voter Initiatives and the Threat of Electoral Reprisal." *University of Colorado Law Review* 65: 733–40.

"Excerpts From the Supreme Court's Decision in Term-Limits Case." 1995. *New York Times*, 23 May, sec. B, p. 8.

Fair, Ray C. 1978. "The Effect of Economic Events on Votes for President." *Review of Economics and Statistics* 60: 159–72.

———. 1982. "The Effect of Economic Events on Votes for President: 1980 Results." *Review of Economics and Statistics* 64: 322–25.

———. 1988. "The Effect of Economic Events on Votes for President: 1984 Update." *Political Behavior* 10: 168–79.

Farah, Barbara G., and Ethel Klien. 1988. "Public Opinion Trends." In *The Election of 1988: Reports and Interpretations*, edited by Gerald Pomper. Chatham, N.J.: Chatham House.

Feldman, Stanley. 1989. "Reliability and Stability of Policy Positions: Evidence from a Five-Wave Panel." *Political Analysis* 1: 25–60.

Fenno, Richard. 1973. *Congressmen in Committees*. Boston: Little, Brown.

———. 1978. *Home Style: House Members in Their Districts*. Boston: Little, Brown.

Ferejohn, John. 1974. *Pork Barrel Politics: Rivers and Harbors Legislation, 1947–1968*. Stanford: Stanford University Press.

Field Research Institute. "California Poll." San Francisco, CA.

Finkel, Steven. 1993. "Reexamining the 'Minimal Effects' Model in Recent Presidential Elections." *Journal of Politics* 55: 1–21.

Fiorina, Morris P. 1977. *Congress: Keystone of the Washington Establishment*. New Haven, Conn.: Yale University Press.

———. 1981. *Retrospective Voting in American National Elections*. New Haven, Conn.: Yale University Press.

———. 1992. *Divided Government*. New York: Macmillan.

Fishkin, James S. 1991. *Democracy and Deliberation: New Directions for Democratic Reform*. New Haven, Conn.: Yale University Press.

Flanigan, William H., and Nancy H. Zingale. 1987. *Political Behavior of the American Electorate*. Newton, Mass.: Allyn & Bacon.

Fountaine, Linda. 1988. "Lousy Lawmaking: Questioning the Desirability and Constitutionality of Legislating by Initiative." *Southern California Law Review* 61: 733–76.

Gamble, Barbara S. 1997. "Putting Civil Rights to a Popular Vote." *American Journal of Political Science* 91: 245–69.

Gamson, W. 1961. "The Fluoridation Dialogue." *Public Opinion Quarterly* 25: 526–37.

Gerber, Elisabeth R. 1992a. "Legislative Politics and the Direct Ballot: Comparing Policy Outcomes across Institutional Arrangements." Ph.D. diss., University of Michigan.

———. 1992b. "Preference Aggregation and the Effects of Institutions: Comparing Legislative and Direct Ballot Outcomes." Paper presented at the annual meeting of the American Political Science Association, September 3–6, Chicago, Ill.

———. 1996. "Legislative Response to the Threat of Popular Initiatives." *American Journal of Political Science* 40: 99–128.

———. 1997. "The Populist Paradox: Interest Group Influence and the Promise of Direct Legislation." Book manuscript, University of California, San Diego.

Gerber, Elisabeth R., and John E. Jackson. 1993. "Endogenous Preferences and the Study of Institutions." *American Political Science Review* 87: 639–56.

Gerber, Elisabeth R., and Arthur Lupia. 1992. "Competitive Campaigns and the Responsiveness of Direct Legislation: Theory and Evidence." Paper presented at the annual meeting of the Western Political Science Association, March 19–21, San Francisco, Calif.

———. 1995. "Campaign Competition and Policy Responsiveness in Direct Legislation Elections." *Political Behavior* 17: 287–306.

Gibson, James L. 1990. "Pluralism, Federalism, and the Protection of Civil Liberties." *Western Political Quarterly* 43: 511–33.

Gibson, James L., and Richard D. Bingham. 1985. *Civil Liberties and Nazis: The Skokie Free Speech Controversy.* New York: Praeger.

Gibson, James L., and James P. Wenzel. 1988. "Cognitive Sophistication and Political Tolerance." Paper presented at the annual meeting of the Midwest Political Science Association, April 18–20, Chicago, Ill.

Giles, Michael W., and Arthur S. Evans. 1986. "The Power Approach to Intergroup Hostility." *Journal of Conflict Resolution* 30: 469–86.

Gillespie, Michael, Elisabeth M. TenVergert, and Johannes Kingma. 1987. "Using Mokken Scale Analysis to Develop Unidimensional Scales." *Quality and Quantity* 21: 393–408.

Gin, Alan, and Jonathan Sandy. 1992. "Evaluating the Demand for Residential Growth Controls." Paper presented at the annual meeting of the Western Economic Association, July 9–11, San Francisco, Calif.

Glickfeld, Madelyn, Leroy Graymer, and Kerry Morrison. 1987. "Trends in Local Growth Control Ballot Measures in California." *UCLA Journal of Environmental Law and Policy* 6: 111–43.

Goetz, J. E. 1987. "Direct Democracy in Land Use Planning: The State Response to Eastlake." *Pacific Law Journal* 19: 793–844.

Goggin, Malcolm, ed. 1993. *Understanding the New Politics of Abortion*. Newbury Park, Calif.: Sage Publications.

Gold, Steven, and Judy Zelio. 1989. "Interstate Tax Comparisons and How They Have Changed over Time." *Legislative Finance Paper*. no. 66. Denver: National Conference of State Legislatures.

Goodwyn, Lawrence. 1978. *Democratic Promise: The Populist Moment in America*. New York: Oxford University Press.

Gorden, James D. III, and David B. Magleby. 1989. "Pre-Election Judicial Review of Initiatives and Referendums." *Notre Dame Law Review* 64: 298.

Gormley, William. 1983. *The Politics of Public Utility Regulation*. Pittsburgh: University of Pittsburgh Press.

Graham, Virginia. 1976. *A Compilation of Statewide Initiative Proposals Appearing on Ballots through 1976*. Washington, D.C.: Congressional Research Service.

Granberg, Donald, and Beth Wellman Granberg. 1981. "Abortion Attitudes, 1965–1980: Trends and Determinants." *Family Planning Perspectives* 12: 250–61.

Granberg, Donald, and Soren Holmberg. 1990. "The Berelson Paradox Reconsidered." *Public Opinion Quarterly* 54: 530–50.

Gray, Virginia. 1976. "Models of Comparative State Politics: A Comparison of Cross-Sectional and Time Series Analysis." *American Journal of Political Science* 20: 235–56.

———. 1990. "The Socioeconomic and Political Context of States." In *Politics in the American States*, 5th ed., edited by Virginia Gray, Herbert Jacob, and Robert B. Albritton. Washington, D.C.: Congressional Quarterly Press.

Gray, Virginia, and David Lowery. 1988. "Interest Group Politics and Economic Growth in the U.S. States." *American Political Science Review* 82: 109–32.

Green, Donald, and Jonathan Krasno. 1988. "Preempting Quality Challenges in House Elections." *Journal of Politics* 50: 920–36.

Green, S., ed. 1992. *California Political Almanac*. 3d ed. Sacramento: California Journal Press.

Gregg, James E. 1970. *Editorial Endorsements: Influence in Ballot Measures*. Davis, Calif.: University of California, Institute of Governmental Affairs.

Grumm, John G. 1971. "The Effects of Legislative Structures on Legislative Performance." In *State and Urban Politics*, edited by Richard I. Hofferbert and Ira Sharkansky. Boston: Little, Brown.

Gunn, P. F. 1981. "Initiatives and Referenda: Direct Democracy and Minority Interests." *Urban Law Annual* 22: 135–59.

Guskind, R. 1990. "Digging Up Dirt." *National Journal* 22 (October 27): 2592–96.

Hackbart, Merl, and James Leigland. 1990. "State Debt Management Policy: A National Survey." *Public Budgeting and Finance* 10.1.

Hadwiger, David. 1992. "Money, Turnout, and Ballot Measure Success in California Cities." *Western Political Quarterly* 45: 539–48.

Hagenaars, Jacques A. 1990. *Categorical Longitudinal Data.* Newbury Park, Calif.: Sage Publications.

Hagle, Timothy M., and Glenn E. Mitchell. 1992. "Goodness of Fit Measures for Probit and Logit." *American Journal of Political Science* 36: 762–84.

Hagstrom, J. 1990. "Squire-Fire." *National Journal* (November 10): 2746–47.

Hahn, Harlan, and Sheldon Kamieniecki. 1987. *Referendum Voting: Social Status and Policy Preferences*. New York: Greenwood Press.

Haider-Markel, D. P. 1997. "From Bullhorn to PACS: Lesbian and Gay Politics, Policy, and Interest Groups." Ph.D. diss., University of Wisconsin.

Haider-Markel, D. and Meier. 1996. "The Politics of Gay and Lesbian Rights." *Journal of Politics* 58: 332–49.

Hamilton, Alexander. [1788] 1961. *Federalist* no. 9. New York: Mentor Book Edition, New American Library.

Hansen, Peter, Melvin Small, and Karen Siune. 1975. "The Structure of Debate in the Danish EC Campaign: A Study of an Opinion-Policy Relationship." *Journal of Common Market Studies* 15: 93–120.

Hayes, Samuel P. 1957. *The Response to Industrialism, 1885–1914.* Chicago: University of Chicago Press.

———. 1964. "The Politics of Reform in Municipal Government in the Progressive Era." *Pacific Northwest Quarterly* 55: 157–69.

Hayes-Bautista, David E., and Gregory Rodriquez. 1994. "Perspective on the Election Fallout: A Rude Awakening for Latinos." *Los Angeles Times*, 11 November, p. 7.

Haynes, George. 1907. "The Education of Voters." *Political Science Quarterly* 22: 484–97.

Helman, Robert A., and Wayne W. Whalen. 1993. "Constitutional Commentary." In Smith-Hurd Compiled [Illinois] Statutes Annotated, Const., art. 14, sec. 3.

Hensler, Deborah, and Carl Hensler. 1979. *Evaluating Nuclear Power: Voter Choice on the California Nuclear Initiative.* Santa Monica, Calif.: Rand Corporation.

Hero, Rodney E. 1992. *Latinos and the U.S. Political System: Two-Tiered Pluralism.* Philadelphia: Temple University Press.

Hero, Rodney E., and Caroline J. Tolbert. 1996. "A Racial/Ethnic Diversity Interpretation of Politics and Policy in the States of the U.S." *American Journal of Political Science* 40 (August): 851–71.

Hero, Rodney E., Caroline J. Tolbert, and Robert Lopez. 1996. "Race/Ethnicity and Direct Democracy: Reexamining Official English and Its Implications." Paper presented at the annual meeting of the American Political Science Association, August 26–September 1, San Francisco, Calif.

Hofferbert, Richard I. 1966. "The Relations between Public Policy and Some Structural and Environmental Variables in the American States." *American Political Science Review* 60: 73–82.

Hofstadter, Richard. 1955. *The Age of Reform: From Bryan to F.D.R.* New York: Vintage Books.

Holbrook, Thomas M. 1994. "Campaigns, National Conditions, and U.S. Presidential Elections." *American Journal of Political Science* 38: 973–98.

Holbrook-Provow, Thomas M., and Steven C. Poe. 1987. "Measuring State Political Ideology." *American Politics Quarterly* 15: 399–416.

Holman, C. B., and Mathew T. Stodder. 1991. "The Fairness Fund: Addressing Spending Imbalances in Ballot Initiative Campaigns." Paper presented at the annual meeting of the American Political Science Association, September 1, Washington, D.C.

Hood, Howard A., ed. 1991. *Abortion in the United States: A Compilation of State Legislation.* Buffalo: William S. Hein & Co.

Horton, J., and W. Thompson. 1962. "Powerlessness and Political Negativism." *American Journal of Sociology* 67: 485–93.

Howe, Frederic C. 1967. *The City: The Hope for Democracy.* Seattle: University of Washington Press.

Huckfeldt, Robert, and John Sprauge. 1987. "Networks in Context: The Social Flow of Political Information." *American Political Science Review* 81: 1197–216.

Jackman, Robert. 1972. "Political Elites, Mass Publics, and Support for Democratic Principals." *Journal of Politics* 34: 753–73.

———. 1989. "An Errors-in-Variance Approach to Estimating Models with Snall Area Data." *Political Analysis* 1: 157–80.

Jackson, John E. 1974. *Constituents and Leaders in Congress: Their Effects on Senate Voting Behavior.* Cambridge, Mass.: Harvard University Press.

Jackson, John E., and David C. King. 1989. "Public Goods, Private Interests, and Representation." *American Political Science Review* 83: 1143–64.

Jacobson, Gary C. 1980. *Money in Congressional Elections*. New Haven, Conn.: Yale University Press.

———. 1987. *The Politics of Congressional Elections*. 2d ed. Glenview, Ill.: Scott, Foresman and Co.

———. 1990. *The Electoral Origins of Divided Government: Competition in U.S. House Elections, 1946–1988*. San Francisco: Westview Press.

Jacoby, WIlliam G. 1991. "Data Theory and Dimensional Analysis." Sage University Paper Series on Quantitative Applications in the Applied Social Sciences, 07–078. Beverly Hills, Calif.: Sage Publications.

Jennings, M. Kent. 1992. "Ideological Thinking among Mass Publics and Political Elites." *Public Opinion Quarterly* 56: 419–41.

Jewell, Malcolm E. 1982. *Representation in State Legislatures*. Lexington: University Press of Kentucky.

———. 1993. "Sources of Support for Term Limitations in State Legislatures." Paper presented at the annual meeting of the Southwestern Political Science Association, March 18–20, New Orleans, La.

Johnson, Charles A. 1976. "Political Culture in the American States: Elazar's Formulation Examined." *American Journal of Political Science* 20: 491–509.

Johnson, Claudius. 1944. "The Adoption of the Initiative and Referendum in Washington." *Pacific Northwest Quarterly* 35: 291–304.

Jost, Kenneth. 1990. "Initiatives: True Democracy or Bad Lawmaking?" *Congressional Quarterly: Editorial Research Reports*. August 17.

Kaiser, H. F. 1958. "The Varimax Criterion for Analytic Rotation in Factor Analysis." *Psychometrika* 23: 187–200.

Karp, Jeffrey A. 1993. "Examining Public Support for Term Limits: A Comparative State Analysis." Paper given at the annual meeting of the American Political Science Association, September 2–5, Washington D.C.

———. 1995. "Explaining Public Support for Legislative Term Limits." *Public Opinion Quarterly* 59: 373–91.

Kazin, Michael. 1995. *The Populist Persuasion: An American History*. New York: Basic Books.

Kehler, David, and Robert M. Stern. 1995. "Initiatives in the 1980s and 1990s." *The Book of the States, 1994–95*. Lexington, Ky.: Council of State Governments.

Kelley, S. 1957. *Professional Public Relations and Political Power*. Baltimore: Johns Hopkins University Press.

Kennerk, Erik. 1992. *1992 State Ballot Listing: A Special Report of the Free Congress Foundation*. Washington, D.C.: Free Congress Foundation.

Key, V. O., Jr. 1936. "Publicity of Campaign Expenditures on Issues in California." *American Political Science Review* 30 (4): 713–23.

———. 1949. *Southern Politics—In State and Nation.* Knoxville: University of Tennessee Press.

———. 1961. *Public Opinion and American Democracy.* New York: Alfred A. Knopf.

———. 1966. *The Responsible Electorate.* Cambridge, Mass.: Harvard University Press.

Key V. O., Jr., and Winston Crouch. 1939. *The Initiative and Referendum in California.* Berkeley: University of California Press.

Kiewiet, D. Roderick, and Kristin Szakaly. 1992. "The Efficacy of Constitutional Restrictions on Borrowing, Taxing and Spending: An Analysis of State Bond Indebtedness, 1961–1990." Paper presented at the annual meeting of the American Political Science Association, September 3–6, Chicago Ill.

———. 1993. "Constitutional Restrictions, Local Borrowing, Taxing, and Spending, 1961–1990." Working paper, California Institute of Technology, Pasadena, Calif.

Kim, Jae-On, and Charles W. Mueller. 1978. *Factor Analysis: Statistical Methods and Practical Issues.* Newbury Park, Calif.: Sage Publications.

Kinder, Donald R. 1983. "Diversity and Complexity in American Public Opinion." In *Political Science: The State of the Discipline,* edited by Ada W. Finifter. Washington, D.C.: American Political Science Association.

Kinder, Donald R., and David O. Sears. 1985. "Public Opinion and Political Action." In *Handbook of Social Psychology,* vol. 2, edited by Gardner Lindzey and Elliot Aronson. New York: Random House.

King, Gary. 1989. *Unifying Political Methodology.* Cambridge: Cambridge University Press.

King, Peter H. 1996. "The Curtain Pulled Back, For a Moment." *Los Angeles Times,* 11 September. Accessed from PoliticsNow, http://politicsnow.com/latimes.199609/11/lat0011.html

Kingdon, John W. 1981. *Congressmen's Voting Decisions.* 2d ed. New York: Harper and Row.

Knight, Kathleen. 1985. "Ideology in the 1980 Election: Ideological Sophistication Does Matter." *Journal of Politics* 47: 828–53.

Knox, Jim, Claire Landry, and Gavin Payne. 1984. *Local Initiative: A Study of the Use of Municipal Initiatives in the San Francisco Bay Area.* San Francisco: Coro Foundation.

Kristol, William. 1993. "Term Limitations: Breaking Up the Iron Triangles." *Harvard Journal of Law and Public Policy* 16: 95–100.

Kuklinski, James H., Daniel S. Metlay, and W. D. Kay. 1982. "Citizen

Knowledge and Choices on the Complex Issue of Nuclear Energy." *American Journal of Political Science* 26: 615–42.

Lascher, Edward L., M. Hagen, and S. Rochlin. 1996. "Gun behind the Door? Ballot Initiatives, State Policies, and Public Opinion." *Journal of Politics* 58: 760–75.

Lau, Richard R. 1986. "Political Schemata, Candidate Evaluations, and Voting Behavior." In *Political Cognition*, edited by Richard R. Lau and David O. Sears. Hillsdale, N.J.: Lawrence Erlbaum.

Lawrence, David G. 1995. California: *The Politics of Diversity*. Minneapolis: West Publishing.

Lazersfeld, Paul, Bernard Berelson, and Helen Gaudet. 1944. *The People's Choice*. New York: Duell, Sloane, and Pearce.

Lee, Eugene C. 1978. "California." In *Referendums: A Comparative Study*, edited by David Butler and Austin Ranney. Washington, D.C.: American Enterprise Institute Press.

———. 1979. "The Initiative: A Comparative State Analysis." *Western Political Quarterly* 28: 248–49.

———. 1997. "Hiram's Dream—"The People's Rule"—and the 21st Century." In *Governing the Golden State*, edited by G. Lubenow. Berkeley: IGS Press.

Legge, Jerome. 1983. "The Determinants of Attitudes toward Abortion in the American Electorate." *Western Political Quarterly* 36: 479–90.

Legislative Council of the Colorado General Assembly. 1992. *An Analysis of 1992 Ballot Proposals*. Denver: Colorado General Assembly.

———. 1994. *An Analysis of 1994 Ballot Proposals*. Denver: Colorado General Assembly.

———. 1996. *An Analysis of 1996 Ballot Proposals*. Denver: Colorado General Assembly.

LeLoup, Lance T. 1978. "Reassessing the Mediating Impact of Legislative Capability." *American Political Science Review* 72: 616–21.

Levitin, Teresa E., and Warren E. Miller. 1979. "Ideological Interpretations of Presidential Elections." *American Political Science Review* 73: 751–71.

Lewis-Beck, Michael S. 1977. "The Relative Impact of Socioeconomic and Political Variables for Public Policy." *American Political Science Review* 71: 559–66.

Lewis-Beck, Michael S., and Tom W. Rice. 1984. "Forecasting U.S. House Elections." *Legislative Studies Quarterly* 9: 475–86.

———. 1992. *Forecasting Elections*. Washington, D.C.: Congressional Quarterly Press.

Liechtling, Gilliam, Jonathon Mazzochi, and Scott Gardnider. 1993. *The Covert Crusade: The Christian Right and Politics in the West*. Portland, Ore.: Western States Center.

Lieske, Joel 1993. "Regional Subcultures of the United States." *Journal of Politics* 55: 888–913.

Limerick, Patricia Nelson. 1987. *Legacy of Conquest: The Unbroken Past of the American West*. New York: W. W. Norton; Cambridge: Belknap Press.

Linde, Hans A. 1989. "When Is Lawmaking Not Republican Government?" *Hastings Constitutional Law Review* 17: 159–73.

———. 1993. "When Initiative Lawmaking Is Not Republican Government: The Campaign against Homosexuality." *Oregon Law Review* 72: 20–39.

———. 1994. "Who Is Responsible for Republican Government?" *University of Colorado Law Review* 65: 709.

Lindsay, H. 1996. "Local School Districts Seek Political Expert for Bonds." *Education Week* May 27, pp. 18–23.

Lockley, L. 1950. "Notes on the History of Marketing Research." *Journal of Marketing* 14: 733–36.

Lowenstein, Daniel Hays. 1982. "Campaign Spending and Ballot Propositions: Recent Experience, Public Choice Theory and the First Amendment." *UCLA Law Review* 29: 505–641.

———. 1983. "California Initiatives and the Single-Subject Rule." *UCLA Law Review* 30: 936–75.

———. 1992. "A Patternless Mosaic: Campaign Finance and the First Amendment After Austin." *Capital University Law Review* 21: 381–427.

———. 1994. "Are Congressional Term Limits Constitutional?" *Harvard Journal of Law and Public Policy* 18 (Fall): 1–72.

———. 1995. *Election Law: Case and Materials*. Durham, N.C.: Carolina Academic Press.

Lowenstein, Daniel Hays, and R. Stern. 1989. "The First Amendment and Paid Initiative Petition Circulators: A Dissenting View and a Proposal." *Hastings Constitutional Law Quarterly* 17: 175–224.

Lowery, David. 1987. "The Distribution of Tax Burdens in American States: The Determinants of Fiscal Incidence." *Western Political Quarterly* 40: 137–58.

Lowery, David, and Virginia Gray. 1993a. "The Density of State Interest Group Systems." *Journal of Politics* 55: 191–206.

———. 1993b. "The Diversity of State Interest Group Systems." *Political Research Quarterly* 46: 81–98.

Lowery, David, and Lee Sigelman. 1981. "Understanding the Tax Revolt: Eight Explanations." *American Political Science Review* 75: 963–74.

———. 1985. "Political Culture and State Public Policy: The Missing Link." *Western Political Quarterly* 38: 376–84.

Lowi, Theodore. 1969. "Four Systems of Policy, Politics and Choice." *Public Administration Review* 32: 298–310.

Lowrie, S. Gale. 1911. "New Forms of Initiative and Referendum." *American Political Science Review* 5: 566–72.

Lunch, William. 1993. "Term Limits in Oregon." Paper presented at annual meeting of the Western Political Science Association, Pasadena, California.

Luntz, Frank. 1988. *Candidates, Consultants and Campaigns: The Style and Substance of American Electioneering.* New York: Basil Blackwell.

Lupia, Arthur. 1992. "Busy Voters, Agenda Control, and the Power of Information." *American Political Science Review* 86: 390–403.

———. 1994a. "The Effect of Information on Voting Behavior and Electoral Outcomes: An Experimental Study of Direct Legislation." *Public Choice* 78: 65–86.

———. 1994b. "Shortcuts versus Encyclopedias: Information and Voting Behavior in California Insurance Reform Elections." *American Political Science Review* 88: 63–76.

Luskin, Robert C. 1987. "Measuring Political Sophistication." *American Journal of Political Science* 31: 856–99.

———. 1990. "Explaining Political Sophistication." *Political Behavior* 12: 331–61.

Luttbeg, Norman R.. 1968. "The Structure of Beliefs among Leaders." *Public Opinion Quarterly* 32: 398–409.

Mackey, Scott R. 1993. "Constitutional Restrictions on Legislative Tax Powers." National Conference of State Legislatures Legisbrief, vol. 1, no. 29. Denver: NCSL.

Macpherson, C. B. 1977. *The Life and Times of Liberal Democracy.* New York: Oxford University Press.

Madison, James. [1788] 1961. *Federalist* nos. 10 and 51. New York: New American Library, Mentor Book Edition.

Magleby, David. 1984. *Direct Legislation: Voting on Ballot Propositions in the United States.* Baltimore: Johns Hopkins University Press.

———. 1986. "Legislatures and the Initiative: The Politics of Direct Democracy." *State Government* 59 (1): 31–39.

———. 1988. "Taking the Initiative: Direct Legislation and Direct Democracy in the 1980s." *PS: Political Science and Politics* 21: 601–11.

———. 1989. "Opinion Formation and Opinion Change in Ballot Proposition Campaigns." In *Manipulating Public Opinion*, edited by Michael Margolis and Gary A. Mauser. Pacific Grave, Calif.: Brooks/Cole Publishing.

———. 1990. "Legislatures and the Initiative: The Politics of Direct Democracy." *State Government* 59: 31–39.

———. 1994a. "Campaign Spending and Referenda Voting." Paper presented at the annual conference of the Western Political Science Association, March 10–12, Albuquerque, N.Mex.

———. 1994b. "Direct Legislation in the American States." In *Referendums around the World: The Growing Use of Direct Democracy*, edited by David Butler and Austin Ranney. Washington, D.C.: AEI Press.

———. 1995. "The United States." In *Referendums around the World*, edited by A. Ranney and D. Butler. Washington, D.C.: American Enterprise Institute.

Magleby, David B., and Kelly D. Patterson. 1996. "Political Knowledge and Term Limits: Can Angry Citizens Be Educated?" Paper presented at the annual conference of the Western Political Science Association, March 14, San Francisco, Calif.

March, James G. 1970. "Power in the City." In *Urban Processes as Viewed by the Social Sciences*, edited by K. Arrow and J. Coleman. Washington D.C.: Urban Institute.

March, James G., and Johan P. Olsen. 1984. "The New Institutionalism: Organizational Factors in Political Life." *American Political Science Review* 78: 734–49.

———. 1989. *Rediscovering Institutions*. New York: Free Press.

Marcus, George E., David Tabb, and John L. Sullivan. 1974. "The Application of Individual Differences Scaling to the Measurement of Political Ideologies." *American Journal of Political Science* 18: 405–20.

Markus, Gregory B. 1979. *Analyzing Panel Data*. Sage University Paper Series on Quantitative Applications in the Social Sciences. Beverly Hills, Calif.: Sage.

———. 1988. "The Impact of Personal and National Economic Conditions on the Presidential Vote: A Pooled Cross-Sectional Analysis." *American Journal of Political Science* 32: 137–54.

Martis, Nancy, and A. G. Block. 1994. "Proposition 187." *California Journal* 26 (December): 20–22.

Mason, Thomas. 1994. *Governing Oregon: An Inside Look at Politics in One American State*. Dubuque, Iowa: Kendal Hunt.

Matsusaka, John G. 1995. "Fiscal Effects of the Voter Initiative: Evidence from the Last 30 Years." *Journal of Political Economy* 103: 587–623.

Mayhew, David R. 1974. *Congress: The Electoral Connection*. New Haven, Conn.: Yale University Press.

———. 1986. *Placing Parties in American Politics*. Princeton, N.J.: Princeton University Press.

———. 1991. *Divided We Govern: Party Control, Lawmaking, and Investigation, 1946–1990*. New Haven, Conn.: Yale University Press.

McClain, Paula D. 1993. "The Changing Dynamics of Urban Politics: Black and Hispanic Municipal Employment—Is There Competition?" *Journal of Politics* 55: 399–414.

McClosky, Herbert. 1984. *The American Ethos: Public Attitudes toward Capitalism and Democracy.* Cambridge, Mass.: Harvard University Press.

McClosky, Herbert, and Alida Brill. 1983. *Dimensions of Tolerance: What Americans Think about Civil Liberties.* New York: Russell Sage Foundation.

McDill, Edward, and Jeanne Ridley. 1962. "Status, Anomie, Political Alienation, and Political Participation." *American Journal of Sociology* 68: 176–87.

McGuire, William. 1969. "The Nature of Attitudes and Attitude Change." In *Handbook of Social Psychology*, vol. 3, edited by Gardner Lindzey and Elliot Aronson. Reading, Mass.: Addison-Wesley.

McIntyre, Robert Douglas Kelly, Michael Ettlinger, and Elizabeth Fray. 1991. *A Far Cry From Fair: CTJs Guide to State Tax Reform.* Washington, D.C.: Citizens for Tax Justice.

McIver, John P., and Edward Carmines. 1981. *Unidimensional Scaling.* Beverly Hills, Calif.: Sage.

McKelvey, Richard D., and Peter C. Ordeshook. 1985. "Elections with Limited Information: A Fulfilled Expectations Model Using Contemporaneous Poll and Endorsement Data as Information Sources." *Journal of Economic Theory* 36: 55–85.

———. 1986. "Information, Electoral Equilibria and the Democratic Ideal." *Journal of Politics* 48: 909–37.

McKenna, Kathy Zimmerman. 1990. "Ballot Bowl: Industries Seek to Undermine Consumer, Environmentalist Initiatives." *California Journal* 21: 376–78.

McWilliams, Carey. 1951. "Government by Whitaker and Baxter." *The Nation*, 14 and 21 April, 5 May.

Meier, Kenneth. 1987. *Politics and the Bureaucracy.* Monterey, Calif.: Brooks Cole.

Meier, Kenneth J., and Joseph Stewart, Jr. 1991. *The Politics of Hispanic Education.* Albany: State University of New York Press.

Meier, Kenneth, Joseph Stewart, Jr., and Robert England. 1989. *Race, Class, and Education: The Politics of Second Generation Discrimination.* Madison: University of Wisconsin Press.

Mendelsohn, Matthew. 1994. Direct Democracy and Political Behavior: The Case of the 1992 Constitutional Referendum. Paper presented at the annual meeting of the Canadian Political Science Association, June 13, Calgary, Alberta.

Merida, Kevin. 1994. "Americans Want a Direct Say in Political Decision-Making, Pollsters Find." *Washington Post,* 20 April, sec. A, p. 19.

Merrill, Samuel, III. 1988. *Making Multicandidate Elections More Democratic.* Princeton, N.J.: Princeton University Press.

Michels, Robert. 1915. *Political Parties: A Sociological Study of the Oligarchical Tendencies of Modern Democracies.* New York: Hearst's International Library Co.

Miller, Warren E., Donald R. Kinder, Steven J. Rosenstone, and the National Election Studies. *American National Election Study: Pooled Senate Election Study, 1988, 1990, 1992* [computer file]. 2d release. Ann Arbor: University of Michigan, Center for Political Studies, 1993. Distributed by Ann Arbor: Inter-University Consortium for Political and Social Research.

Miller, Warren, and Donald Stokes. 1963. "Constituency Influences in Congress." *American Political Science Review* 57: 45–56.

Minger, Marilyn E. 1991. "Putting the 'Single' Back in the Single-Subject Rule: A Proposal for Initiative Reform in California." *UC Davis Law Review* 879: 899–900.

Moncreif, Gary F., and Joel A. Thompson. 1991. "The Term Limitation Movement: Assessing the Consequences for Female (and Other) State Legislators." Paper presented at the annual meeting of the Western Political Science Association, March 21–23, Seattle, Wash.

Moncrief, Gary, Joel A. Thompson, Michael Haddon, and Robert Hoyer. 1992. "For Whom the Bell Tolls: Term Limits and State Legislatures." *Legislative Studies Quarterly* 17: 37–47.

Mondak, Jeffrey J. 1995. "Elections as Filters: Term Limits and the Composition of the U.S. House." *Political Research Quarterly* 48: 701–27.

Mooney, Christopher Z. 1993. "Citizens, Structures, and Sister States: Influences on State Legislative Professionalism." Paper presented at the annual meeting of the Southwest Social Science Association, March 18–20, New Orleans, La.

Morehouse, Sarah M. 1982. *State Politics, Parties and Policy.* New York: Holt, Rinehart and Winston.

Mueller, John E. 1965. "Reason and Caprice: Ballot Patterns in California." Ph.D. diss., University of California, Los Angeles.

———. 1969. "Voting on the Propositions: Ballot Patterns and Historical Trends in California." *American Political Science Review* 63: 1197–213.

Mulligan, Kenneth. 1996. *Statewide Initiatives on the 1996 General Election Ballot: A Special Report of the Free Congress Foundation.* Washington, D.C.: Free Congress Foundation.

Mulligan, Kenneth, Stephen Lillienthal, and John Gesmundo. 1994. *1994 Statewide Ballot Measures: A Special Report of the Free Congress Foundation.* Washington, D.C.: Free Congress Foundation.

Myrdal, Gunnar. 1944. *An American Dilemma: The Negro Problem and Modern Democracy.* New York: Harper and Bros.

National Abortion Rights Action League. 1991, 1992, 1993. *Who Decides? A State by State Review of Abortion Rights in America.* Washington, D.C.: National Abortion Rights Action League.

National Conference of State Legislatures (NCSL). 1989. *Interstate Tax Comparisons and How They Have Changed over Time.* Legislative Finance Paper no. 66.

National Gay and Lesbian Task Force. 1994. "Survery on Voter Attitudes." Washington, D.C. June.

Neal, Tommy. 1993. "The Voter Initiative." *Legisbrief,* vol. 1, no. 38. Denver: National Conference of State Legislatures.

Neiman, Max, and M. Gottdiener. 1985. "Qualifying Initiatives: A Heuristic Use of Data to Command an Unexplored Stage of Direct Democracy." *Social Science Journal* 22: 100–109.

Neuman, W. Russell. 1986. *The Paradox of Mass Politics.* Cambridge, Mass.: Harvard University Press.

Nie, Norman H., and Kristi Anderson. 1974. "Mass Belief Systems Revisited: Political Change and Attitude Structure." *Journal of Politics* 36: 540–87.

Nie, Norman H., Sidney Verba, and John R. Petrocik. 1979. *The Changing American Voter.* Cambridge, Mass.: Harvard University Press.

Niemi, Richard G., and Herbert F. Weisberg. 1974. "Single-Peakedness and Guttman Scales: Concept and Measurement." *Public Choice* 20: 1306–15.

Niskanen, William A. 1971. *Bureaucracy and Representative Government.* Chicago: Aldine, Altherton.

Noah, Rebecca L. 1995. "The Limited Legislature: The Arizona Case." Paper presented at the annual meeting of the Western Political Science Association, 17 March, Portland, Ore.

———. 1996. "The Legislative Term Limits Research Agenda: A Status Report." Paper presented at the annual meeting of the Western Political Science Association, 14 March, San Francisco, Calif.

Nunn, Clyde Z., Harry J. Crockett, and J. Allen Williams, Jr. 1978. *Tolerance for Nonconformity.* San Francisco: Jossey-Bass Publishers.

Olson, David J. 1992. "Term Limits Fail in Washington: The 1991 Battleground." Chap. 4 in *Limiting Legislative Terms,* edited by Gerald Benjamin and Michael J. Malbin. Washington, D.C.: Congressional Quarterly Press.

Olson, Mancur. 1965. *The Logic of Collective Action.* Cambridge, Mass.: Harvard University Press.

Ordeshook, Peter. 1986. *Game Theory and Political Theory.* Cambridge: Cambridge University Press.

———. 1992. *A Political Theory Primer.* New York: Routledge.

Oregon Secretary of State, Elections Division. Various years. "Summary of Campaign Contributions and Expenditures."

Osgood, Charles E., and Percy Tannenbaum. 1955. "The Principle of Congruity in the Prediction of Attitude Change." *Psychological Review* 62: 42–55.

Owens, John, and Larry Wade. 1986. "Campaign Spending on California Ballot Propositions, Trends and Effects, 1924–1984." *Western Political Quarterly* 39: 675–89.

Page, Benjamin I., and Calvin Jones. 1979. "Reciprocal Effects of Policy Preferences, Party Loyalties and the Vote." *American Political Science Review* 73: 1071–89.

Page, Benjamin I., and Robert Y. Shapiro. 1992. *The Rational Public.* Chicago: University of Chicago Press.

Pateman, Carole. 1980 *Participation and Democratic Theory.* New York: Cambridge University Press.

Peffer, William A. 1992. *Populism: Its Rise and Fall.* Lawrence: University of Kansas Press.

Peterson, L. 1986. "The Wizards of Cause: California Campaign Consultants Prefer Initiative Campaigns over Candiatates because Propositions Produce More Profit and Less Hassle." *Golden State Report* 2 (6): 33–38.

Petracca, Mark P. 1993a. "A New Defense of State-Imposed Congressional Term Limits." *PS: Political Science and Politics* 24: 1700–1705.

———. 1993b. "Do Term Limits Rob Voters of Democratic Rights? An Evaluation and Response." *Western State University Law Review* 20: 547.

———. 1994. "Predisposed to Oppose: Political Scientists and Term Limitations." *Polity* 24: 657–72.

Petracca, Mark P., and Darcy Jump. 1992. "From Coast to Coast: The Term Limitation Express." *National Civic Review* 81: 352–65.

Petracca, Mark P., and Kareen Moore. 1993. "Testing Limits: The Experience with Municipal Term Limits in Orange County, CA." Paper presented at the annual meeting of the Western Political Science Association, Pasadena, Calif.

Phillips, Kevin. 1993. *Boiling Point: Democrats, Republicans and the Decline of Middle-Class Prosperity.* New York: Random House.

Pitkin, Hannah. 1967. *The Concept of Representation.* Berkeley: University of California Press.

Plotnick, Robert D., and Richard F. Winters. 1985. "A Politico-Economic Theory of Income Redistribution." *American Political Science Review* 79: 458–566.

Polsby, Nelson W. 1993. "Some Arguments against Congressional Term Limits." *Harvard Journal of Law and Public Policy* 16: 101.

Popkin, Samuel L. 1991. *The Reasoning Voter.* Chicago: University of Chicago Press.

Pound, William T. 1993. "Legislatures: Our Dynamic Institutions." *State Legislatures* 19: 22–25.

Price, Charles M. 1975. "The Initiative: A Comparative State Analysis and Reassessment of a Western Phenomenon." *Western Political Quarterly* 27: 243–62.

———. 1988. "Big Money Initiatives." *California Journal* 19: 481–88.

———. 1992a. "The Guillotine Comes to California: Term-Limit Politics in the Golden State." In *Limiting Legislative Terms,* edited by Gerald Benjamin and Michael J. Malbin. Washington, D.C.: Congressional Quarterly Press.

———. 1992b. "Signing for Fun and Profit." *California Journal* 23 (November): 545–49.

———. 1994. "Initiative Reform." *California Journal* 25 (April): 33–37.

Price, Charles, and Charles Bell. 1996. *California Government Today.* Pacific Grove, CA: Cole Publishing.

Pritchell, R. 1959. "The Influence of Professional Campaign Management Firms in Partisan Elections in California." *Western Political Quarterly* 12: 278–300.

Public Affairs Research Institute of New Jersey, Inc. 1992a. "Initiative Petitions." *Initiative and Referendum Newsletter.* June, issue 3. Princeton: Public Affairs Research Institute of New Jersey, Inc.

———. 1992b. "Initiative and Referendum Analysis." *Initiative and Referendum Newsletter.* June, issue 2. Princeton: Public Affairs Research Institute of New Jersey, Inc.

———. 1992c. "Initiatives and Voter Turnout." *Initiative and Referendum Newsletter.* July, issue 4. Princeton: Public Affairs Research Institute of New Jersey, Inc.

———. 1992d. "Statewide Initiatives." *Initiative and Referendum Newsletter.* June, issue 2. Princeton: Public Affairs Research Institute of New Jersey, Inc.

———. 1992e. "Why Initiative and Referendum Contributions and Expenditures Cannot Be Limited." January, issue 1. Princeton: Public Affairs Research Institute of New Jersey, Inc.

Quattrone, George A., and Amos Tversky. 1988. "Contrasting Rational and Psychological Analyses of Political Choice." *American Political Science Review* 82: 719–36.

Quinn, Tony. 1978. "The Specter of 'Black Wednesday': How the Establishment Destroys Unwanted Initiatives like Jarvis." *California Journal* 9: 153–54.

Rahn, Wendy M., John H. Aldrich, Eugene Borgida, and John L. Sullivan. 1990. "A Social-Cognitive Model of Candidate Appraisal." In *Information and Democratic Processes,* edited by John A. Ferejohn and James H. Kuklinski. Urbana and Chicago: University of Illinois Press.

Ranney, Austin, ed. 1981. *The Referendum Device.* Washington, D.C.: American Enterprise Institute for Public Policy Research.

Rapaport, R. 1989. "In the beginning . . . A History of California Political Consulting." *California Journal* 20 (July): 418–24.

Rausch, John David. 1993. "The Politics of Legislative Term Limitations: A Comparison of Four States." Paper presented at the annual meeting of the American Political Science Association, September 4, Washington D.C.

———. 1994. "Anti-Representative Direct Democracy: The Politics of Legislative Constraint." *Comparative State Politics* 15: 1–16.

Reed, Robert W., and Eric D. Schansberg. 1995a. "The House under Term Limits: Focusing on the Big Picture." *Social Science Quarterly* 76: 734–40.

———. 1995b. "The House under Term Limits: What Would It Look like." *Social Science Quarterly* 76: 699–716.

Regens, L., and T. Lauth. 1992. "Buy Now and Pay Later: Trends in State Indebtedness, 1950–89." *Public Administration Review* 52: 146–56.

Reich, Kenneth. 1987. "Insurance Lobby Study Cites Large Gifts to Politicians by Trial Lawyers." *Los Angeles Times,* 20 June, sec. 1.

———. 1988. "Bid to Qualify Five Insurance Initiatives Is in High Gear." *Los Angeles Times,* 30 November, sec. 1.

Renisch, Paul. 1912. "The Initiative and Referendum." *Political Science Quarterly* 25: 155–61.

Rhyme, Nancy. 1994. "What's Up with Term Limits." *State Legislatures* 20: 19.

Riker, William. 1982. *Liberalism against Populism: A Confrontation between the Theory of Democracy and the Theory of Social Choice.* San Francisco: W. H. Freeman.

Ripley, Randall, and Grace Franklin. 1987. *Congress, the Bureaucracy and Public Policy.* Chicago: Dorsey Press.

Rivers, Douglas. 1988. "Heterogeneity in Models of Electoral Choice." *American Journal of Political Science* 32: 737–57.

Robinson, Will, and David Dixon. 1992. "How We Short-Circuited the Terminators in Washington State." *Campaign Magazine,* February.

Robson, C., and B. Walsh. 1974. "The Importance of Positional Voting Bias in the Irish General Election of 1973." *Political Studies* 32: 144–54.

Roche, John. 1961. "The Founding Fathers." *American Political Science Review* 55 (December): 799–816.

Rosenthal, Cindy. 1990. "How Long Is Enough?" *State Legislatures* 16: 27–28.

Rothenberg, Stuart. 1992. "How Term Limits Became a National Phenomenon." *State Legislatures* 18: 35–39.

Sabatier, Paul, and Daniel Mazmanian. 1983. *Can Regulation Work? The Implementation of the 1972 California Coastal Initiative.* New York: Plenum Press.

Sabato, Larry. 1981. *The Rise of Political Consultants.* New York: Basic Books.

Samish, A., and B. Thomas. 1971. *The Secret Boss of California.* New York: Crown.

Sayrs, Lois W. 1989. *Pooled Time Series Analysis.* Newbury Park, Calif.: Sage.

Schlitz, Timothy D., and R. Lee Rainey. 1985. "The Geographic Distribution of Elazar's Subcultures among the Mass Population: A Research Note." *Western Political Quarterly* 38: 410–415.

———. 1989. *Citizen Lawmakers: The Ballot Initiative Revolution.* Philadelphia: Temple University Press.

Schmidt, David. 1989. *Citizen Lawmakers: The Ballot Initiative Revolution.* Philadelphia: Temple University Press.

Schultz, Jim. 1996. *The Initiative Cookbook: Recipes and Stories from California's Ballot Wars.* San Francisco: Democracy Center.

Schwartz, Thomas. 1986. *The Logic of Collective Choice.* New York: Columbia University Press.

Scott, Steve. 1996. "Ballot Bulge." *California Journal* 27: 12–19.

Sears, David O., and Jack Citrin. 1982. *Tax Revolt: Something for Nothing in California.* Cambridge, Mass.: Harvard University Press.

Sears, David O., Carl P. Hensler, and Leslie K. Speer. 1979. "Whites' Opposition to 'Busing': Self-interest or Symbolic Politics?" *American Political Science Review* 73: 369–84.

Sharp, E., and D. Elkins. 1987. "The Impact of Fiscal Limitations: A Tale of Seven Cities." *Public Administration Review* 47 (September/October): 385–92.

Shepsle, Kenneth A., and Barry R. Weingast. 1993. "Positive Theories of Congressional Institutions." *Legislative Studies Quarterly* 19: 149–79.

Shockley, John S. 1980. The Initiative Process in Colorado Politics: An Assessment. Boulder: University of Colorado, Boulder Bureau of Governmental Research and Service.

———. 1985. "Direct Democracy, Campaign Finance, and the Courts: Can Corruption, Undue Influence and Declining Voter Confidence Be Found?" *University of Miami Law Review* 39: 377.

Shogan, Robert. 1990. "Bush Gives Impetus to Term Limits." *Los Angeles Times*, 13 December.

———. 1994. "Public Discontent for Lawmakers New High; Drastic Reforms Gain Favor." *Los Angeles Times*, 10 March, sec. A, p. 5.

Simon, Herbert A. 1957. *Models of Man: Social and Rational.* New York: Wiley.

Siune, Karen. 1993. "The Danes Said No to the Maastricht Treaty." *Scandinavian Political Studies* 16: 93–103.

Skowronek, Stephen. 1982. *Building the New American State: The Expansion of National Adaptive Capacities, 1877–1920.* Cambridge: Cambridge University Press.

Smith, Daniel. 1996. "Faux Populism: Populist Entrepreneur Douglas Bruce and the Anti-Tax Crusade in Colorado, 1986–1996." Paper presented at the annual meeting of the Western Political Science Association, San Francisco, Calif.

Smith, Eric R. A. N. 1980. "The Levels of Conceptualization: False Measures of Ideological Sophistication." *American Political Science Review* 74: 685–96.

———. 1989. *The Unchanging American Voter.* Berkeley: University of California Press.

Smith, Richard A. 1995. "Interest Group Influence in the US Congress." *Legislative Studies Quarterly* 20: 89–140.

Smith, Rogers M. 1993. "Beyond Tocqueville, Myrdal, and Hartz: The Multiple Traditions in America." *American Political Science Review* 87 (3): 549–66.

Sniderman, Paul M. 1994. "The New Look in Public Opinion Research." In *Political Science: The State of the Discipline,* edited by Ada W. Finifter. Washington, D.C.: American Political Science Association.

Sniderman, Paul M., Richard A. Brody, and James H. Kuklinski. 1984. "Policy Reasoning on Political Issues: The Problem of Racial Equality." *American Journal of Political Science* 28: 75–94.

Sniderman, Paul M., Richard Brody, and Philip E. Tetlock. 1991. *Reasoning and Choice: Explorations in Political Psychology.* Cambridge: Cambridge University Press.

Sniderman, Paul M., Thomas Piazza, and Anne Kendrick. 1991. "Ideology and Issue Persuasibility: Dynamics of Racial Policy Attitudes." In *Reasoning and Choice,* edited by Paul M. Sniderman, Richard A. Brody, and Philip E. Tetlock. Cambridge: Cambridge University Press.

Squire, Peverill. 1992a. "Legislative Professionalization and Membership Diversity in State Legislatures." *Legislative Studies Quarterly* 17: 69–79.

———. 1992b. "The Theory of Legislative Institutionalization and the California Assembly." *Journal of Politics* 54: 1026–54.

———. 1993. "Professionalization and Public Opinion of State Legislatures." *Journal of Politics* 55: 479–91.

Stansel, Dean. 1994. *Taming Leviathan: Are Tax and Spending Limits the Answer?* Washington, D.C.: Cato Institute for Policy Analysis.

Steinmo, Sven. 1989. "Political Institutions and Tax Policy in the United States, Sweden, and Britain." *World Politics* 41: 500–534.

Steinmo, Sven, Kathleen Thelen, and Frank Longstreth, eds. 1992. *Structuring Politics: Historical Institutionalism in Comparative Analysis.* Cambridge: Cambridge University Press.

Stimson, James. 1975. "Belief Systems, Constraint and the 1972 Election." *American Journal of Political Science* 19: 393–417.

———. 1986. "Regression in Space and Time: A Statistical Essay." *American Journal of Political Science* 30: 914–47.

Stodder, Mathew T. 1992. "Controlling the Agenda through Confusion: The Rise of the Counter Initiative in the California Ballot Measure Process." Paper presented at the annual meeting of the Western Political Science Association, March 19–21, San Francisco, Calif.

Storing, Herbert. 1981. *What the Anti-Federalists Were For.* Chicago: University of Chicago Press.

Stouffer, Samuel C. 1955. *Communism, Conformity, and Civil Liberties.* New York: Doubleday.

Struble, Robert, Jr. 1993. "Second Time a Charm: Term Limits in Washington State." Paper presented at the annual meeting of the Western Political Science Association, March 18–20, Pasadena, Calif.

Sullivan, John L., James E. Pierson, and George E. Marcus. 1978. "Ideological Constraint in the Mass Public: A Methodological Critique and Some New Findings." *American Journal of Political Science* 22: 233–49.

Sundquist, James L. 1988. "Needed: A Political Theory for the New Era of Coalition Government." *Political Science Quarterly* 103: 613–36.

Sussman, Glen, Nicholas P. Lovrich, Byron W. Daynes, and Jonathan P. West. 1994. "State Legislators' Attitudes toward Term Limits: A Seven-State Study." Paper presented at the annual meeting of the Western Political Science Association, March 10–12, Albuquerque, N.Mex.

Sutro, Stephen. 1994. "Interpretations of Initiatives by Reference to Similar Statutes." *Santa Clara Law Review* 34: 945–64.

Tatalovich, Raymond. 1995. *Nativism Reborn? The Official English Movement and the American States.* Lexington, Ky.: University Press of Kentucky.

"Tax Advocates Enlist Radio." 1928. *Los Angeles Times*, 11 January.

Tedin, Kent, and Richard Murray. 1981. "Dynamics of Candidate Choice in a State Election." *Journal of Politics* 43: 435–55.

Thomas, Sue. 1984. "A Comparison of Initiated Activity by State." *Initiative Quarterly* 3: 8–10.

Thomas, Tom E. 1991. "Campaign Spending and Corporate Involvement in the California Initiative Process." In *Research in Corporate Social Performance and Policy,* vol. 12, edited by James Post. Greenwich, Conn.: JAI Press.

Thompson, Joel A., and Gary F. Moncrief. 1993. "The Implications of Terms Limits for Women and Minorities: Some Evidence from the States." *Social Science Quarterly* 74 (2): 300–309.

Thurber, James A., and Candice J. Nelson, eds. 1995. *Campaigns and Elections American Style.* Boulder, Colo.: Westview Press.

Tolbert, Caroline J. 1992. "Citizens Take the Initiative: The Politics of State and Local Tax Reform." Paper presented at the annual meeting of the Western Political Science Association, March 13, San Francisco, Calif.

———. 1993. "Hit the Road Jack: The Politics of State Term Limitation Reform." Paper presented at the annual meeting of the Midwest Political Science Association, April 18, Chicago, Ill.

———. 1994a. "Direct Democracy and A Second Generation of State Tax Reforms." Paper presented at the annual meeting of the Western Political Science Association, March 10–12, Albuquerque, N.Mex.

———. 1994b. "Direct Democracy and State Governance Policies." Paper presented at the annual meeting of the American Political Science Association, September 1, New York, N.Y.

———. 1996. "The New Populism: Direct Democracy and State Governance Policy." Ph.D. diss., University of Colorado, Boulder.

Tolbert, Caroline J., and Rodney E. Hero. 1996. "Race/Ethnicity and Direct Democracy: An Analysis of California's Illegal Immigration Initiative." *Journal of Politics* 58: 806–18.

Tucker, Harvey J. 1982. "It's about Time: The Use of Time in Cross-Sectional State Policy Research." *American Journal of Political Science* 26: 176–96.

———. 1985. "Legislative Logjams: A Comparative State Analysis." *Western Political Quarterly* 38: 432–46.

Tufte, Edward R. 1975. "Determinants of the Outcomes of Midterm Congressional Elections." *American Political Science Review* 69: 812–26.

Tversky, Amos, and Daniel Kahneman. 1986. "Rational Choice and the Framing of Decisions." *Journal of Business* 59: 251–78.

U.S. Bureau of the Census. 1991. *Statistical Abstract of the United States.* Washington, D.C.: GPO.

Verba, Sidney, and Norman Nie. 1972. *Participation in America*. New York: Harper and Row.

Warner, Daniel M. 1995. "Direct Democracy: The Right of the People to Make Fools of Themselves." *Seattle University Law Review* 19: 47–100.

Washington Secretary of State. 1994. "History of State Measures Filed with the Secretary of State." Olympia, Wash.: Office of the Secretary of State.

Weberg, Brian. 1988. "Changes in Legislative Staff." *Journal of State Government* 61: 190–97.

Weingast, Barry. 1979. "A Rational Choice Perspective on Congressional Norms." *American Journal of Political Science* 23: 245–62.

Weingast, Barry, and William Marshall. 1988. "The Industrial Organization of Congress, or, Why Legislatures, like Firms, Are Not Organized as Markets." *Journal of Political Economy* 96: 123–63.

Weingast, Barry, Kenneth Shepsle, and Christopher Johnsen. 1981. "The Political Economy of Benefits and Costs: A Neoclassical Approach to Distributive Politics." *Journal of Political Economy* 89: 624–64.

Weisberg, Herbert. 1980. "A Multidimensional Conceptualization of Party Identification." *Political Behavior* 2: 33–60.

Weisberg, Herbert F., and Jerrold Rusk. 1970. "Dimensions of Candidate Evaluations." *American Political Science Review* 64: 1167–85.

Weissberg, Robert. 1978. "Collective versus Dyadic Representation in Congress." *American Political Science Review* 72: 535–47.

Willhoite, Fred, Jr. 1977. "Evolution and Collective Intolerance." *Journal of Politics* 39: 667–84.

Wilson, James Q. 1980. *The Politics of Regulation.* New York: Basic Books.

Wilson, James Q., and Edward C. Banfield. 1963. *City Politics.* Cambridge: Harvard University Press.

———. 1964. "Public-Regardingness as a Value Premise in Voting Behavior." *American Political Science Review* 58: 876–87.

Witt, Stephanie, and Suzanne McCorkle. 1997. *Anti-Gay Rights: Assessing Voter Initiatives.* Westport, Conn.: Praeger.

Wolfinger, Raymond E., and F. I. Greenstein. 1968. "The Repeal of Fair Housing in California: An Analysis of Referendum Voting." *American Political Science Review* 62: 753–69.

Woodward, Calvin. 1995. "Language Laws Spur a War of Words." *Associated Press*, 18 October.

Woodward, Steve. 1996. "It's Not Always the Money That Matters." *The Oregonian*, 9 November, p. 1.

Wright, Gerald C., Robert S. Erikson, and John P. McIver. 1985. "Measuring State Partisanship and Ideology with Survey Data." *Journal of Politics* 47: 469–89.

Young, Amy E. 1993. "The Money behind the Movement." *Common Cause Magazine* 19 Summer: 37ff.

Zaller, John. 1987. "The Diffusion of Political Attitudes." *Journal of Personality and Social Psychology* 53: 821–33.

———. 1989. "Bringing Converse Back In: Information Flow in Political Campaigns." *Political Analysis* 1: 181–234.

———. 1990. "Political Awareness, Elite Opinion Leadership, and the Mass Survey Response." *Social Cognition* 8: 125–53.

———. 1991. "Information, Values and Opinion." *American Political Science Review* 85: 1215–38.

———. 1992. *The Nature and Origins of Mass Opinion.* Cambridge: Cambridge University Press.

Zax, Jeffrey. 1989. "Initiatives and Government Expenditures." *Public Choice* 63: 267–77.

Zimmerman, Joseph F. 1986. *Participatory Democracy: Populism Revived.* New York: Praeger.

Zisk, Betty. 1987. *Money, Media, and the Grass Roots: State Ballot Issues and the Electoral Process.* Newbury Park, Calif.: Sage.

# Index

# Contributors

**Susan A. Banducci** is a research fellow with the New Zealand Election Study, Department of Political Science and Public Policy, University of Waikato. Her research has appeared in *American Politics Quarterly*.

**Shaun Bowler** is an associate professor of political science at the University of California, Riverside. He is co-author, with Todd Donovan, of *Demanding Choices: Opinion and Voting in Direct Democracy* (University of Michigan Press). His articles have appeared in such journals as *Comparative Politics, Political Behavior, American Politics Quarterly,* and *Journal of Politics.*

**Todd Donovan** is an associate professor of political science at Western Washington University. He is co-author, with Shaun Bowler, of *Demanding Choices: Opinion and Voting in Direct Democracy* (University of Michigan Press). His research on direct democracy has appeared in such journals such *American Politics Quarterly, Journal of Politics, Political Research Quarterly,* and *Political Behavior.*

**Ken Fernandez** is a Ph.D. candidate in political science at the University of California, Riverside. His research on direct democracy has been published in the *European Journal of Marketing.*

**Elisabeth R. Gerber** is an assistant professor of political science at the University of California, San Diego. Her research has appeared in such journals as the *American Political Science Review, American Journal of Political Science,* and *Political Research Quarterly.*

315

**Rodney E. Hero** is a professor of political science at the University of Colorado. He is the author of *Latinos and the U.S. Political System: Two-Tiered Pluralism* (Temple University Press). His research has appeared in such journals as *Social Science Quarterly, American Journal of Political Science,* and *Journal of Politics.*

**Jeffrey A. Karp** is a research fellow with the New Zealand Election Study, Department of Political Science and Public Policy, University of Waikato. His research has appeared in such journals as *Public Opinion Quarterly* and *American Politics Quarterly.*

**Daniel H. Lowenstein** is a professor of law at the University of California, Los Angeles. He is the author of *Election Law, Cases and Materials* (North Carolina Academic Press). His research has appeared in such journals as the *Harvard Journal of Law and Public Policy, Hastings Constitutional Law Quarterly,* and *UCLA Law Review.*

**David McCuan** is a Ph.D. candidate at the University of California, Riverside. His dissertation research examines the politics of initiative campaigns.

**Caroline J. Tolbert** is an assistant professor of political science at Kent State University. Her research on direct democracy has appeared in such journals as the *American Journal of Political Science* and the *Journal of Politics.*

**James Wenzel** is an assistant professor of political science at the University of California, Riverside. He received his Ph.D. from the University of Houston.